MUIRHEAD LIBRARY OF PHILOSOPHY

An admirable statement of the aims of the Library of Philosophy was provided by the first editor, the late Professor J. M. Muirhead, in his description of the original programme printed in Erdmann's *History of Philosophy* under the date 1890. This was slightly modified in subsequent volumes to take the form of the following statement:

'The Muirhead Library of Philosophy was designed as a contribution to the History of Modern Philosophy under the heads: first of Different Schools of Thought—Sensationalist, Realist, Idealist, Intuitivist; secondly of different Subjects—Psychology, Ethics, Political Philosophy, Theology. While much had been done in England in tracing the course of evolution in nature, history, economics, morals and religion, little had been done in tracing the development of thought on these subjects. Yet "the evolution of opinion is part of the whole evolution".

'By the co-operation of different writers in carrying out this plan it was hoped that a thoroughness and completeness of treatment, otherwise unattainable, might be secured. It was believed also that from writers mainly British and American fuller consideration of English Philosophy than it had hitherto received might be looked for. In the earlier series of books containing, among others, Bosanquet's *History of Aesthetic*, Pfleiderer's *Rational Theology since Kant*, Albee's *History of English Utilitarianism*, Bonar's *Philosophy and Political Economy*, Brett's *History of Psychology*, Ritchie's *Natural Rights*, these objects were to a large extent effected.

'In the meantime original work of a high order was being produced both in England and America by such writers as Bradley, Stout, Bertrand Russell, Baldwin, Urban, Montague, and others, and a new interest in foreign works, German, French and Italian, which had either become classical or were attracting public attention, had developed. The scope of the Library thus became extended into something more international, and it is entering on the fifth decade of its existence in the hope that it may contribute to the mutual understanding between countries which is so pressing a need of the present time.'

The need which Professor Muirhead stressed is no less pressing today, and few will deny that philosophy has much to do with enabling us to meet it, although no one, least of all Muirhead himself, would regard that as the sole, or even the main, object of philosophy. As Professor Muirhead continues to lend the distinction of his name to the Library of Philosophy it seemed not inappropriate to allow him to recall us to these aims in his own words. The emphasis on the history of thought also seemed to me very timely; and the number of important works promised for the Library in the very near future augur well for the continued fulfilment, in this and other ways, of the expectations of the original editor.

H. D. LEWIS

MUIRHEAD LIBRARY OF PHILOSOPHY

General Editor: H. D. Lewis

Professor of History and Philosophy of Religion in the University of London

Action by SIR MALCOLM KNOX

The Analysis of Mind by BERTRAND RUSSELL

Brett's History of Psychology edited by R. S. PETERS

Clarity is Not Enough by H. D. LEWIS

Coleridge as a Philosopher by J. H. MUIRHEAD

The Commonplace Book of G. E. Moore edited by C. LEWY

Contemporary American Philosophy edited by G. P. ADAMS and W. P. MONTAGUE

Contemporary British Philosophy first and second Series edited by J. H. MUIRHEAD

Contemporary British Philosophy third Series edited by H. D. LEWIS

Contemporary Indian Philosophy edited by RADHAKRISHNAN and J. H. MUIRHEAD 2nd edition

Contemporary Philosophy in Australia by ROBERT BROWN and C. D. ROLLINS

The Discipline of the Cave by J. N. FINDLAY

Doctrine and Argument in Indian Philosophy by NINIAN SMART

Essays in Analysis by ALICE AMBROSE

Ethics by NICOLAI HARTMANN translated by STANTON COIT 3 vols

The Foundations of Metaphysics in Science by ERROL E. HARRIS

Freedom and History by H. D. LEWIS

The Good Will: A Study in the Coherence Theory of Goodness by H. J. PATON

Hegel: A Re-examination by J. N. FINDLAY

Hegel's Science of Logic translated by W. H. JOHNSTON and L. G. STRUTHERS 2 vols

Hegel's Science of Logic translated by A. V. MILLER

History of Aesthetic by B. BOSANQUET 2nd edition

History of English Utilitarianism by E. ALBEE

History of Psychology by G. S. BRETT edited by R. S. PETERS abridged one volume edition 2nd edition

Human Knowledge by BERTRAND RUSSELL

A Hundred Years of British Philosophy by RUDOLF METZ translated by J. H. HARVEY, T. E. JESSOP, HENRY STURT

Ideas: A General Introduction to Pure Phenomenology by EDMUND HUSSERL translated by W. R. BOYCE GIBSON

Identity and Reality by EMILE MEYERSON

Imagination by E. J. FURLONG

Muirhead Library of Philosophy

EDITED BY H. D. LEWIS

MEANING IN THE ARTS

MEANING IN THE ARTS

BY

LOUIS ARNAUD REID
D.Litt.

*Professor-Emeritus of Philosophy of Education
in the University of London*

LONDON : GEORGE ALLEN & UNWIN LTD
NEW YORK: HUMANITIES PRESS

FIRST PUBLISHED 1969

© George Allen & Unwin Ltd., 1969

SBN 04 701004 5

PRINTED IN GREAT BRITAIN
in 11 on 12 point Imprint type
BY UNWIN BROTHERS LIMITED
WOKING AND LONDON

To
YEHUDI MENUHIN
*in whose devoted playing
the embodiment of musical meaning
is so perfectly shown*

PREFACE

This book is a continuous argument, the later parts depending logically upon the earlier. But since readers' interests are various, some indication of the different emphases in different places may be useful.

After distinguishing, and relating, the functions of Criticism and Aesthetics in Part I, Part II develops the basic thesis of the book, which is that the central defining characteristic of the aesthetic is 'embodiment' rather than 'expression'. Part III tests this out in examples from the different arts, 'representative' and 'abstract', with very special attention to music (as an 'abstract' art), in which the problem of art's apparently contradictory characters—of being both autonomous and yet expressive of life outside art—is seen in its most acute form. The Chapter on 'Feeling' in this Part is essential to the understanding of the idea that the experience of art—and not only of music—is a *sui generis* kind of *knowing*. Part IV is a philosophical analysis of the main concepts so far involved—meaning, symbolism, knowledge, truth, standards—in art as distinct from other, discursive knowledge. It concludes with a discussion of the question whether art is in any sense a 'revelation'. Part V considers the bearing of the arguments of the book on aesthetic education.

I am indebted to Mr. Harold Osborne, who suggested that I should write another book on aesthetics, and whose comments led me to cut out some excesses. I am indebted too to my wife for critical comments, to Professor P. H. Hirst, who read portions of an early draft, and whose pointed and always relevant remarks were immensely suggestive, and to Professor H. D. Lewis, whose own views on revelation led me to rewrite completely the whole chapter on the subject. Finally, I am deeply grateful to Professor L. R. Perry, who read the whole typescript in its nearly-final form, making many suggestions of great profit.

L. A. R.

June 1969

CONTENTS

PART I

INTRODUCTORY—ON TALKING ABOUT THE ARTS

CHAPTER I

CRITICISM AND AESTHETICS

CHAPTER I

CRITICISM AND AESTHETICS

§1 *Introductory: the crucial importance of the aesthetic*

The title of this Part and Introduction might better be set down as: 'Some kinds of talking about the arts'—for there are very many ways in which we may talk about art and the arts. I am going to be concerned with the *aesthetic* emphasis of two main kinds of talk—criticism, and aesthetics, or, more accurately, that part of aesthetics which is philosophy of art.

The subject-matter of 'aesthetics' is, of course, much wider than what are called 'the fine arts'. It would probably be agreed that there can be 'aesthetic' enjoyment of many things not art in a strict sense. Watching, or playing, a stroke in cricket or a swing in golf, looking at a natural scene or a 'found object', can be an aesthetic experience. An 'aesthetic object' may be described as anything which is contemplated and enjoyed in a certain way, with attention to its form or to selected aspects of its form. (The meaning of 'contemplation', 'enjoyment', 'a certain way', 'form' of course require explication.) The part of aesthetics which is philosophy of art is concerned mainly (*a*) with the making, and (*b*) the contemplation and enjoyment, of the artifacts which are art-objects.

If the subject-matter of aesthetics is wider than the arts, so talk about art has a much wider scope than the purely aesthetic. It is important to be clear about this at the start—otherwise the attention to the aesthetic side which will be stressed in this book might be misunderstood, and talk about art be thought to be identical with the aesthetics of art. But of course 'the arts' are far wider than the aesthetic aspects of them: the arts themselves are part of a whole cultural context, and in turn influence it. Sometimes this has not been recognized, and the purely aesthetic side of art has been given exclusive attention: the aesthetic has appeared in isolation. Extreme examples are the extravagant aestheticism of the nineties or some of the one-sided statements of Clive Bell in the early nineteen-hundreds. Bell said, for example, that to apprehend aesthetic form 'we need bring with us nothing from life, no knowledge of its ideas and affairs, no familiarity with its emotions'.[1] That the arts spring out of a vastly complex

---

[1] Clive Bell, *Art*, p. 25.

cultural background I shall take for granted without enlarging upon it here. The study of the arts in the fullest sense—dance, drama, music, literature, the visual arts and crafts (plastic and otherwise), architecture—may draw from the understanding of magic, myth, religion; archaeology, anthropology, social and political history, 'conscious' and 'depth' psychology, in fact from all the sources of human experience and culture. So, if we talk chiefly of the aesthetic, it is as the *focus* of a field which is vastly larger than the aesthetic.

But the term 'focus' is metaphorical and, although useful, may suggest an inadequate view of the importance of the aesthetic in any full discussion of the arts. If one focuses a camera or a pair of field glasses, a sharp image of an area on a plane is picked out; the rest is blurred, or 'out of focus'. The picking-out aspect is again brought out if, less accurately, one speaks of the beam of a torch or a searchlight as 'focused' on a small area. Both these (connected) senses of 'focus' are combined when we talk of focusing our eyes physically, or our minds mentally, upon a field of attention. We—so to speak—direct a 'beam' on a small area which is the 'focus' of attention, whilst the periphery or the background is blurred.

This is all obvious: and the aesthetic can be a focus of attention within the wider field of art. But it is not enough to say this—or so I shall maintain. One can, at will, focus upon anything: what one focuses on may be determined by chance, or by some unregulated impulse of temperament, interest, attention. (But I shall argue) when one is talking about the arts seriously, the focus upon the aesthetic aspect of art, the keeping of it constantly in mind, is not just a matter of temperamental interest, but is *logically* necessary if the talk is really to be about *art*. We need not prejudge questions of the logical importance of other kinds of talk about art—for example the anthropological, historical, sociological, psychological. It is quite certain that they all contribute to the fullest understanding of the arts. Nevertheless the *constant* keeping in mind of the aesthetic aspect of art is essential and crucial in a way which is not true to the same extent of any of the other modes of discussion. The aesthetic is a differentiating characteristic of art as the others are not.

To keep hold of the aesthetic factor in art as a kind of master key is, then, important both in criticism and in aesthetics. But our view of the meaning of the 'relevance' of the aesthetic will depend upon what we think of the nature and function of criticism and aesthetics respectively.

§2   Criticism and its relation to the aesthetic

Schools of criticism are many, and the controversies between them sometimes fierce. I have nothing original to say on this subject: nevertheless it is necessary to remind ourselves (1) that 'criticism' is not a monolithic conception, and (2) that if criticism is to be valid it must be related to the *aesthetic* aspects of art.

Criticism involves interpretation and evaluation of schools and individual works of art. Interpretation and evaluation (the judgment of 'good' or 'bad') overlap all the time, and are inseparable. They involve the giving of some sort of reasons or grounds, the setting up of standards or criteria. These are of various sorts— but again they are not neat and isolated; in practical criticism they overlap and criss-cross. To be a member of this or that 'school' usually means that certain things are being specially emphasized, sometimes to the exclusion of others.[1]

Traditionally, from Aristotle onwards, and notably in the sixteenth to eighteenth centuries in the 'Neoclassical' movement there was a strong emphasis on *rules*—the supposed Aristotelian 'unities' for drama, canons for the different forms of literature, e.g. the epic, the sonnet, the elegy. The rules were sometimes rigidly, but more often flexibly interpreted, by, for example, Dryden, Pope and Johnson.

Contextualist criticism, as the term obviously suggests, implies reference to the many and complex factors of the setting in which a work of art is created. This may be an *historical* setting, either in a wide sense of 'history', or in the more specific sense of history of art—the influences of predecessors, styles, techniques, etc. Or the context may be *sociologically* interpreted, either ideologically or otherwies theoretically worked out as a kind of determinism, as in Marx or Taine. Or the work of the artists themselves—e.g. Ibsen or Synge or Shaw—may be strongly influenced by social problems and social reform, and can only properly be understood by the critic through some knowledge of the social influences on the works. There is, again, the *psychological* approach, which may study either the effects of works of art upon the percipient (as in the work of I. A. Richards in the twenties) or the psychological

[1] Jerome Stolnitz, in *Aesthetics and Art Criticism* gives a penetrating résumé of the schools, to which I am indebted.

mechanisms of the creative artist (as in Freudian or Jungian critics). In some ways allied to this, in other ways distinct from it, is criticism which studies the artist's biography in order to discover if possible the artist's intentions in making the work. This has been called 'intentionalist' criticism. There are, again, those who strongly stress the importance of the *moral* context and influence of art. Irving Babbitt and the Leavises come to mind.

Other critics have thought Contextualism of any kind much too external an approach to art and have stressed the impressions—sense-impressions, images, ideas, feelings, evoked in the critic's own experiences—as all-important. Stolnitz quotes Anatole France: 'The good critic is he who relates the adventures of his own soul among masterpieces'. And Debussy: 'To render one's impressions is better than to criticize, and all technical analysis is doomed to futility'. Walter Pater's *Renaissance* is a typical example of this *impressionist* criticism. Wilde expounded and exemplified it in *The Critic as Artist*. George Saintsbury was—among many other things—an impressionist.

Rejecting all contextualist criticism as too external, and impressionism as too subjective, the most influential contemporary movement, 'The New Criticism', attempts to study the work itself apart from what lies outside it, the work in its *intrinsic* nature. It is associated with the names of Richards, Eliot and Leavis in England and with Ransom and Cleanth Brooks in the United States. This criticism stresses the uniqueness of each work and the concreteness and individuality of its working out. It tends towards formal analysis of structure though it rejects general formal rules. As with all criticism, the theory and practice vary considerably as between practitioners.

This catalogue is simply a fly-leaf reminder that 'criticism' is a polemical word, and the purpose of it is to stress that if any criticism is properly to be called *art* criticism, it must relate whatever it has to contribute, to the aesthetic in art.

Assessment of the types of criticism is clearly impossible here. Every one contains *some* important truth, and every one can contribute something to criticism. But only on one condition. That is that each must be made relevant to, and in one way or another illuminate, the *aesthetic* experience and understanding of art. Whatever is learnt from outside art must somehow be assimilated so that it gets into the very experience of art, making it more aesthetically intelligible. If it does not do this it may be learnèd or emotionally exciting, or psychologically interesting—or many other things. But it will not be *art* criticism; it will be a reduction of art to something else. If knowledge of rules, or sociology, or psychology, is not made relevant to the aesthetic discernment of art, it will be talk *round* but not talk *about* art. 'Intrinsic' criticism has the merit of concentrating on the work itself. On the other hand if it is really denying the possibility of illumination through contextual studies (and it would seem impossible entirely to exclude all contextual reference) it is questionable whether it is not avoiding the paradox of art, that art is *in* the world yet not *of* it, by denying one side—that art is indeed within the world.

A main end-function, then, of any kind of criticism, is to develop discriminating aesthetic appreciation of art. Complementary to this is the function of educating this discrimination in others as well as in oneself.

§3   Criticism and Aesthetics

The critic's business is, finally, with individual works of art. The business of the philosopher of art is more general; he is concerned with principles or categories. There is an important division between the two of function and interest. This does *not* mean that the critic can do without principles or categories, or that the philosopher of art can carry on his job at all, can talk relevant sense about 'art', without first-hand discriminating experience of works of art, that he can be anything but vague and doctrinaire if he is not checking his generalizations by constant reference back (at least in his own mind) to particular examples of this or that art. This aesthetic knowledge and experience is the very stuff he is talking about, and he must have it at first hand. The important difference between the critic and the philosopher of aesthetics is, as I say, a difference of function, interest, emphasis.

The critic cannot talk at all without making general assumptions; his statements involve them. But for the critic as such, they are assumptions. They may never become explicit (though when certain fundamental controversies arise, it is hard to see that he can get far without trying to make them explicit), but he makes them all the same, and they affect all the much more particular things he may be saying for most of the time. He is not, as such, a philosopher, and he is not called upon to expound his general ideas about art in any systematic philosophical way. But he has these general ideas, and he is in a healthier state even as critic if he is aware of them and has given at least some thought to their formulation. If his particular talk as a critic is not held together in some general framework (even if it be a flexible one) it will tend to degenerate into loose talk about personal impressions (or other matters). Sensibility above all he certainly must have, but sensibility alone does not make a critic coherently articulate.

On his side, the philosopher *is* concerned directly with general principles and categories underlying all the arts, the notion of art itself, of appreciation, beauty and ugliness, expression, form and configuration. This study of principles and categories is intellectual work. Its primary aim is to understand these things, and to understand the assumptions and language of the critic. On the other hand, since criticism involves assumptions which are the subject-matter of aesthetics, and these assumptions of the critic inevitably affect what he does and says, clearer thinking about the assumptions (or at least the reduction of muddled, incoherent thinking) must have practical effects too. Aesthetics in itself is theoretical, not normative, but it can have indirectly normative effects, on the practice and understanding of the critic.

There are, to repeat and sum up, two expert, and different, jobs, criticism and aesthetics. Each is autonomous in the exercise of its own function, yet each is, in another relationship, dependent on the other. The critic does not get his critical ideas *from* the philosopher—heaven forbid! But he does need either to be *something of a philosopher*, or else to get help from the philosopher in making clearer and more explicit his basic aesthetic assumptions— which will involve critical scrutiny and possibly modification of them. But unless the philosopher, the aesthetic philosopher, knows from the inside what the critic is experiencing and talking about, unless, that is, he is at least something of a first-hand (if not a first-rate) aesthetic expert, he will be of worse than no help to the critic.

Let us now look more carefully at the tension which I referred to—the tension between the discriminating experience of the work of art with its sheer individuality, and the language used respectively by criticism and aesthetics. Both the critic and the philosopher use language, and using language must employ general words. But the character of the language used by the critic is different from the character of the language used by the philosopher of aesthetics.

§4 *The Languages of Criticism and Aesthetics*

Consider first the language used by the critic, the critic talking directly about works of art not round them. It varies, of course, very much with different types of criticism. It may be directly descriptive, of a general or a particular kind, or it may be a mixture of description and evaluation, again of a general or particular sort. (Or, as we shall see later, it may be importantly metaphorical.) The purely descriptive language need not delay us. One can descriptively classify in a general way different kind of arts by using different words—this is a sonata, a fugue, a tragedy, a comedy, an epic or a lyric. Or more particularly, we can describe this or that work of art—this picture with figures in the foreground and landscape in the background, colour predominantly pale green and grey, dance which is of gay or sombre kind, a poem which is about an ocean voyage. Such descriptive language may have accessory uses in talking about works of art, but is of no aesthetic interest in itself. It is aesthetically evaluative language (it can be descriptive too) which is of interest here. Examples might be, again, of a more general kind (say, about types of artistic treatment) or more particular. I choose two short passages from Roger Fry's essay—descriptive-evaluative—on Van Gogh to illustrate each.[1] First, the more general: 'Cezanne's great preoccupation was always with construction in depth. With regard to the contour, what concerned him almost painfully was its function as a disappearing plane. That is the opposite of Van Gogh's interest in the contour as silhouette, as part of the organization of the picture on a flat surface as a decorative unity. This was, no doubt, in part due to the influence of Japanese prints aided by his desire for pure positive colour.' The other quotation, more particular, is about one work of Van Gogh—the 'Sunflowers'. 'It has supreme exuberance, vitality, and vehemence of attack, but with no sign of that loss of equilibrium which affects some of the later work. . . . This is a harmony based almost entirely upon yellows. Against a pale, almost lemon, yellow background the heads of the sunflowers show as dusky masses of heavy burnished gold. . . . Such a use of yellow is rare in European art.' I take one more example of speech directed upon individual works of art though it is not exactly criticism—the (remembered) words of Menuhin on TV whilst giving a lesson on the playing of Beethoven's Violin Concerto:

[1] In *Transformations*.

'It can sound like scales and arpeggios—but in Beethoven there are really no scales and arpeggios, there is a flow. . . .' 'One has to realize the significance of this passage in relation to the whole work' . . . 'Don't underline that phrase; think, then forget, and having thought, you will do it differently.' 'The music in this Concerto is cumulative, like a snowball; don't interrupt the pace. . . .' 'You weren't quite completely aware of its place in the Concerto.'

This illustrates the kind of critical language which critics and artists sometimes use, when they have either particular works in mind or are making more general statements about artists and their work. I want to contrast them now with words which, though always relevant to art, are unlike the specific critical language just illustrated, and are of a fundamental, general, universal kind. Examples are: 'The meaning of a work is wholly inseparable from the form as presented so that it cannot be translated into any other terms, or put into ordinary language in any adequate way: form and matter are inseparable.' 'A work of art is not a piecing together of parts, but is an emergent creative unity.' 'Art has "living form".' 'Art possesses configuration so that every part is organically related to every other part.' 'Art possesses unity.' Some or all of these sentences *might* be used by critics on some occasions— though they are too general to be typical utterances. But they are just the stock-in-trade of the philosopher of aesthetics; he formulates them from his reading of criticism, or from his own experience of the arts, and he subjects them to critical examination and considers their relationships and validity. If the critic does in fact use them, they are uttered in the immediate context of criticism. When the aesthetician uses them he is thinking of them in a general way, as abstract categories.

Broadly speaking, then, there are two distinguishable sets of language and words. There is the more particular language of the critic, focused on this or that work, or if not, derived from consideration of particular works and used in critical references to works of art in a more general kind of way. And there is the very general language of the aesthetician. The two sets are very different in kind and function.

The main questions of the rest of the chapter are, in a sense, opposite sides of the same coin. One is: How can philosophical aesthetics, being general, be relevant to criticism and to particular works of art, which are essentially individual? and (secondly) How can criticism, being concerned with individuals, ever accommodate the general? I will take the questions in that order.

§5   How can Aesthetics be relevant to Individual Works of Art?

(1) The first question is: How are the categories of aesthetics, being very general concepts, related to the judgment of always-individual works of art? Are they not too general to be relevant to the individuality of particular works of art with which the critic is concerned? What the critic on the job is doing, surely, is to give his full attention to the individual work in its internal aesthetically implicative structure? He is a sensitive perceiver, attending to *this*. He must give all he has to it in order that his responses may be complete; and his utterances are relevant to that total perceptive experience. If he starts listening to the philosopher, if he imports into criticism general conceptions from philosophy outside, he will be distracted from his proper job. Instead of devoting himself to what is before him he might be tempted, in a muddled sort of way, to treat this individual as if it were merely an instance of an abstract class. The sort of intellectual activity which is aesthetics and the sort of activity which is criticism may interfere with one another unless in the critical moments philosophy is kept outside in its proper place. The critic must work from inside, and such questions as he asks must arise from the inside knowledge.

This is a real problem; any answer which we give to it must accept in full what has been claimed of the critic, that he gives his full attention to individual works of art, each of which is unique and none of which is merely an instance of anything. And the answer depends upon the reply to three subsidiary questions. First (*a*), *are* the principles of aesthetics, though general, so divorced from the critical experience of individual art as all that? Secondly (*b*), how is a general principle of aesthetic applied to an individual work? Thirdly (*c*), it will be important to ask whether and how particular *critical* judgments may perhaps depend internally for their validity upon the assumption of general aesthetic categories.

(*a*) Are the general categories of aesthetics as extraneous as they have just been made out to be? No, they are not. The thing to hold on to is what has been insisted on already, that these categories are formulated from or arise out of aesthetic experience itself of the arts. From the perception of the presentational fields of works of art, apprehended in their internal relationships and unity, appreciated in the way that works of art are appreciated, arises the philosophical reflection (repeated and checked again and again) upon their nature which forces us to claim that, in spite of the unlimited differences between individuals, they do all possess what can properly be called some general characters (instanced above) in common. They are all (it can be claimed) created artifacts in which meaning is inseparably united with perceived form, and which possess a unity of configuration which can only be called 'aesthetic' and which is exactly like nothing else.[1]

If any such generalizations are valid, if all works of art do have these specified characters and nothing but works of art have them (all of which has to be defended in a systematic treatment of aesthetics), then, if *this* artifact possesses these characters, it comes into the category of being a 'work of art'. Note here that I am talking about aesthetics, about a way in which it is possible to speak. One *can* say of a work of art, 'This work, having certain characters which all known works of art possess and only they, is a work of art'. It is not suggested that the critic—even if he does have at the back of his mind some general concepts about art— would use language like this, or works in this highly intellectual and artificial way, or that all is now complete. To say that 'this comes into the category of being a work of art' could only be a pre-condition of criticism. The critic is concerned with individual aesthetic judgments, with the sometimes long, detailed, particular reflection and talk that is inseparable from them.

Further, the aesthetician himself, though he is interested in generalizing, does not recognize an 'instance' of art in the simple easy casual way in which one might recognize that this is red, or a triangle, or an example of the conventional sonata form. He cannot even 'recognize' that this is an 'instance' of art without giving himself with all his aesthetic attention to the individual embodied form of *this* work.[2] As we have said, the aesthetic categories are formulated out of aesthetic experience in depth. Whatever its legitimacy in some sorts of discourse, simple logical subsumption is never in the realm of aesthetics a *substitute* for attentive aesthetic perception. The aesthetician cannot give a single instance of

[1] These pronouncements will be expounded in the course of the book.

[2] The common separation between the philosopher of art as concerned in a second order ('meta') occupation (see Morris-Jones, *Brit. Journal of Aesthetics*, Vol. 5, No. 1) and the first-hand experience of art is far too sharp.

any of his generalizations without being more than a philosopher.

This is very important. The properties which are common to all art can be verbally articulated (e.g. that form and matter are inseparable), or perhaps better, indicated. But that the properties *are* common can be known only by a wide personal experience of the arts, of which there are many kinds, and which in each case is experience of an individual work. This, that, the other . . . possesses unity of form and matter; each is individual; yet it makes sense in the context of aesthetics to say that each *and all* possess unity of form and matter. The logical account of this is quite different from that of the matter-of-fact impersonal description of the dimensions and form of a house (which might be a pattern not individual but multipliable), which any Tom, Dick or Harry can see, and which is formulable abstractly. The aesthetic generalization of the aesthetic philosopher depends upon a special kind of personal experience. It is not merely subjective, for we can communicate about it to others. But one must be or must have been aesthetically involved in a great many individual experiences in order to understand the generalization.

One more comment. Though aesthetic categories are generalizations about art as such, and therefore about 'all art', this does not imply any claim to infallibility, incorrigibility, completeness. Like all philosophical generalizations, general aesthetic categories are provisional and open. Art is always changing; today in particular we are living in an age of experimental art; almost weekly new forms are appearing—some of which at least do not seem to fit well into the categories which we have instanced. What then are we to do? Abandon all our categories hitherto accepted, and tolerate anything which claims to be art? Certainly not. Aesthetic categories, if seriously constructed and close to the best critical judgments, are to be seriously maintained and not lightly thrown overboard, or even modified. On the other hand, there has to be openness and humility, for the fact of creative art is that upon which all criticism and all aesthetics depends, and if aesthetic categories now in operation are tested ideas with which we come to confront new experiences of art, they are not a procrustean bed into which the products of the creative experimental artist must be fitted at all costs. New forms of art may compel us, if conservatively, to reconsider our aesthetic categories. The 'tension' between thinking and aesthetic experience is acutely operative here.

There is no simple answer; neither can be overthrown lightly. There is a dialectic or dialogue which is always going on, and which is never quite or finally conclusive.

In the light or what has been said, the answer to the second question (*b*) above, can be short. The question was, How is a general principle of aesthetic *applied* to an individual work, e.g. the 'unity of form and matter'? The answer has been given. It is that it can only be seen to be an instance of an aesthetic principle by *aesthetic* entry into the work. As aesthetic principles can only be *extracted* from first-hand aesthetic experience, so can instances of them only be *recognized* in aesthetic experience.

§6 *Critical Judgments and Aesthetic Categories*

(*c*) The answer to the third question whether and how *particular* critical judgments depend for their validity upon *general* aesthetic categories, is of great importance, because critics and philosophers alike tend to ignore it. If a critic refers, say, to Botticelli's 'graceful lines', Rembrandt's *chiaroscuro*, spondees which give weight to this line in this poem, the restraint or the urgency of this passage of music, the 'rightness' of the slight staccato here—these particular judgments, if valid, are valid only in assessing each individual work, this work. There is an intense aesthetic perception of the passage in this particular context, which is, in the final count, the content of the *whole* work. Now the very assumption of this is the assumption in fact of an aesthetic category which is claimed as applying universally to all works of art. It is the assumption that works of art, as such, are single systematic aesthetic individuals, in which the artistic significance of any part is inseparable from its relation to the whole. It is the principle of configuration, of artistic unity, of the system of aesthetic meaning which is often called 'organic'. These connected *general* aesthetic categories are logically presupposed, I am saying, in the claim that the *particular* critical judgments are valid. The critic, however properly his attention is given to the particular observations in their context, is thinking within a general categorial assumption of the individuality and unity presupposed in all art. The work of art is a complex but continuous and single system within which the parts fall into place, and without which the particular judgments can have no validity.

One can put the same thing in a slightly more general way. Stuart Hampshire is one of the people who are sceptical about aesthetic generalization. 'When attention is directed to the particular features of the particular object, the point is to bring people to see these features, not simply to lead them to say: "That's good." There is no point in arguing that the object is good *because* it possesses these qualities if this involves the generalization that all objects similar in this respect are good. If one generalizes in this manner one looks away from the particular qualities of the particular thing and is left with some general formula or recipe, useless alike to artist and spectator.'[1] And he concludes his essay: 'Neither an artist nor a critical spectator unavoidably needs an aesthetic. And when in aesthetics one moves from the particular to the general, one is travelling in the wrong direction.'

Hampshire is perfectly right in his emphasis on the individuality of art. But his conclusion is wrong. He confuses aesthetics and criticism. Directing attention to particular features is the work of criticism, not of aesthetics as such, and it is a complete travesty of aesthetics to suppose that what aesthetics does is to generalize the *particular* judgments of criticism in order to produce a 'general formula or recipe'. This would be fatuous. But what Hampshire does not see is that in his very proper insistence on particularity, the particularity of criticism, he is assuming an inescapable aesthetic category, the universal category of artistic individuality. It is this very generalization which Hampshire is assuming when he insists that we can't make generalizations out of particular critical judgments. All his observations depend upon this; it is an important example of the aesthetic generalization which he illogically denies to be necessary. Critics and philosophers alike, in their emphasis on the 'particular' critical judgment, are apt to ignore the universal categorial assumption.

§7 *Generality, and the Nature and Functon of Critical Language*
(2) We now turn to the question which is the opposite side of the same coin. How is it that criticism, being concerned with the individual, can accommodate the general? (And what kind of 'general' is it?) I will quote Isenberg.[2] Speaking of those who argue against critical standards (Croce, Dewey, Richards, Prall), he says: 'In one way or another they all attempt to expose the absurdity of presuming to judge a work of art, the very excuse for whose existence lies in its *difference* from everything that has gone before, by its degree of *resemblance* to something that has gone

---

[1] *Aesthetics and Language* (Ed. Elton), p. 166.
[2] Elton, *op. cit.*, p. 136 *et seq.*

before.' Criticism is concerned with the individual. But if so, how can one use critical appraisements validly, since, if they are concerned with the individual, they can only have an internal reference, whereas language used always includes reference to ideas which are outside the work and have something of a general flavour.

One form of criticism we know, 'intrinsic' criticism, for which a phrase of Matthew Arnold's (quoted by Stolnitz) can be taken as the motto: 'to see the object in itself as it really is'. In this school of criticism the whole emphasis professes to be upon the work; considerations outside the work are to be avoided. The positive emphasis of this is, certainly, sound. On the other hand I hinted earlier that it is 'virtually impossible' to avoid contextual reference. Whether or not *contextual* reference is always implied ('contextual' in a straightforward sense), it is quite certain that there is some *generality* in all talk about art. The critic does not just point to works of art—though he does point: he uses language; and the words of his language *always* contain references to meanings 'beyond' or 'outside' the particular work which is referred to.

What kinds of language does the critic use on the actual job, and what are their functions? I am assuming that such language as is used is intended to illuminate and enhance the appreciation of the works it refers to. It is not the general language of aesthetics as the philosopher uses it, but a language more pointed, more suggestive, more metaphorical. Such generality as it has (and being language must have) seems to be entirely instrumental, having the function of directing our attention to what is individual in the work. John Holloway,[1] arguing that the critic's problem is to draw attention to the work, speaks of 'figurative' language (for example 'a glittering style'), and of the 'writing which itself manifests those features of the subject-work to which the critic is drawing attention', often called 'evocative criticism'. He speaks, too, of describing one's own reactions to a work with the intention of causing the reader to scan the work more attentively to see what he gets out of it. Again, 'reading a description of a state of mind often evokes a faint trace of it, and this evocation of the critic may may be carried on by something in the work—which thereby reveals itself'. So 'the vocabulary of criticism largely hangs in suspension between a psychological interpretation, and an "objective"—that is, one which gives a sense to the words by

[1] Aristotelian Society, Supplementary Volume XXIII, pp. 173-4.

referring to features of works of art recognizable independent of the feelings they tend to evoke'.

The language of criticism is of a very curious kind, and if the critic seems to 'argue' he is not doing so in any usual sense. Isenberg, who writes very interestingly on this topic, refers[1] to a criticism of a work of El Greco which includes the following: 'Like the contour of a violently rising and falling wave is the outline of the four illuminated figures in the foreground: steeply upwards and downwards about the grey monk on the left, in mutually inclined curves about the yellow of the two saints, and again steeply upwards and downwards about . . . the priest on the right. . . .' This kind of thing, Isenberg says, has the same quality ('a steeply rising and falling curve') as could be found in any of a hundred lines one could draw on a board in three minutes. 'It could not be the critic's purpose to inform us of the presence of a quality as obvious as this. It seems reasonable to suppose that the critic is thinking of another quality, no idea of which is transmitted to us by his language, which he *sees* and which by his use of language he *gets us to see*. This quality is, of course, a wave-like contour. Any object which has this quality will have a wave-like contour; but it is not true that any object which has a wave-like contour will have this quality.' To put this in another way (not Isenberg's), the aesthetic quality to which the critic is referring, something which has to be aesthetically perceived to be known, is an aesthetic 'emergent'; emergent from forms which can be described in matter-of-fact non-aesthetic language. In the above case ('mutually inclined curves') the words refer to the matter-of-fact structural pattern, the perception of which is the condition for the experience of the emergent aesthetic quality. Isenberg puts it as follows: 'It seems that the critic's *meaning* is "filled in", "rounded out", or "completed" by the act of [aesthetic] perception, which is performed not to judge the truth of his description but in a certain sense to *understand* it. And if communication is a process by which a mental process is transmitted by symbols from one person to another, then we can say that it is a function of criticism to bring about communication at the level of the senses; that is, to induce a sameness of vision, of experienced content.' But 'there is a contrast, therefore, between critical communication and what I may call normal or ordinary communication. In ordinary communication, symbols tend to acquire a footing rela-

[1] Elton, *op. cit.*, p. 138 *et seq.*

tively independent of sense perception'. They have a common, neutral meaning. But the words used in criticism can only be understood by going to that which they suggest. It is a little—though not exactly—like describing the expression on a friend's face; after some attempts you may have to say 'You would have to have seen him to understand what he looked like. Unless you know him, I can't adequately convey my meaning'.

Two other writers reinforce this. In the same (Elton) volume, Margaret Macdonald suggested that 'the task of the critic resembles those of the actor and executant rather than those of the scientist and logician'.[1] She supplements this by saying[2] that 'to justify a verdict is not to give general criteria as "reasons", but to "convey" the work as a pianist might "show" the value of a sonata by playing it'. (Yes, but the critic does have to use words of some general import, as the pianist does not.) John Holloway says: ' "His work is good because harmonious", for example, is not an inference like "this object is sweet because rosy and apple-like". It is not an inference from observed to unobserved and indeed not an inference at all. The value-judgment finds its proof directly in the object; but what validates it can be seen only by a sensitive observer whose attention is properly directed.'[3]

§8   *The convergence of inadequate language—and the aesthetic 'leap'*

In aesthetics and criticism alike we might consider an inversion of Spinoza's dictum: *Omnis determinatio est negatio*, saying instead, *Omnis negatio est determinatio*. Thinking is aesthetics and criticism we use in succession a number of concepts and images provisionally, none of which are quite right. We say, 'That, but no, not quite that', 'this instead, but not quite that either . . .'.

Take aesthetics first. In aesthetics we are concerned with the nature of art in general. But since each work of art is unique, and its concrete character is only known in experience, no general concepts which we formulate will quite fit. What we seem to be doing is to consider a number of them in turn, and say, 'That is getting some way towards it, but it won't do'—and so on, moving on towards a more illuminated understanding of art itself, art which is seen to have a structure because we have been trying to think discursively in concepts about it, none of which, admittedly, are quite right. If such tentative thinking had not taken place, we

---

[1] Elton, *op. cit.*, p. 127.   [2] *ibid.*, p. 129.
[3] Aristotelian Society, *op. cit.*, p. 175.

should have no intelligent understanding whatever of the nature of what we apprehend in art. (I am *not*, of course, saying that without such philosophical thinking we should have no discrimination of art.)

Consider, for example, Susanne Langer's essay on 'Expressiveness' in her *Problems of Art*. She is expounding the idea of form. What does she do? She considers 'form' in various senses, none of which are just what she wants. There are the ordinary classifications of 'forms' within art—the sonnet, the ballad, the sonata... but these, though they have to do with art, do not tell us anything of the inner form of art. She then speaks of shape, which is an obvious example of form and gives an inkling of what artistic form might be, but is not, of course, adequate. She then moves to structure in the sense of logical form, the formulation of relationships, taking as examples maps on a flat surface projected from a sphere. She considers the opposite but corresponding forms of the two hands, and of mirror images, the forms of the dissolving mushroom of an atom-bomb explosion, of a flowing river. From these she works towards the conception of artistic form as form which is not discursively communicable or in the strict sense logically thinkable, yet can be known in experience. Genuine knowledge, she rightly says, is considerably wider than the range of our discourse. And yet—and this is the point I would make here—our conceptual discourse, though to some degree inept, is necessary in order that our minds may be prepared to come to understand the nature of form which is experienced in art. Without the half-negative, half-positive approaches of thought, we should have no intellectual understanding at all—even understanding of the reasons why we cannot adequately formulate the concept of artistic form. The concepts 'have their day and cease to be', but the form of art is more than they. Yet the mind's understanding could not have been achieved if it had not been for the mind's imperfect negated concept.

The same kind of thing is true, though it functions in a different way, of the work of the critic. He (though as we have said, he assumes some general categories) is more directly concerned with the particular ideas and canons, and with their bearing on this or that work. In criticism the language, not so much of pure concepts but of metaphor and analogy and suggestion, moves towards illumination of the work. As before, the language is never exactly right; it is (as we say) suggestive. The words are like the rungs of

B

a ladder on which we climb in order to look through an upper window into a room which belongs to a dimension which is other than that of our common existence. The ladder can be kicked away when we reach the right level; yet it was necessary to reach that level. Or—to use another image; from inadequate indispensable language we make a leap towards aesthetic illumination. Less metaphorically, the language, having done its work, can be forgotten. Nevertheless forgetting is not eliminating: it did its work, which was not to produce any mirror image or duplicate of the work of art, but to lead us towards it in a new experience.

This can be related to some further very interesting remarks of Isenberg and to others by William Righter. Speaking[1] of vagueness and precision in relation to critical statements, Isenberg writes: 'For the last twenty or thirty years the right thing to say about the metaphysical poets is this: "They think with their senses and feel with their brains." One hardly knows how to verify such a dictum: as a psychological observation it is exeedingly obscure. But it does not follow that it is not acute criticism; for it increases our awareness of the difference between Tennyson and Donne. Many words—like "subtlety", "variety", "complexity", "intensity"—which in ordinary communication are the vaguest in the language, have been used to convey sharp critical perceptions. And many expressions which have clear independent meaning are vague and fuzzy when taken in relation to the content of a work of art.'

William Righter makes the same point in his book *Logic and Criticism* (Routledge, 1963). He also argues that 'reasons', in the logical sense, don't support judgments about art at all; rather they explain them, showing what we mean in an aesthetic judgment. When we argue about aesthetic matters 'we are not moving from hypothesis to conclusion or in any other formally logical way, but we show, point, compare, draw attention to, and generally try to make others see what it is that we mean by offering alternative descriptions or suggesting different ways of looking at a particular work' (p. 24). 'Full justification' for an aesthetic judgment (a very dubious idea) is seldom asked for and, in strictness, could never be given; to 'justify', or to follow through justification, we have to go and look. And the relative failure of critical concepts to take on logical character indicates a different picture of critical language, 'a language made up of the many things which can

[1] Elton, *op. cit.*, p. 141.

relate to a work of literature, and where method consists more in a developed sensibility to the weight of different kinds of language and of their conflicting claims on our attention.' The autonomy of criticism 'consists not in its possession of a discipline of its own, but in its preserving of this open character, in its refusal to be assimilated into any of the other studies which make claims upon it' (p. 116). And because of all this, what is called 'vague' and what is called 'exact' have different meanings in criticism, and in common sense or logic or science. We may say of an elusive characterizaton that it strikes the 'exact' note. Righter refers to Wittgenstein, who pointed out that the instruction 'stand roughly here' may work out perfectly for the particular circumstance. The 'exact' of normal argument may have no serious role in criticism—though criticism has its own goals and 'can carry them out with that definitiveness, that perfect suiting of means to ends that we can only call "exact". "The vague word has its precise use."' (All p. 118.)

We may perhaps add one more comment by saying that in criticism vague language is effective because it gathers together, without trying to separate them conceptually, a number of significant ideas which converge all at once. We saw how, in aesthetic philosophizing, we try to get clearer by asserting, then discarding, this idea, then that. In the effectively vague language of criticism there is no conscious attempt to do this. Rather the process is telescoped or fused. We may then get the force of a number of suggestions gathered into a few phrases none of which has precise, but all of which together may have a cumulative fused meaning. Clear, definite language is wrong because it is far too abstractly simple, too cut-and-dried. The advantage of a clear concept is that you can rest in it. But when you are talking about art you can never rest, or stop, in a concept. The value of vague suggestive writing is that it leads us on to the experience, and not only leads us on to the experience, but contributes to the illumination of the experience by the cumulative effect of a criss-crossing of ideas in our freshly attentive minds.

§9 *Conclusion: The Opposite Tensions of Criticism and Aesthetics*
To conclude, the language of criticism, and the language of aesthetics, although both have to employ general words and ideas, are different, yet complementary. The critic works within general aesthetic categories, but most of his emphasis is upon a skilful

fusing of many kinds of concepts, images and metaphors in a way which is relevant to the particular work and which draws us into seeing it with greater aesthetic penetration. The aesthetician goes back, through criticism, to attempted universalization or generalization. Like the critic, he is a servant of two disciplines pulling in different directions. For the critic, the pull is towards the work, and this being so, he may forget his linkage with the ideas which lie beyond the work. For the aesthetician, the pull is towards the general, and *he* may forget his linkage with the critic and ultimately with the experience of individual works of art. If the critic entirely repudiates, in word and deed, his linkage with what is beyond the work—general aesthetic categories and all the thoughts, images, reference to different aspects of culture which belong to life beyond art—he will have to stop talking altogether. He will be wordless. If the philosopher forgets his linkage with the basic fact which is the aesthetic experience of art, he will indeed not be wordless, but his words will be empty—as so much *a priori* aesthetics of the past has been.

PART II

THE NATURE OF THE AESTHETIC: FROM 'EXPRESSION' TO 'EMBODIMENT'

CHAPTER II

EXPRESSION, SENSA, AND FEELINGS

CHAPTER II

EXPRESSION, SENSA, AND FEELINGS

§1 *Introduction*

One of the central problems of this book will be how the experience, meaning and knowledge of life outside the arts influences, 'enters', 'gets into' art and is at the same time transformed by the aesthetic into a new dimension. The general problem, in one form or another, is as old as art and the thinking about art; most aesthetic theories—imitationism, formalism, expressionism—have been attempts to answer it. They tend to fail by leaning over too much in one of two directions—towards making art a mirror of life, or towards isolating it from life-influences outside art. The problem of trying to achieve an understanding of art which does justice to both sides, presents itself in many forms. It can be, as we have seen a problem of language, or of the character of 'representative' and 'abstract' arts and their relationship, of the nature of artistic 'meaning', 'symbols', 'truth', 'reality', 'knowledge'.

In order to tackle these problems, very complex and not often attended to by British philosophers, we have to try at the outset to construct a basic working hypothesis of the aesthetic in art which is sufficiently clear in itself and which can be tested by its application to the various questions mentioned. The meaning, as well as the degree of truth of the hypothesis can only emerge gradually as the discussion goes on. The test will be whether the hypothesis is plausible and coherent in itself, and whether it can throw light on, help us to understand better, some of the perennial puzzles. The best general hypothesis in aesthetics will be one which is internally coherent and sufficiently comprehensively based on knowledge and experience of a wide range of the different arts, and which throws most light on the many-sided problems tested throughout this wide range. Some philosophers (e.g. Professor Morris Weitz and others) have doubted the possibility of definitions and general hypotheses of art, holding that the so-called general theories of aesthetic are but passing reflections of their time, historical reactions to this or that one-sided view (either of the theory of art or its practice), and are themselves similarly relative and one-sided. There is certainly some basis for this relativism—and I have already advocated a conservative open-endedness. But the charge of historical relativism can be levelled at all philosophical thinking

B*

whatever. I do not think we should let it dismay us or inhibit at least the resolute search for more permanent truth.

One of the most prevalent and influential theories of the modern era is that the key to understanding art is *expression*. This theory has its historical setting; it is, by and large, a 'romantic' or post-romantic view—and some of its forms may be as evanescent as some of the other theories of art. Nevertheless in its serious working out it properly claims to be *true* theory of art. I do not myself think, for reasons which I shall state very fully, that it is an adequate view. Expression is certainly an important element in some, perhaps all art, but it is not sufficient to differentiate it. I believe it needs to be transcended in a more comprehensive idea, the idea of *embodiment*. For this reason I have called this *Part* "From "expression" to embodiment" '.

The *Part* is a continuous argument. Chapter II will deal generally with the idea of 'expression' in life and art, including some discussion on the relation of sensa and feelings, necessary to the understanding of expression as 'objectified feeling'. Chapter III will work towards a constructive theory arising in part out of a critical examination of some of Susanne Langer's later work, which treats art as a form expressive of feeling, and as—up to a point at least—a symbol. Chapter IV will discuss (again with many references to Mrs Langer) the relation of expression to something else, 'creative embodiment', and will maintain that 'creative embodiment' is an emergent not reducible to that from which it emerges.

§2 *'Expression' in life and art*

I shall, then, be exploring in these three chapters the uses of the word 'expression' in their aesthetic contexts. And since traces and influences (or more) of non-aesthetic uses can be discerned in the aesthetic use and may invade thinking in aesthetics, it is important to start by looking, quite briefly, at some of these extra-aesthetic uses, beginning with the very crudest ones.

The most literal sense of 'expression' is of squeezing or pressing out water (or other liquid) from a cloth or sponge, where in squeezing, the water, exactly the same water, flows forth. Through the use of metaphor and analogy the same image often underlies popular psychological talk. We speak of the discharge or expression of emotion in behaviour (as if through a pipe, from inside to outside). We talk of 'expression' as the 'relief' of feelings by talk or action as if it were like opening a boil to relieve the pus. We speak of a person's behaviour as being a 'symptom' of his internal state, as though the outer were some sort of expressive revelation of the inner.

This is no place to criticize in detail the limits of the analogy—as though feelings were entirely internal and through expression are 'got out'. We know that although there may be (and I think certainly is, in spite of certain contemporary philosophers) some sense in distinguishing feelings as internal from behaviour as external, what is 'outside' (say in emotional behaviour) is not sharply separated from what is 'inside'; emotions and feelings are psycho-physical. And we know, of course, that behaviour which is 'outside' is not exactly the same as what is felt 'inside'—as the water which is expelled is the same water. Again, expressive behaviour changes feeling. And so on. It is obvious that the analogy between the merely physical and the psycho-physical events breaks down very soon and that metaphors can mislead if their literal meaning obtrudes.

It can mislead in simple-minded—or not so simple-minded—thinking in aesthetics too. We may say, 'The artist expresses his emotions' in his work, or that 'he got his emotions out' in that painting. We say that making works of art can be a 'relieving' process. Or we say that artistic expression reveals feelings. To quote a very sophisticated writer indeed, R. G. Collingwood: 'When a man is said to express emotion, what is being said about him comes to this. At first, he is conscious of having an emotion, but not conscious of what that emotion is: "I feel . . . I don't know what I feel." From this . . . he extricates himself by doing something which we call expressing himself.' And later, 'The act of expressing is therefore an exploration of his own emotions. He is trying to find out what these emotions are.'[1] Again, we say the *work* is 'expressive' because we think that feelings or emotions are somehow articulated in the work. We go further: we say that through their articulation in the work we as spectators become aware of the artist's emotion. So (in this language) the artist is expressing, the work is expressive, and we in turn become aware of what the artist was experiencing, through the work. In all this there is a very distinct image of something which is substantially the same, flowing from inside to outside and so ultimately reaching us. Sophisticated writing (and of course Collingwood himself)

[1] *Principles of Art*, pp. 109 and 111.

does not put it in this crude way—and there is much more to be said about aesthetic expression than this; yet the influence of the analogy is there.

Apart from the analogy, there is something queer about Collingwood's idea of expression of emotion, and of art as expression of emotion. A man is said to be having an emotion, not to be conscious of what that emotion is, but to be able to discover this by 'expressing himself'. But how, if he does not know what his emotion is or was before it is expressed, can he be said to be expressing that emotion and know that he is expressing it? After expressing he knows something, but he cannot know that it is an expression of a particular emotion which, by definition, he could not know before expression. 'Expression' for Collingwood seems to be a new discovery, and this is quite comprehensible: what is not comprehensible is that if it is a new discovery, it can be known to be an expression of an emotion which existed before expression. For if this were known, it would not be a discovery, and if the previous emotion is not known, it cannot be confidently affirmed to an expression of that emotion. There is contradiction here—which suggests that we should be very cautious in saying that by means of expression we discover what our emotions are or were. And I shall go on to argue that if we are thinking of artistic expression, as Collingwood is, it is very misleading to say that art is an exploration of one's own emotions.

I do not mean that there is nothing in what Collingwood says, or that he is talking nonsense. It is up to a point true that expressing reveals emotion and the character of an emotion, both in life and in art. Take the case of a life-emotion, say, jealousy. A person may be jealous without being aware of it: 'I feel . . . I don't know what I feel.' Then by some sudden impulsive action—a spiteful gesture, word or action, the 'expression'—he may become aware, perhaps with horror: 'I'm jealous!' Again, in art, an artist might draw black jagged lines which express and reveal feelings of which he was not aware or fully aware. But what is not quite accurate—and in the case of art dangerously *in*accurate—is the suggestion that what is discovered in or after the expressive act is *what was there all the time*. ('He is trying to find out what these emotions are.') He couldn't know that it was, though he might 'feel' it. In the case of the jealousy we have no right to assume that the revelation of jealousy in doing the spiteful act, say of hurting a rival, is the same as what was felt before doing the act in the external world. The very horror which

we are supposing our own act to evoke shows that we did not feel
or know exactly the jealousy we now know. The expression is not
strictly a revelation of what we 'felt all the time'. The expression
in fact changes something, brings something new into being which
is known for the first time and actually comes into being for the
first time. So expressing is not just an 'exploration' of one's own
emotions but produces a new situation.

In the case of the artistic expression the jagged line, and the
feeling of jagged line, is again a new thing. Certainly the drawing
of the jagged line may express some feeling that is there already (as
the jealous act similarly does). But the feeling-of-the-jagged-line
is a new event, and we have no right to assume that it 'expresses'
exactly what the artist felt before he began to draw. (He in fact
probably now feels very different.) And it is highly questionable
to say that the function of *art* is to explore and reveal 'the artist's
emotions'.

The above uses of 'expression' all refer to expression of feeling
or emotion in ordinary behaviour or artistic activity, and my suggestion is that they are tinged with the 'in-out' metaphor. But
feelings and emotions are not the only things we can be said to
express; the content of 'expression' can be broader; it can include
images and ideas, and sometimes very complex organizations of
them. Or we can be said to express 'experience'—not necessarily
highly emotional experience. A good many years ago Lascelles
Abercrombie wrote that 'the moment of imaginative experience
which possesses our minds the instant the poem is finished, possessed the poet's mind the instant the poem began'. The inspiration of the poem is that which 'the verbal art exists to convey'.[1]
And Harold Osborne, expounding the expressionist theory of art
(with which he does not agree) writes[2] 'The underlying theory (of
art as expression) is, in its baldest form, that the artist lives
through a certain experience; he then makes an artifact which in
some way embodies that experience; and through appreciative
contemplation of this artifact other men are able to duplicate in
their own minds the experience of the artist. What is conveyed
to them is . . . an experience of their own as similar as possible to
the artist's experience in all its aspects. . . .' Note the emphasis
here on duplication: first some sort of duplication through the
artifact, of an experience which occurred before the artifact, and

---

[1] *The Theory of Poetry*, p. 58. Cf. my *A Study in Aesthetics*, pp. 198–201.
[2] *Aesthetics and Criticism*, p. 143.

secondly, the duplication by means of the artifact of the artist's experience in the mind of the person who sees the artifact.

The content of this expression is a wide one, 'experience'. But most of the emphasis in the theory of art as expression is upon feelings and emotions: as such it has come under severe criticism.

Hospers sums up much of it in a paper to the Aristotelian Society in 1946.[1] He points out, for instance, that expression of emotion is not necessarily involved in art-making and that some artists—e.g. Edgar Allen Poe and T. S. Eliot—explicitly deny that artistic expression involves emotion. Again, emotional turmoil does not necessarily produce good art. As Osborne says: 'All the characteristic phenomena of inspiration are described in indistinguishable terms by bad and good artists alike. Nor has the most penetrating psychological investigation succeeded in detecting any general differences between the mental processes which accompany the creation of a masterpiece and the inspirations of a third-rate botcher.'[2] It is the work which we judge, and there is no inference from the work to the psychological processes which go to the making of the work. The characters which the work seems to have are aesthetically independent of the feelings of the artist. As Hospers says: if we know that Mozart was not feeling joy when he wrote a rondo, we would not retract our judgment that the rondo is joyful music.

This remark is a bridge to a further development of the idea of expression. There seems to be something very peculiar about the feeling or emotion which is said to be expressed in a work. Being expressed, it acquires a character which it did not have as a psychological event. It is often said that, for instance, the alleged 'sadness' of a piece of music is very different from the sadness which we experience in real life. If sadness is a permissible word (which we shall discuss later) it is sadness in some special sense 'enjoyed'. These and similar phenomena lead us on to look more carefully at what could be meant by the 'objectification' of feeling in expression: it has long and strong roots in the romantic movement, and cannot be dismissed lightly. So let us now consider the claim of expression to objectify feeling, with the accompanying claim that feeling in being objectified is in some ways changed, standing on its own right so that it is feeling in a special sense, not to be identified with the psychological feelings which existed

[1] 'The Concept of Artistic Expression', by John Hospers, *Proceedings of the Aristotliean Society*, 1954–55, pp. 313 *et seq.*   [2] *Op. cit.*, p. 161.

before the making or during the making. There is, it is said, a communication of something new, fused into the work itself.

§3 'Feeling objectified' (Santayana)

A step towards this—but only a step, I think—is Santayana's. In a familiar passage he writes:[1] 'In all expression we may thus distinguish two terms: the first is the object actually presented, the word, the image, the expressive thing; the second is the object suggested, the further thought, emotion or image evoked, the thing expressed.' And 'the expression depends on the union of the two terms'. They must, as Santayana says, 'lie together in the mind'. 'Not until I confound the impressions, and suffuse the symbols themselves with the emotions they arouse, and find joy and sweetness in the very words I hear, will the expressiveness constitute a beauty.' It is important to notice that this 'fusion' and 'confounding' is aesthetic confusion and aesthetic confounding; it is not an analytic or intellectual confusion (as Hospers seems mistakenly to hint in the article quoted from).

Santayana's phrase, extracted from its context: 'find joy and sweetness in the very words I hear' expresses a true insight into the nature of poetry. But it is, I suggest, inconsistent with all the rest. The postulated two-term basis—of the object presented, and the object suggested—does not lead to the conclusion. Taking the stock example of music which is called (or miscalled) 'sad', it does not appear to be true that there is a projection of subjective feeling, fused, or 'suffused', into the music (elsewhere described by Santayana generally as 'pleasure objectified'), nor 'confounded' with it, nor that the two things 'lie together in the mind'—though admittedly the words 'suffused', 'union' and 'confound' are vague. The so-called 'sadness' of music is something quite new, which is not just an existing feeling of sadness projected and fused in the music. Sadness is a psychological life-condition and, although we certainly do apply the word to music, it is not that kind of sadness which belongs to music; life-sadness, indeed, with all its extra-musical implications, is—at least in part—alien to the enjoyment of pure music. The word 'sad' may have *some* sort of relevance (which we shall discuss very fully later),[2] but it does not exactly fit even if there be some underground connection with life-sadness. The 'sadness' of the music is not like sadness in any other sense; it is a new character, a concrete character of the music

[1] All from *The Sense of Beauty*, pp. 147-9.   [2] Below, Chapters IX-X.

itself, a musical character. It is important to insist that it is a *concrete* character, in view of the fact that there is a school of thought which, admitting that it is not straight ordinary life-sadness which gets into the music, argues that it is some sort of extracted, or abstracted 'essence' of sadness which gets in. This, however, will not do, for even the most abstract definition of life-sadness is life-bound—there still remains the notion of a transfer of life-feeling into art, and the characteristic newness of the art-content is being denied. Whatever may be the relation between what we apprehend in music (or other art) and the life-feelings outside it, the character of what we apprehend belongs immediately to the art: in Santayana's phrase, we must find 'joy and sweetness in *the very words*' (or other sounds) we hear. This is here necessarily stated in a dogmatic way: I hope to defend it in what follows.

§4   *Sensa, 'aesthetic surface', and feelings*

Since I myself a great many years ago put forward a 'two-term' theory (in *A Study in Aesthetics*, 1931), which has been ably and at length criticized by Vincent Tomas in an article 'The Concept of Expression in Art'[1], I must now spend a little time looking at the defects of this 'two-term' assumption. I am glad to accept Tomas' substantial criticisms and had already, before seeing Tomas' article, corrected in a later book, *Ways of Knowledge and Experience*,[2] some epistemological errors of the earlier work. An idea of the distinctions which are necessary can be made plain by a few quotations.

It would seem, says Tomas, that 'the concept of expression is a concept of something such that if, for a contemplator C, A expresses B, B is presented "in" A, though A is something given, and B is not given, but suggested or evoked. The problem is to explain how this is possible. The central problem of the aesthetic attitude, Bosanquet said, is "how a feeling can be got into an object".[3] As Reid puts it (his italics), '*How* do perceived characters come to *appear* to possess, for aesthetic imagination, qualities which as bare perceived facts they do not possess? How does body, a non-mental object, come to "embody" or "express", for our aesthetic imagination, values which it does not literally contain? Why should

---

[1] Reprinted in Joseph Margolis, *Philosophy looks at the Arts*, pp. 30–44.
[2] Part I, pp. 35–100, esp. pp. 53–6.
[3] *Three Lectures on Aesthetic*, p. 74.

colours and shapes and patterns, sounds and harmonies and rhythms, come to *mean* so very much more than they *are*?'[1] This problem, to which Santayana, Reid, and others have devoted so much attention and ingenuity, is, I submit, a pseudo-problem. It presupposes something false, namely, that (Reid's italics) 'The embodiment of value in the aesthetic object is of such a nature that the value "embodied" in the perceived object or "body" is *not literally* situated in the "body". The "joy" expressed in the music is not literally in the succession of sounds.'[2] To see why this is false, let us ask what exactly are the two terms of aesthetic expression: 'the object actually presented . . . the expressive thing', on the one hand, and 'the object suggested . . . the thing expressed', on the other.[3]

One thing is clear at once—and of course I agree with Tomas— namely that the first term is *not* a physical thing or event. It is the object-as-experienced, that which appears to us, which is presented in aesthetic contemplation. We may, if we like, call this the *phenomenal* object. The second term is what is suggested by the phenomenal object, often called the 'feeling import'. 'On this view, the first term in the sad music we hear is a pattern of sounds, *devoid of feeling import*; and the second term is its sad-feeling import, *devoid of sensuous embodiment*.'[4]

Now it is clear also that this distinction can be made only by an effort of abstraction. 'The idea of what Reid refers to as "bare perceived facts" is, as Collingwood says, "the product of a process of sterilization".'[5] I agree; this is quite right: it *is* a process of sterilization. It is an account which represents experience as having sterilized out of its data what has sometimes been called a 'tertiary' quality of affective value or affective meaningfulness. (The term used by Tomas and many others is 'feeling import'. I shall hardly be able to avoid using this term at present though I have some doubts about it.[6]) And I fully admit that this representation is wrong, is a misrepresentation of ordinary experience as it naturally occurs. But all this can be said without denying that it may be entirely legitimate to affirm that the aesthetic datum, un-'sterilized', single and indivisible as *aesthetically* experienced, has two aspects, conceptually distinguishable, derived from two distinguishable but not sharply divided sources, one of them what we call broadly

[1] *A Study in Aesthetics*, pp. 62–3.   [2] *ibid.*, p. 60.
[3] Tomas, *op. cit.*, p. 33.   [4] *Op. cit.*, p. 34.
[5] *The Principles of Art*, p. 163.   [6] See below, pp. 192–4.

speaking the senses (though there is much more than sensation in it)—the colours, shapes, sounds, rhythms and patterns of them which are, in part, the materials of art—and the other coming from 'inner' and more 'mental' sources—ideas, images, feelings and emotions, dispositions to feelings and emotions, joy, sorrow, mental tension, apprehension, longing, frustration, happy fulfilment, peace. . . . This is a motley list and meant to be so. And it is difficult to make this rough dual classification without being unjustly thought to be drawing far too sharp a line between 'sensation' and the 'mental'. My defence for talking in this way is to say that I am of course acutely aware of the interplay between the two in the psychophysical, but that we all, unless we are extreme behaviourists, first make these distinctions, and that they are necessary now.

I was saying that the single indivisible aesthetic datum has two conceptually distinguishable aspects derived from, roughly, these two sources. It is of the greatest importance to emphasize that the aspects, and their derivation, are apprehended only when we are in a sophisticated, analytic, intellectual mood. In *aesthetic* experience itself (as distinct from reflection on it, even immediately afterwards) the values or meanings of what we apprehend are quite indistinguishable from what is given in sensation. In spite of the shortcomings which Mr Tomas rightly castigates, I think I have never failed to recognize this, and could substantiate it by many quotations. One might be: 'In aesthetic experience we perceive meaning as invading, pervading, as inherent in, as indwelling in . . . the texture and pattern of the work of art. The poetic meaning *belongs* to the spoken poem; the musical meaning with all its vitality and movement, its unfolding and development, *belongs* to the actual music which we hear.'[1] The 'mistake' to which I confess is not a failure here, but rather a failure to see clearly enough that in quite ordinary, and not necessarily aesthetic, experience, sensa and affective meanings are indistinguishable too. Illegitimately importing the habit of philosophical analysis, I assumed that in ordinary perceptual experience there are (as Tomas quotes from me) 'bare perceived facts' stripped of all 'feeling import'. Assuming that, I then had to try to show how 'feelings' could—sometimes at least—'get into' the supposed bare perceived facts: and I did it (in this one respect like Santayana) by an imputation theory, of fusion into the bare datum of an

[1] *Ways of Knowledge and Experience*, p. 55.

imported 'feeling'. This is wrong because it puts the cart before the horse. What we start with (in all probability) is what we can only describe, if we have to use words, as 'perceptual facts-charged-with-affective-meaning'—complex as verbally described, but not in typical immediate perception, discerned as complex. It is only upon subsequent sophisticated reflection that we discern the complexity, can name it as having two aspects, and can then, if we are so inclined, proceed to trace the sources of the two aspects, and to explain why, when we go forward to a new sophisticated look at the perceptual datum, we use such words as 'sense' aspect and 'affective meaning' aspect. This, I think, is the sound order: we start with the experientially indivisible; upon reflection find it complex. To sum it up: my previous order was wrong because I started from the sophisticated end, thought mistakenly that it was the naïve end, and then had artificially to reconstruct the naïve (and the aesthetic) position by the imputation and fusion theory, the fusion of what were, in fact, two abstractions. But there is, indeed, no need to do the fusing, for the indivisibility of the two intellectually distinguishable aspects was given at the very start.

(I do not apologize for these autobiographical reminiscences since their subject-matter is basic to aesthetics.)

Santayana's (and the earlier Reid's) theories are unsatisfactory, then, in that they have to talk of 'feeling' (the abstracted feeling) as objectified through projection and imputation and fusion, in relation to the supposed bare perceived object. Collingwood and Tomas (the latter with the aid of Charles Hartshorne) are right in attacks they make on this kind of theory, for the reasons I have mentioned.

§5 Aiken: are 'surface' and 'feeling-import' divisible?

The motive behind all this discussion is the desire to find a firm basis for a sensible theory of aesthetics. Such a theory, as I said earlier, is one which explains and relates a variety of aesthetic phenomena systematically, in a coherent and comprehensive way, and which is confirmed by aesthetic testing. I feel sure that a theoretic account of the aesthetic object as indivisible (but implicitly complex) is the true one. But this account can only be validated on the one hand (i) by examining and reporting with the utmost care aesthetic experience itself, and (ii) (as has just been said) by showing the report of it to be a key idea in the systematic explanation of other aesthetic phenomena. The first is a direct appeal; the second can only be worked out properly on a large scale.

It is by these methods only that one can meet a contentious claim of H. D. Aiken, criticized by Tomas in the last part of his paper.[1] The point at issue is Aiken's observation that when several, people 'perceive the same, or closely similar, sensory surfaces these do not succeed in evoking in each of them the same degree or even the same kind of emotional feeling'. I.e., the 'surface' is the same, and the felt import different. Tomas replies to this in Hartshorne's words: 'the assumption that persons whose sense of the meaning of a piece of music differs can yet have the very same sense of perception of sounds is, so far as I know, devoid of all evidence'.

Put in *that* way, it would be hard, perhaps impossible, to find clear evidence *either* that different people with different 'senses of the meaning' of a piece of music are having 'the very same' perception of sounds *or* that they are having different ones. But put in another way, I do not see that 'evidence' need be so difficult to find, and being found it should enable us to decide on an issue which is absolutely crucial for aesthetics.

One need not ask *two* (or more) people listening to, say, a piece of music with a brisk tempo whether what they are having is the very same perception with a different 'feeling import'—or whether what they actually hear is different. The question here is difficult or impossible to decide or answer because experiences of different people cannot be directly and objectively examined and compared. But I can ask *myself* the question whether the *same* pattern of sounds with the same tempo sounds differently to me at *different* times when my subjective feelings are different. Or it might be that my experiences in between an earlier and a late hearing, including what has been happening in my musical education, have made a difference.

This is the first test mentioned as (i) on p. 51 above, the careful examination of aesthetic experience. Personally I have not the slightest doubt that the same pattern of sounds with the same tempo *does* 'sound' and 'feel' different at different times, and that this is borne out by common (aesthetic) experience. It is, I would say, just a familiar fact of developing artistic appreciation that things 'sound' and 'look' different as we progress. And this is

[1] *Op. cit.*, pp. 41–3. Also Henry D. Aiken, 'Art as Expression and Surface', *The Journal of Aesthetics and Art Criticism*, December 1945, p. 91.

entirely in accord with the general view that in our experience of art what is perceived and 'affective import' are, aesthetically speaking, indivisibly one, or conceptually distinguishable aspects of an aesthetically indivisible unity. This is borne out by the findings of Gestalt psychology.

Then ((ii) above) we can ask whether this is not an illuminating key-idea for a systematic theory of aesthetics, and a better one than any known alternative hypothesis. I believe it is so and shall try to show it.

CHAPTER III

SUSANNE LANGER, AND BEYOND

CHAPTER III

SUSANNE LANGER, AND BEYOND

§1   *Art as form expressive of feeling: Mrs Langer's views*

Mrs Susanne Langer has, through many years, developed her own views of art as expression, perhaps further and more subtly than any other living writer; for this reason alone they deserve special attention. There is a further reason why I shall give them a good deal of space in a book intended to be constructive rather than critical. It is that I have learned much from her: in some ways my own position is very close to hers: and she has been kind enough more than once to suggest some influence of my earlier writings upon her own earlier ones. On the other hand there are important differences: consideration of these differences will be one of the best ways of leading towards a positive thesis.

Mrs Langer's best known works are perhaps her earlier book *Philosophy in a New Key*, and her later *Feeling and Form*. It what follows I shall quote from and consider parts of a volume of her Essays, *Problems of Art*, as well as Volume I of her current work *Mind: an Essay on Human Feeling*.

'The work of art,' she says[1] 'is an expressive form created for our perception through sense or imagination, and what it expresses is human feeling. The word "feeling" must be taken here in its broadest sense, meaning *everything that can be felt*, from physical sensation, pain and comfort, excitement and repose, to the most complex emotions, intellectual tensions, or the steady feeling tones of a conscious human life.' Again, works of art are 'images of the forms of feeling. . . . The art symbol sets forth in symbolic projection how vital and emotional and intellectual tensions appear, i.e. how they feel.'[2]

A work of art is an expressive *form*. The word 'form' needs consideration. It has many meanings, all legitimate in different circumstances. There are set forms, like the sonnet form in poetry or the sonata in music; there is form which means simply shape, or something like it. But more important is the abstract sense of form, meaning 'structure, articulation, a whole resulting from the relation of mutually dependent factors, or more precisely, the way

[1] *Problems of Art*, p. 15.
[2] *Mind: An Essay on Human Feeling* (hereafter referred to as *Mind*), p. xix.

that whole is put together'.[1] It is this sense, sometimes called 'logical form', which is involved in Mrs Langer's idea of the expression that characterizes art.

Further—and this is vital—artistic forms 'are not abstractable from the works that exhibit them. We may abstract a shape from an object that has this shape, by disregarding colour, weight and texture, even size; but to the total effect that is an artistic form, the colour matters, the thickness of lines matters, and the appearance of texture and weight. . . . Form, the sense in which artists speak of "significant form", or "expressive form", is not an abstracted structure, but an apparition; and the vital products of sense and emotion that a good work of art expresses seem to the beholder to be directly contained in it, not symbolized but really presented. The congruence is so striking that symbol and meaning appeal as one reality.'[2]

It is *what*-is-felt by the artist which is expressed. But art, as Mrs Langer says repeatedly, is not merely expression of private personal feeling; it is an expression of 'the *life* of feeling, not the feelings an artist happens to have'.[3] The expression is 'an "expression" in the logical sense, presenting the fabric of sensibility, emotion, and the strains of more concerted cerebration for our impersonal cognition—this is, in abstracto'.[4] Nor is this expressiveness limited to pictures, poems, or other compositions that make a reference to human beings. A wholly non-representational design, a building or a pot, can be as expressive as a love sonnet or a religious picture. 'It has an import which is, I think, a wordlessly presented conception of *what life feels like*.'[5] 'Felt life' is 'objectified in the work, made amenable to our understanding. In this way and in no other essential way a work of art is a symbol.'[6]

§2 Critical Comments

Mrs Langer is certainly right in denying that art is merely expression of feeling as a symptom is expressive (though art may certainly sometimes indicate something about the artist). But the whole idea of art as the symbolic projection of the 'life' or 'form' of feeling, a 'conception presented to our understanding' of 'what life feels like'—is shot through and through with difficulties.

I must postpone fuller discussion of the nature of 'feeling' until later, but some preliminary observations are necessary. 'Feeling'

---

[1] *Problems of Art*, p. 15.   [2] *ibid.*, pp. 25–6.   [3] *ibid.*, p. 80.
[4] *ibid.*, p. 126.   [5] *ibid.*, p. 59.   [6] *ibid.*, p. 60.

is an ambiguous word. In its primary, most natural and ordinary
use it has a more purely subjective flavour than any other term,
indicating what includes a private and personal realm of direct,
immediate experience, strictly unshareable with others. The
meaning of the word 'feeling' can be indicated rather than defined;
we all know what it means in its primary sense, and if pressed, we
give examples. 'I feel—toothache, not-very-well, fighting-fit, peace-
ful, interested, excited, in love, baffled, carried away. . . .' My
feelings of these states or processes are, on the one hand, known
directly as something which is happening to me all the time I am
alive and conscious: I just *am* immediately aware of these things
in the sense of feeling them, 'living through' them. On the other
hand, although everyone knows what is being referred to (namely,
a subjective experience) when it is said 'I am feeling . . .', there is
no such thing as pure feeling existing by itself, without *content*
which is in some degree particular, concrete, specific. Feeling,
according to Mrs Langer, is 'whatever is felt'.

I agree that this is so—though I do not think the statement is
clear without further distinction. If I have a toothache or am in
love, *what* I feel is the feeling *of* toothache or being in love, certainly. But it is also true that *I am feeling* toothache or being in
love. It is clearer, therefore, to say, 'There is feeling, and always
feeling is feeling *of something* (of "whatever is felt")'. The verb 'to
feel' is logically, though not grammatically transitive: feeling (as
I have argued elsewhere, and shall return to below) is a form of
cognition, or has a cognitive aspect. As we cannot cognize without
cognizing something, we cannot feel without feeling something—
even if it is the obscurest organic or mental stirring.

Feeling then is, in its primary sense, a subjective word, referring
to immediate experience of our own essentially private states. But
although this is true, by itself it gives an entirely artificial picture
of the cognitive function and range of feeling. We can, by attending
to them, become in some degree introspectively aware of our in-
ward feelings of being alive in various ways. But this attention is a
very unnatural thing: the life of feeling takes place in a context
of ordinarily outward-looking consciousness of the world we live
in. We can, and do, immediately feel our own inner states, but,
since, normally, what we are attending to are objects and situations
(of all sorts) in the world about us, what we are feeling is (speaking
generally) the world-as-we-know-and-respond to it. Some of our
most clearly recognized and specific feelings are feelings of our

cognitive-conative responses to objective situations.[1] We feel sad
or disturbed about the loss or absence of a well-known friend,
disturbed in different ways about loss of an opportunity, angry
about insult or frustration, happy about being in love with X.
The feeling-*of* is specific to the total cognitive-conative-organic
relationship of the person to the particular situation in the world
in which he happens to be placed. Feeling isolated from such
feeling-*of* is as much a nonentity as any other cognition which is
not cognition of anything in particular.

Even mood-feelings are not real exceptions to this. One may
certainly feel well, energetic, tired, generally depressed, vaguely
anxious, without these mood-feelings being 'about' anything in
particular; they can be general, without specific objects in the
external world. But the feelings are all (at least) feelings *of* states
of body and mind. Moreover, if they do not have very specific
objects in the independent world, they tend to colour our outlook
on the world so that everything is tinged with the mood. Not only
this; they tend at least in some cases to select their own appropriate
objects. A mood of depression has a miserable way of attracting
one's mind, one's memory and attention, to all the gloomy things
that ever were; vague anxiety may become concrete by fastening
on the most trifling things.

If feelings are feelings-of, the character of any feeling is in this
sense concrete and particular; it can have no character except in
so far as it is the feeling-of—*this*. If so, no particular feeling or
complex of feelings can be 'projected' in any strict sense. Feelings
exist as particulars, and are what they are. Even if a purely personal feeling—say of anger or fear—is 'expressed' non-aesthetically,
symptomatically, the feeling itself is not, strictly speaking, projected. I may act angrily or fearfully, express and project and so
show my feelings to you in that sense. But it is you who see a
fearful or angry man, and I who have the particular feeling of
fear or anger of which only I can know the feeling directly. If you
are sympathetic and can imagine what I am afraid of or angry
about, you may feel some fear or anger too in sympathy: but this
is another particular feeling-event and a more complex one:
obviously *you* do not, feel *my* fear or anger. This is trite and
self-evident.

Mrs Langer does not, of course, hold that art is the expression

---

[1] This must be left rather vague and obscure for the moment; I shall return
to it below.

or projection of merely personal feeling; she expressly denies it. For her, what the artist does is to project the *form* of feeling, to set forth in symbolic form what feelings are *like*, 'how vital and emotional and intellectual tensions . . . feel'.[1]

This 'form' of the feeling which art is said to be 'like' is the form of vital feeling, the feeling of the life which is much wider than art. We come to know something of this feeling in two sorts of connected ways. We know it, first, by living life, knowing it in experience as it flows along, and second, by reflecting upon it, introspecting and retrospecting, doing introspective psychology, trying to understand the components and the interrelations of the components of the flux. Knowledge obtained in this way, Mrs Langer says, is vague and elusive, and psychologists have thrown little light upon it.[2] She is very definite that the artist 'is not a psychologist, interested in human motivation and behaviour; he simply creates an image of that phase of events which only the organism wherein they occur ever knows'.[3] All the same, one must suppose that if the artist is to make an image of feeling, he must know the original pretty intimately. Indeed she says: 'He knows something of how feeling rises, develops, tangles or reverses or breaks or sinks, spent in overt action or buried in secrecy.'

The artist, it is said, makes an image of feeling; art is 'the form of feeling'. But if all feelings or complexes of feeling are feelings-*of*, are concrete and particular, how can their 'forms' be other than concrete and particular too? And if so, how can the 'form' of one kind of concrete feeling or complex of feelings, the feelings of 'life', be projected into another form, the form of art? The feelings (and the 'forms' of the feelings) of life outside art and the feelings (and the 'forms' of the feelings) inside art are, concretely, different. The form of the feeling in any individual work of art (accepting *pro tem* this language) is as special to that work as, in a different way, the form of any particular complex of life-feelings is special to a particular life situation. Strictly speaking, the forms of the feelings of life-situations *cannot* be expressed or projected into art-situations. 'Expression' and 'projection' seem to be the wrong words and the wrong ideas for formulating the *essential* nature of art. What happens is that in creating a work of art a new complex object comes into being, and in our aesthetic experience of it we come to have new feelings, and new structures of feeling, which are not projections of the forms of life-feelings but new vital

---

[1] *Mind*, p. xix.   [2] *ibid.*, p. 57 *et seq.*   [3] *ibid.*, p. 54.

feelings themselves, not just 'how vital and emotional and intellectual tensions feel . . .' but new and fresh vital tensions relevant and specific to the meaning specifically embodied in this thing here before us, nowhere else and never before.

'Projection', of course, does happen—and Mrs Langer mentions several senses.[1] Although, as we said, it is self-evidently impossible for me to 'project' my feeling so that you can experience my feeling exactly as I experience it, a mechanism of projection may enable me to convey to you something of what I feel, so that the 'form' of your feeling has some resemblance to mine. If I am filled with horror and pity by the sight of war-refugees, I may be able to induce feelings of horror and pity in you by projecting, by making a projection (say by photograph or film)—if I cannot lead you to the place to see for yourself.

This kind of projection is, certainly, included in the processes of making some kinds of art. Artists 'project' by making realistic paintings or telling stories realistically in order to evoke similar feelings about their subject-matter in you and me. But, although projection in this sense may be involved in some art making, projection does not *differentiate* it as art. Art is not duplication in a projection, but a new created image embodied in a medium, derived perhaps from life experience but not photographing it.

No one, of course, knows this better than Mrs Langer. The work of art is a '*metaphorical* symbol'; every symbolic projection is a 'transformation' (pp. 104–5). Visual art is not 'optical' but imaginative.[2] Citing Bosanquet with reserved approval she avers that feeling is 'organized, plastic or incarnate'. Quoting him: 'We must not suppose that we first have a disembodied feeling, and then set out to find an embodiment adequate to it. In a word, imaginative expression creates the feeling in creating its embodiment, and the feeling so created not merely cannot be otherwise expressed, but cannot otherwise exist, than in and through the embodiment which imagination has found for it.'[3]

Here, I think, *is* the very centre of the aesthetic. And if indeed it is so, my complaint against Mrs Langer is that some of her other emphases are misleading if not actually wrong. Art 'images' the forms of feeling, setting forth what feelings are *like*. Feeling is 'like' the dynamic and rhythmic structures created by artists (or their structures 'like' feeling). Art is a 'projection'—of something else? Yes: art projects the 'form of feeling'. The artist,

---

[1] *Mind*, p. 74.   [2] *ibid.*, pp. 104–5.   [3] *ibid.*, p. 112.

'though not a psychologist, . . . creates an image of that phase of events which only the organism wherein they occur ever knows', and this reveals not only his own private feeling but the basic forms of feeling common to most people.[1] An expressive form represents 'some other whole whose elements have analogous relations'. And though art does not lead to scientific psychological knowledge—for important and good reasons—'it is not unreasonable to expect some formulation of psychological basic facts to come from art'.[2]

I do not deny that there is truth contained in all this. Art springs out of life-experience, and there are important questions about the movement from life-feelings to art-feelings, about the 'resemblance' (as well as the non-resemblance) between the two. Understanding of art might contribute to understanding of substantive psychology. Life-feelings may in some measure be shown through the medium of the constructed objects of representative art. The vital, emotional and intellectual tensions of a non-representative art like pure music may have something in common with, may in some respect be like, the tensions of life. How this and similar things happen is a legitimate part of the psychology of aesthetics and it may throw incidental light on the nature of feeling. But though legitimate, it is off-centre. The centre is that the artist imaginatively constructs a *new* object in terms of a medium, an object of which he and we have feeling-experience. Our feeling-experience of it is new and individual, concrete because it is feeling of *that* total situation and no other. Feeling-import and 'surface' are as we saw, in aesthetic experience so inseparably one that in this context it sounds artificial to say that art is projecting or expressing something else—'feeling'. If art reveals human feeling it is neither (as we know) just the artist's feelings before making; nor is it even anything so general (if indeed there *is* anything so general) as 'the form' of human feeling; what is experienced is the particular individual affective import of *that* work—however dependent the intelligent apprehension of it may be upon other felt life-experiences. It is dangerous, too, to speak as if art presents an 'essence' of feeling. Mrs Langer quotes Mrs Ivy Campbell-Fisher:[3] 'If I could be as sad as certain passages in Mozart, my glory would be greater than it is. . . . The fact that I know as much as I do of the essence of pathos comes from meeting with such music. . . . My grasp of the essence of sadness . . . comes

[1] *Mind*, p. 64.   [2] *ibid.*, p. 65   [3] *ibid.*, p. 88

not from moments when I have been sad, but from moments when I have seen sadness before me released from entanglements with contingency.' Again, 'In what actual person have we ever experienced the inevitability of passionate pattern that Oedipus and Lear present to us?' I do not for a moment deny the immensely important truth expressed in this passage. But, though there is release from 'the entanglements with contingency' it is the contingency of *life* from which we are released. We move, however, into another 'contingency', the contingency of the world of the play—of the 'passionate pattern' of Oedipus and Lear—or the music. The universal is not an abstract universal, but a new individual concrete universal.

It is constantly difficult, too, to think of art as presenting the form of *feeling*. 'Feeling', though it is feeling-*of*, is (as we said) primarily a subjective word. But in art our attention is to the object rather than to the 'feeling'. It is strained to say philosophically that when I contemplate Oedipus, or Lear, or Mozart's music, I contemplate feeling. I contemplate the works themselves; I get (mediately, in a complex way) the feeling *of* them through attending to them wholly. It is their meaning, as known through feeling, rather than a structure or form of feeling which I apprehend. To speak in this way is more natural, and seems to set the problem of aesthetic more clearly. Mrs Langer indeed often eloquently stresses this attention to the unique and untranslatable work itself. But it is difficult to see that some of her other language about feeling coheres clearly with it.

§3   Symbols and Art: Langer

The use of the word 'symbol', again, requires special scrutiny. In order to make this scrutiny, I must spend a little more time in expounding carefully Mrs Langer's very fine account of it in the chapter of her book called 'The art symbol and the symbol in art'. But in this Chapter I can only touch the fringe of the complex problem of symbolism. I hope to deal with it rather more fully below.

If one wants to understand elaborate structures, one has to have a model which is not an instance but 'a symbolic form which can be manipulated, to convey, or perhaps to hold' one's conceptions. The symbolism of ordinary language, as we know, gives us no model of the primitive forms of feeling; she holds that only art does this. Yet there are obvious difficulties in speaking, as she did in *Feeling and Form*, of the 'Art Symbol'. 'This roused a

flood of criticism from two kinds of critics—those who misunderstood the alleged symbolic function and assimilated everything that
I wrote to some previous, familiar theory, either treating art as a
genuine language or *symbolism*, or else confusing the art symbol
with *the symbol in art* as known to iconologists or to modern
psychologists; and secondly, those critics who understood what I
said but resented the use of the word "symbol" that differed from
accepted usage in current semantical writings.'[1] In *Problems of
Art* she admitted the difficulties and adopted a more cautious line:
it brings out the difference between the function of what logicians
call the 'genuine' symbol, and a work of art. The art symbol, she
said, is not *exactly* a symbol but is 'more like a symbolic function
than anything else. A work of art is expressive in the way a
proposition is expressive—as the formulation of an idea for conception'. Since Nagel objected to her calling that which art expresses
its 'meaning', because it is not 'meaning' in any of the precise
senses known to semanticists, she substituted the word 'import'—the import of the expressive form. This is the more important as the work may have *meanings* besides. As 'a work of art is
an expressive form somewhat like a symbol, and has import which
is something like meaning, so it makes a logical abstraction, but
not in the familiar way of genuine symbols'. It is a 'pseudo-
abstraction', and aesthetics is concerned with 'pseudo-semantics'.
There follows an interesting comparison between art-symbols
and other symbols.

The 'genuine' symbol is defined by Nagel as 'any occurrence
(or type of occurrence), usually linguistic in status, which is taken
to signify something else by way of tacit or explicit conventions
or rules of language'. But (Mrs Langer says) the words of ordinary
language are not habitually used in isolation, but in complex concepts and states of affairs. They don't simply name things: they
express ideas about things. A thing can't be asserted by a name; it
can only be mentioned. 'As soon as you make an assertion you are
symbolizing some sort of relation between concepts of things, or
maybe things and properties, such as: "The grapes are sour".'
So symbols do not simply refer to things or communicate facts;
they express ideas. This involves the formulation of ideas, or conception itself, the conception which gives form and connection,
clarity, to the contents of our experience.

---

[1] All quotations from here to the end of § 3 are from *Problems of Art*, pp. 126–
139.

'The great importance of reference and communication by means of symbols has led semanticists to regard these uses as the defining properties of symbols—that is, to think of a symbol as essentially a sign which stands for something else and is used to represent that thing in discourse. This preoccupation has led them to neglect, or even miss entirely, the more primitive function of symbols, which is to formulate experience as something imaginable in the first place . . . to articulate ideas.' According to the usual definition of 'symbol', as something which stands for something else apart from it, perhaps the most important office of symbols is overlooked—'their power of formulating experience, and presenting it objectively for contemplation, logical intuition, recognition, understanding. That is articulation, or logical expression. And this function every good work of art does perform. It formulates the appearance of feeling . . . which discourse, the normal use of words, is peculiarly unable to articulate. And whereas a genuine symbol ("genuine" only in Nagel's too limited sense), such as a word, is only a sign, an instrument, our interest reaching beyond it to the concept, the work of art does not point us to a meaning beyond its own presence. What is expressed can't be grasped apart from the sensuous or poetic form that expresses it'. The work seems 'to be imbued with the emotion or mood or other vital experience that it expresses. That is why I call it an "expressive form" and call that which it formulates for us not its meaning, but its *import*.'

Now comes the vital distinction between the Art Symbol and the Symbol in Art. The work as a whole is 'the image of feeling, which may be called the Art Symbol. It is a single organic composition, which means that its elements are not independent constituents, expressive in their own right, of various emotional ingredients, as words are constituents of discourse, and have meanings in their own right, which go to compose the total meaning of the discourse. Language is a *symbolism*, a system of symbols with definable though fairly elastic meanings, and rules of combination whereby larger units . . . may be compounded . . . Art, contrariwise, is not a symbolism. The elements in a work are always newly created with the total image, and although it is possible to analyse what they contribute to the image, it is not possible to assign them any of its import apart from the whole. That is characteristic of organic form. The import of a work of art is its "life", which, like actual life, is an indivisible phenomenon.' The Art Symbol is a single symbol, and its import is not compounded of partial symbolic values. It is 'the absolute image'.

But this is not to deny that symbols may be incorporated in works of art. In poems or pictures, novels or dances, they certainly are. 'Some artists work with a veritable riot of symbols; from the familiar halo of sacrosanct personages to the terrible figures of the *Guernica*, from the obvious rose of womanhood or the lily of chastity to the personal symbols of T. S. Eliot. . . .' All these elements are genuine symbols, and their meanings can be stated. They 'enter into the work of art as elements, creating and articulating its organic form'. The symbols used in art lie on a different semantic level from the work that contains them. Their meanings are not *part* of the import, but elements in the form that *has* import, the expressive form. 'The meanings of incorporated symbols may lend richness, intensity, repetition or reflection or a transcendent unrealism.'. . But they function in the normal manner of symbols.' But the use of these symbols is a 'principle of construction—a device'—to be distinguished from a 'principle of art'. 'The principles of art are few . . . the achievement of organic unity or "livingness", the articulation of feeling.' The principles of construction, on the other hand, are many—such as representation in painting, diatonic harmony in music, metrical versification in poetry, etc. But they are not indispensable. So the difference between Art Symbol and Symbol used in Art is a difference not only of function but of kind. Symbols occurring in art are symbols in the usual sense; the art symbol, on the other hand, *is* the expressive form. 'It is not a symbol in the full familiar sense, for it does not convey something beyond itself. Therefore it cannot strictly be said to have a meaning; what it does have is import. It is a symbol in a special and derivative sense, because it does not fulfil all the functions of a true symbol.' It formulates and objectifies experience. 'But it does not abstract a concept for discursive thought. Its import is seen in it; not, like the meaning of a genuine symbol by means of it but separable from the sign.'

§4 *Symbols and Art: some questions*

This is a most penetrating exposition of the uses of the word 'symbol' in art theory, and the exposition of the distinction between the 'art-symbol' and the 'symbol in art' is an important one. Yet the question—whether art is or is not a 'symbol', and in what senses either might be so—is a good deal more complex than is shown here. In the present section I shall simply make some comments and open up some more questions, leaving the problem to be dealt with more fully in Chapter XI. The answer to the question whether or not art can properly be called a symbol depends upon a thorough understanding of what—for me—is the key conception of aesthetics, *embodiment*; it can better be expounded after a fuller exposition and testing out of the principle of embodiment in various examples. With this explanation, the comments here, and in Chapter XI (§§ 5 and 6) form a continuous series.

Everything Mrs Langer says (pp. 64–7 above) about the contrast between ordinary language, as a symbolism having constituent parts, and art as being a whole of newly created elements, is true, and of the greatest importance. It is true, too, that the work 'seems to be imbued with the . . . vital experience that it expresses'. This is in contrast with the use of ordinary symbols whose instrumental function seems to be to express meaning distinct from the symbols themselves. Mrs Langer is right, again, in pointing out that the view of a symbol as sign standing for something else is far too limited; symbols *articulate* ideas—and if art is a symbol it must at least do that.

But I think that the affirmation that the art symbol is not 'exactly a symbol', though it is 'more like a symbolic function than anything else', is too vague, and is not made crystal-clear by adopting Melvin Rader's 'expressive form'. Nor do I see why she should defer to the self-limited view of meaning held by Nagel and other semanticists, deciding to use the word 'import' instead. Perhaps there is some value in the change of word; if you want to stress internality and autonomous structure, the first syllable of the word '*im*port' may help. But kow-towing to the logicians doesn't do them, or aesthetics, any good. 'Meaning' is a word with a rich variety of content, and should not be used in one logical context only. There are contexts in which aestheticians and art critics ought to use 'meaning'; aesthetic meaning is one of the facts of life, and if logicians do not yet understand this, they have, as the saying goes, 'something coming to them!'.

Mrs Langer says that art is 'not a symbol in the full familiar sense' because it doesn't have meaning, but import. But we ought to ask unambiguously: Is the work of art in *any* sense clearly a symbol? And, Is the work of art in *any* sense clearly *not* a symbol? It may be that in some ways it seems to be, and in others not.

Perhaps the term 'work of art' is ambiguous, and is being used in at least two different senses?

The term 'work of art' is indeed in a very obvious sense ambiguous. It can mean (a) the physical objects (e.g.) that hang on walls or are otherwise displayed in galleries, and which may be looked at in various unaesthetic ways—e.g. by the servitor in the gallery as so much weight to be lifted about, or by some meticulous scientist who wants for some reason to measure areas of colour or formulate geometrical forms, in pictures or sculptures. *Mutatis mutandis*, the same could be said of other kinds of art. (b) Although such a use of 'art' is quite common and understandable, it is also quite inadequate. 'Works of art' are not just physical objects to be observed or shifted about casually; they are consciously-made artifacts to be enjoyed aesthetically. In this sense, everything under heading (a) might be described not so much as art, but as physical conditions—perceived or otherwise—for the existence of 'art' in any full sense.

These conditions for the full existence of art might be called 'symbolic' conditions—though as actually described under heading (a) they are not even that: the supposed servitor or scientist does not think of them as symbols but as perceived material objects. They *could*, however, be counted as 'symbols'. Let us call, for short, by the name 'perceptua' what is presented to our senses when ordinary words and sentences are used, or when we look at pictures or listen to pieces of music. In the case of meaningful words and sentences the perceptua are, clearly, taken as symbolic. In the case of pictures or pieces of music, it may be argued that the perceptua again have to be taken as symbols. Although pictures and music *can*, as we have said, be taken as just occupying so much space or filling the air, they can also be taken as aesthetically meaningful, and therefore, it might be argued, symbolic. I say 'might be argued', because, since the perceptua are (aesthetically) meaningful, they would appear to be 'symbols'. One usually assumes that, where there is meaning, there are perceptua which mean, and these are what we call 'symbols'. But although it is quite clear that the perceptua involved in the use of ordinary meaningful words and sentences are 'symbols', and it looks as though exactly the same reasoning should be applied to the perceptua of art, the perceptua of art have a relation to their aesthetic meaning which is so different from the relation of the perceptua (heard or written words and sentences) or ordinary language to *their* meaning, that the word 'symbol'—which seems entirely appropriate in the latter case—cannot be assumed without argument to apply to the perceptua of art in the same or even in an analagous way. There is a difficult question and a problem which can be suppressed by the too-easy use of the word 'symbol' as applied to art perceptua.

A plausible case *for* a distinction between perceptua and aesthetic meaning may seem obvious. Patterns of paint or sound are in one sense quite distinguishable from their aesthetic meaning and can be pointed to; meaning is *not* just patterns of paint or sound. As a piece of analysis, this seems self-evident. It is a piece of analysis, however, and when we think of 'art' in the sense (*b*) above, the opposite and apparently contradictory fact emerges. There is the inseparability of 'surface' and 'meaning'. In *aesthetic* experience of art (as distinct from a philosophical analysis) there seems to be no distinction between patterns of paint or sound and their meaning. We do not see or hear (*a*) patterns of paint or sound, *and* (*b*) say or think or suppose or know that they 'mean' so and so. This is why Mrs Langer prefers 'expressive form' rather than 'art symbol'. I prefer it too, but I prefer to say that we apprehend patterns of paint or sound, not as 'meaning something' or expressing something, but as *meaningful*: in other words, as I shall argue in the chapters which follow, there is a unique thing, *embodied meaning*. This is quite different from the relations of words and sentences to *their* meanings. The words and sentences refer to things or concepts or propositions which are their meanings and— although one cannot apprehend clearly concepts or propositions without some words and sentences—words and sentences have a meaning which is distinct from themselves. It must be so, because the same meaning can be stated in different languages, written in different-looking alphabets (English, Russian, Greek . . .). In art, there is no such distinct meaning: aesthetic meaning is so bound up, (as ordinary verbal meaning is not), with the particular individual shape, form, colour, etc., of the perceptua that it cannot be stated adequately in any other way but the one. *This* exact meaning can be said in no other 'language'. Watch yourself (or, if that is impossible, remember it) actually appreciating this picture—the relation of the grey moonlit house to the green shadows in contrast to the almost black background, the way the shadows lick, like tongues, over the grass slopes in front of the houses, the way in which the complex details of the patterns weave into a whole with a kind of liquid unity—and you find it is quite impossible to distinguish between the experience of the painted shapes, and their meaningfulness; their meaning is embodied in them. In contrast to this, other symbols are not only clearly distinguishable from their meanings but are separable from them. The sentence is separable from the proposition.

Of both words and sentences, then, and of the perceptua of art, it can be said that they 'have meaning'. But 'have meaning' is quite different in the two cases. The meaning, expressible in any language, of words and sentences, is distinct and even separable (because several languages *will* do for one meaning) from particular words and sentences. The meaning of the perceptua of art is certainly not separate from them and, in aesthetic experience, not even distinguishable. It is this which makes the use of the word 'symbol' very questionable as applied to art. To anticipate an analogy of the next chapter: we would not say (except very pedantically) of an obviously angry man that, when he throws things about, his movements 'mean' that he has certain feelings, or that his movements 'symbolize' angry feelings: we just *see* him as angry.

But these arguments can only be developed and understood more fully when the central concept of aesthetics, *embodiment*, has been expounded and tested out.

CHAPTER IV

EXPRESSION, AND THE EMERGENCE OF 'CREATIVE EMBODIMENT'

C*

CHAPTER IV

EXPRESSION, AND THE EMERGENCE OF 'CREATIVE EMBODIMENT'

In a work of art, something entirely new is brought forth. Before it is made, there are ideas, feelings, agitations, discomforts, partial formulations, schematic forms, floating images. But the whole is a new creation. This we may hold in common with Mrs Langer and most other philosophers of art.

What I now want to suggest is that the proper word for all this is 'embodiment' rather than 'expression'. It is true that 'embodiment' is often used interchangeably with 'expression',[1] and that 'expression' is, in part at any rate, often intended to mean what I now exclusively call 'embodiment', or more fully, 'creative aesthetic embodiment'. But I have already hinted, and shall try to show further, bit by bit, that the word 'expressive' has so many misleading contra-aesthetic undertones that it is almost impossible to continue to use it as the main keyword of aesthetics.

The change is partly a verbal one and I do not think that even 'embodiment' is an ideal term. Since it refers to something unique, *sui generis*, it really needs a unique word which has meaning only in the context of total aesthetic discourse. Somebody might invent one; I cannot think of anything which is not hideous or open to other objection; 'creative aesthetic embodiment' will have to do. But if it is to be used, we must make clear all over again that the embodiment which is aesthetic and creative is different from any other sort. 'Embodiment' here must be a special technical term.

There are, of course, non-aesthetic uses. We speak of 'embodying' a principle in an action or invention, 'the embodying' of an

---

[1] I have so used 'expression' myself in the past, although the intention was towards what I am now calling embodiment. In her earlier books Mrs Langer has sometimes referred to my views of expressiveness. In *Problems of Art*, p. 119, she quotes me as having said, 'Beauty is just expressiveness' and she adds, 'upon the definition of art, proposed at the beginning of this lecture—"Art is the expression of forms expressive of human feeling"—Reid's dictum comes almost as a scholium and, moreover, it has the pragmatic values by which I advertise my own theory'. In proposing now to distinguish more sharply between the ideas of expression and embodiment and to limit the use of each in a more defined way I am not throwing overboard all I formerly wrote but am rather (to change the metaphor) re-examining parts of the foundation, strengthening the superstructure and doing a bit of reconstructing with some new additions—all with the help of much valuable writing by many authors in recent years, of whom a chief is Mrs Langer.

idea in a formula, or in a memorandum or resolution. It may be said that the Mace 'embodies' a facet of English history. Or in the ordinary use of words to express concepts or propositions, the word 'embody' *can* be used as an alternative to 'express'. If I use the word 'table' or say 'The Prime Minister has to tackle the problem of inflation', noises or marks on paper, or a pattern of them, used as symbols, are absolutely necessary in order to grasp the ideas clearly. We cannot do any explicit conceptual thinking at all without employing these 'material' symbols. Their 'body' is in this sense essential to explicit thinking and understanding, and it can be said quite sensibly that they 'embody' ideas. Nevertheless the function of the 'body' here, and its relation to the meaning 'embodied', is quite different from the function and relation of body to meaning in aesthetic embodiment. In the written or sounding sentences just given, marks or sounds and their sensuously-perceived relationships are necessary instruments to the grasp of conceptual meaning, but their particular individual forms as perceived are not essential to, and are not a part of, what they mean. What they mean could be said (as we noticed before) in *any* different sounding—or looking—language. In *aesthetic* embodiment, on the other hand, perceived sounds, shapes, rhythms, etc., are not only instrumental to the grasp of aesthetic meaning; the experience of attentive perception to them is an essential part of the apprehension of the meaning. The attention to perceived forms is both instrumental *and* intrinsic to the understanding of aesthetic meaning. Conversely, in an art which uses words (say a poem) the pattern of said, heard words *embodies* poetic meaning in a sense in which words expressing ordinary propositions do not. 'Content' and medium are indivisibly and uniquely united. This is true not only of poetry but of all the arts, as I shall try to suggest.

Indivisibility of 'content' and 'medium' is known in our confrontation with an embodied person. To 'see' character in a person's face, in his posture and gesture, is neither to perceive his body only nor to apprehend his character through his body, but to apprehend one single embodied person with distinguishable aspects. If I apprehend someone as sad, or wistful, or angry, I am not aware just of ideas, or feelings or a body behaving, but of a person—sad, wistful, angry.

To feel happy, or angry, at ease or in anxiety, is neither mental only nor physical only, but psycho-physical. The aspects are indivisible and convey the idea of meaningful embodied experience.

This experience is not aesthetic, or is not necessarily so; yet psycho-physical embodiment is not only a good analogue of aesthetic embodiment, but one of the conditions of its existence. It is, at least in part, because our whole meaningful existence (with the possible exception of paranormal phenomena) is psycho-physical, and lived dynamically in a coloured, tactile, resonant, spatio-temporal world, that all the variety of the art forms can appear so profoundly significant to us: those philosophers who have conceived of the aesthetic as a purely 'spiritual' phenomenon have committed about the worst blunder it is possible to make. So, though psycho-physical experience is not, as such, aesthetic, the aesthetic is closely bound up with it, and the good analogy is perhaps something more than an analogy.

But the aesthetic—in art at any rate—is related to an *artifact* as psycho-physical experience is not. The embodiment in the artifact which is art is characterized, I have been arguing, by an internality of relationship between content and form which is not found in the other types of expression or 'embodiment'—in sentences or formulae. The artist discovers in creating. It is a unique kind of discovery—not of something which was there all the time ready-made, like an article discovered in a drawer. Nor is it the 'discovery'—if that is the right word—of seeing realized in material forms a fully worked-out design or plan which has taken time to complete, seeing for instance, with tremendous pleasure of achievement, a sailing dinghy one has made, long in the planning and making, now 'real' at last before our very eyes. Art—though sometimes it may include much planning, is much more than carrying out a plan. It is in fact discovery of a new dimension of being, a new dimension that can only come into being through the creative manipulation of a material medium—words, paint, clay . . . tones, melody, rhythm . . . actions, gestures, and other bodily movements . . . The artist shapes and forms these with the hopeful purpose that he may achieve this discovery through making a final material form which (as far as possible) satisfies him as being, for his imaginative mind, in its very perceived form charged with meaning.

It is better to call this aesthetic 'embodiment' of meaning rather than 'expression' for a number of reasons, of which the following are a specimen first three. First, 'embodiment' suggests the thing directly before us, while 'expression' has the unfortunate tendency, already criticized, to direct our thoughts otherwards to feelings or ideas which are expressed. Secondly, 'expression' suggests, at least in some of its uses, events which had some sort of complete existence before they were expressed and became known in expression, whereas the aesthetic meaning which is embodied has no complete existence till it is born in embodiment. Thirdly, 'embodiment' stresses the importance of the actual presence of what we are *sensibly* aware of, and attending to—the sounding music, the plastic forms, the dramatic action. (It is also true that 'embody' must be stretched to include the whole range of what we can imagine.) 'Expression', as used by professional aestheticians such as Croce and Collingwood, has scandalously underrated the actual manipulation and perception and imagination of the material medium, regarding it as merely instrumental, or even accidental and unnecessary. 'Body', and our incarnate experience of it, is central to the aesthetic and the artistic.

The stress here is on sensible awareness and the physical medium of embodiment, and it is intended to counteract a one-sided emphasis in some forms of expression theory upon the extra-aesthetic meanings which 'expression' claims to 'express'. 'Embodiment' better than 'expression suggests that meaning is part of the medium-involved *substance* of the aesthetic.

At this point, two things have to be said: (*a*) The stress has been on the sensible awareness of physical media: this is right, and it will be maintained. On the other hand, although always an essential part of the aesthetic in art, it must not be given exclusive importance.

Typical examples of embodiment are the visual arts and music; there the medium of embodiment is, clearly, sensibly perceived (though that is not the whole story). In all the arts this happens too, though not so obviously in every one. In reading a novel our main attention is, naturally and normally, to ideas, images, character development, etc., rather than to the form of words. The form of words, the style ... are vitally important; and it is through them, as it were, that we apprehend everything else. At times, as critics or students, we may attend to them closely, finding out how important they are as constituent of the art. But, however essential this aspect of embodiment may be, it is not the only important aspect. Sensible perceptua are not the sole media of embodiment. There is imaginative 'seeing' too, of new individual embodied meaning. There is the union of things usually thought of as apart in a vivid image, the 'similitude in dissimilitude' of which Wordsworth wrote. Shakespeare's union of the two contrasting images of a defined, straining constricting mesh or sieve and the 'dropping of the gentle rain from heaven', and their combined illumination of the concept of the quality of mercy would be one illustration.

> The quality of mercy is not strain'd
> It droppeth as the gentle rain from heaven
> Upon the place beneath . . .

Donne's relation of the contrasting ideas of life and death in the vivid

> A bracelet of bright hair about the bone

is another.

All arts cannot employ metaphor, or at least employ it in the same way, as others; each has to exploit its own special media of embodiment in its own way. The point I wish to make here is the simple one that the aesthetic concept of embodiment is not exclusively confined to the media which can literally be sensibly perceived.

(b) Again, the stress on 'embodiment' can help to correct an imbalance of some limited interpretations of *formalistic* theories of art. As some kinds of expression-theory come dangerously near to reducing the aesthetic to terms of extra-artistic life-contents, so some types of formalism can attenuate the content of the aesthetic by overemphasis on a limited idea of form—as was done by the famous Bell–Fry theory of 'significant form'. 'To the apprehension of form we need bring with us nothing from life, no knowledge of its ideas and affairs, no familiarity with its emotions.'[1] Bell's theory was of course only a sketch and was never worked out philosophically. Fry on the other hand was a seminal thinker, and his struggles (e.g. in *Transformations*) with the idea of 'significant form' were largely an attempt to make it compatible with other than formalistic 'content'. For Fry and Bell—with visual art in mind—'form' referred mainly to line, two and three-dimensional shape, colour . . .; 'significance' was, very vaguely, perhaps in a viciously circular way, conceived in terms of the 'aesthetic emotion'.

[1] *Art*, p. 25.

This is, pretty clearly, too limited a conception of form and significance to be acceptable. On the other hand, my emphasis upon the 'body' component of 'embodiment' (the physical medium, etc.) may well be thought one-sided too, over-emphasizing the sensuous side of perception of the medium to the neglect of the formal. I do not intend to do this. As far as medium-emphasis is concerned, 'embodiment' means embodiment in *formed* medium. There is no medium without form, and the working up of the medium into art is, from beginning to end, the discovery and construction of form. The employment of media—paint, stone, words in literature, words and action in drama, gesture in dance, patterns of sound, etc., in music—is inseparable from the formulation of these and the construction of the final form of a work. On the other hand, forms and form in art include a great deal more than this—and if, continually, I stress material forms, it is because they are essential and can be neglected, not because they are everything. 'Form' is a very wide conception indeed, and much wider than what can be apprehended through the senses. The concepts and images of art have form; we rightly talk of the conceptual structure of *Lear*, or *Pride and Prejudice*, or of the ambitions of Becky Sharp. A work of art as embodied has always a physical structure, but its structure or 'shape', or the way it appears, or the perspective of it, requires all the powers of mind to apprehend fully. This is very obviously true of arts like literature and drama, but it is equally true, though in different ways, of an art like pure music.

In that sense, art is meaningful 'form'. On the other hand, in spite of—perhaps in some ways because of—its ambiguity, I think that the word 'embodiment' is more robust than 'form', avoiding some of the one-sided and at times misleading emphases of 'expression' on the one hand and 'form' on the other. But of course no single word could ever adequately symbolize the many-sidedness of art. The only value which a word like 'embodiment' can have is in its application and use.

I spoke earlier of 'creative manipulation' of a material medium—using 'manipulation' in a wide sense to include the 'manipulation' of words in poetry or of the body in dance. I think there is no harm in this; but if we do keep the term, it is important not to yield to the tendency and temptation to *identify* too simply the 'creative manipulation' of the medium with a deliberate fully consciously planned *act* of embodiment, with an embodying activity. In strictness, although meaning is embodied and there is embodied meaning, this is the new resultant of an exploratory movement which because humanly creative is not completely visualized beforehand. Embodiment, the created new embodied meaning, is something which *happens* when the creative manipulation of a medium is complete and successful. Further, though the artist, with his creative manipulation, is the cause, or a cause (or maybe an agent, like a psychic 'medium', moved by something beyond himself) the embodiment is something which when it happens is appreciated, rather than made. An observation about the playing of music (which being a performing art is admittedly a special case) may suggest what I mean. In playing music it is important to *listen* to oneself whilst playing: by so doing one finds out, so to speak, what is 'happening'. And in the making of any art there tends to be a rhythmic alternation between the activity of making, and of enjoying critically and contemplatively what has been done, part or whole. Generally speaking, the new embodied meaning in the completed artifact appears almost as a kind of magic in which the artist enjoys as a discoverer. At that point he is spectator rather than actor, and in that respect like ourselves when we see or hear his work. There must always of course be differences of content between the experiences of different persons; the artist sees his work with his background of the experience of making, whereas we see it only as completed. But in both cases it is the appreciation of meaning as embodied.

There is a kind of dialectic in the argument I have been putting forward. The importance of the medium has to be insisted upon as against those who treat it as merely instrumental or unnecessary. But art-making is not just the purposeful manipulation of a medium; it is the creation of something new which is the outcome of successful artistic manipulation. This looks like mere instrumentality over again. It is not so; it is not mere instrumentality which is being asserted, but the coming into being of new embodied meaning which is both distinct from, and of a piece with, inseparable from, the formed medium. The new thing, the creation, is integral with the formed medium and yet transcends it (the Light that never was . . .).

§2   Langer on 'creation'

The word 'creation' and the kind of creation it is, is crucial. The word 'creation' is of course something often conjured with, and badly overworked. Although I have been using it in an evaluative way—and creation is, when it occurs, always moving and surprising—it is important as a basis of any evaluation to understand it descriptively. Mrs Langer writes about it as follows. 'The difference between creation and other productive work is this: an ordinary object, say a shoe, is made by putting pieces of leather together; the pieces were there before. The shoe is a construction of leather. It has a special shape and use and name, but it is still an article of leather, and is thought of as such. A picture is made by deploying pigments on a piece of canvas, but the picture is not a pigment-and-canvas structure. The picture that emerges from the process is a structure of space, and the space itself is an emergent whole of shapes, visible coloured volumes. Neither the space nor the things in it were in the room before. Pigments and canvas are not in the pictorial space; they are in the space of the room, as they were before, though we no longer find them there by sight without a great effort of attention. For touch they are still there. But for touch there is no pictorial space. The picture, in short, is an apparition . . . The whole picture is a piece of purely visual space. It is nothing but a vision.'[1] Continuing, she speaks of this as 'virtual' space. But as distinct from the virtual space, say behind a mirror, which is an indirect appearance of visual space, 'the virtual space of a painting is *created*. The canvas existed before, the pigments existed before; they have only been moved about, arranged to compose a new physical object, that the painter calls "my big canvas" or "that little new canvas". But the picture, the spatial illusion, is new in the sense that it never existed before, anywhere, nor did any of its parts. The illusion of space is created.' This illusion is the stuff of art. 'To call the art-image illusory is simply to say that it is not material; it is not cloth and paint-smooches, but space organized by balanced shapes with dynamic relations, tensions and resolutions, among them. Actual space is not like that; it has no organic form, like pictorial space.' In another place,[2] speaking of the apparition created out of paint deployed on a ground, she says 'The paint and the ground themselves disappear. One does not see a picture as a piece of spotted canvas, any more than one sees a screen with shadows on it in a movie . . . it presents volumes in a purely created space.' All this is further worked out in a distinction between the *materials*

---

[1] *Problems of Art*, p. 28. The other references are between pp. 28 and 34.
[2] *ibid.*, pp. 127–8.

(which she here identified with medium) and the elements of an art. In the case of music, 'Sonorous, moving forms . . . are the elements of music. The *materials* of music, on the other hand, are sounds of a certain pitch, loudness, overtone mixture, and metronomic length. In artistic production, the composer's materials must be completely swallowed up in the illusion they create, in which henceforth we find only illusory elements, but not—except through technical interest and workmanlike attention—the arrangement of materials.'[1]

§3   *Critical Comment: her too-sharp division between medium and creation*

This in my view is original and profound writing. The substance of it is of the utmost importance. The distinctions made are valid. Yet I think the emphases at times do real injustice to the integral relation between material medium and aesthetic meaning.

The affirmation and the distinctions referred to in such words as 'apparition', 'virtual', 'illusion', 'elements' *versus* materials, I am bound to accept. And since the affirmation logically imply denials, I am bound to accept these also. In fact, in her text the affirmations and the denials are usually set side by side. But to leave it at that, is to consent to a bifurcation, logically understandable, but aesthetically not viable. I shall try to explain what I mean.

The affirmations are acceptable. The dance is an apparition—a 'display of interacting forces . . .'. Picture space is a creation, 'an emergent whole of shapes, visible coloured volumes'. It has no acoustical properties. All this is very true and important. Logically, the denials that are implied in all these affirmations must be accepted too. If these objects are like that, they are not like something else. Logically, if what you see is the virtual image of the dance, you do not see people running around twisting their bodies. The picture is not a pigment and canvas structure, the art image is not cloth and paint smooches. Music is not the arrangement of materials.

These are logical distinctions, validly made, acceptable, about the experience of art. And yet, being analytic, they are necessarily abstract, and partial. Mrs Langer is affirming a valid point about aesthetic experience, in which, as logically stated, A excludes B. But the fact that the mode in which A is an apparition is one in which, *qua* apparition, it is not smooches of paint, does not imply

[1] *Problems of Art*, p. 39.

a denial that in the total *aesthetic* experience the apparition and the smooches of paint are two aspects of one larger concrete whole. The distinction of 'apparition', though legitimate, is a conceptual distinction—and as conceptual must be opposed to the 'material'. But this does not imply that the conceptual distinctions stand for separate ontological objects, that the virtual image of the dance ('a display of interacting forces', etc.) is something cut off from the motions of the dancers ('People running round or twisting their bodies'). Nor does the emergent whole of shapes, 'visible coloured volumes', imply space which is cut off from 'the space of the room', from the colours of pigments, from the suggestions of ordinary space—volumes, of tactile values. Nor have the sonorous, moving forms of music—though logically and on a partial view of aesthetic experience distinguishable from sounds of a certain pitch, loudness, etc.—existence apart from those same sounds. We can, it is true, attend separately to the illusions, apparitions, elements and to their oppositely distinguished numbers (though I would say it takes about as much or more effort, though maybe of a different kind, to think of pure apparitions as it does to think of 'paint smooches'). But this is an intellectual attention. And even the unspoken suggestion that there are two sorts of things (even if one 'thing' is called virtual) existing side by side, to which we can attend, one or the other, seems to me to be highly misleading. The logical analysis is correct as far as it goes, but it is incomplete and needs to be supplemented in an adequate account of aesthetic. In the total aesthetic experience, the distinctions are of features within a single whole. In assessing the nature of the experience, the distinctions must be taken up again into the whole: the logical negations must be cancelled in a positive aesthetic affirmation. This is one of the dangers of *talking* about art. For if we stick to logic, we remain in the world of distinctions. If we do not go back constantly to the indivisible experience from which the distinctions are made and to which they must again be re-related, we get the 'either-or' or the 'side-by-side' mistake. Once again, I think that the logician tends to dictate to the aesthetician in Mrs Langer—the logician interested in pure forms, abstractions, distinctions, the aesthetician close to experience, affirming all the time the indivisibility of form and content.

§4   *Creative embodiment an 'emergent'*
She uses the word 'emergent'. ('The picture that emerges from

the process . . . The space itself is an emergent . . .') This word if taken seriously—taken more seriously than Mrs Langer takes it— is about the best word we can get. It is not perfect, since the aesthetic is unique, and the word 'emergent' as used by its inventors Lloyd Morgan and Alexander was intended to apply to cosmic evolution. But its use can illuminate aesthetics.

With certain organizations of the medium (together of course with other factors, such as the presence of the discriminating per-cipient, which we need not now bother with), the 'quality' of aesthetic embodiment emerges. The new quality has its own 'laws' and 'logic' (of a very peculiar and concrete kind) but as emergent inseparable from the organization of the material medium from which it does emerge; the emergent aesthetic 'quality' is a quality of that organization. Again, we can *attend* (with various kinds of effort) to the laws and logic of the different levels—to the techniques of the medium and its organization, or to the pure aesthetic 'logic' of embodied meaning, of the 'appari-tion', the 'virtual image', etc., and in doing so we need not always be thinking of the other; each has its own autonomy. But ontolo-gically and implied in our aesthetic experience, the different levels are compresent. The quality of aesthetic embodiment is always found together with a certain organization of the medium, and we cannot think or feel aesthetically in that particular way without perceiving that particular material organization.

The 'apparition' language, again is too attenuated: the word 'virtual' is still more ghostly. The apparition is the appearance of something. We can (as has been repeatedly said) recognize—by a difficult and admittedly important kind of abstraction—what is referred to by the words 'virtual' and 'apparition': we are well-advised to do this. It is quite another thing to be advised that the total object of aesthetic perception is the virtual; the aesthetic object, on the contrary, is rooted and grounded in heard sounds, painted canvas, vibrant words, physical action in dance or drama. Moreover, it must be insisted that we attend to these things, or give them a proportion of our total attention; it includes them as ingredients of the whole. (What would appreciation of Van Gogh be, if it excluded enjoyment of vibrant 'paint-smooches'?) That we can so attend to them can be suggested by an argument some-what analogous to that used by Harold Osborne.[1] In writing of the

---

[1] *The Philosophical Quarterly*, July 1964, 'Artistic Unity and Gestalt', pp. 220-1.

contrast between aesthetic perception and ordinary Gestalt perception, he points out that in aesthetic perception the (Gestalt) figure-ground process is restrained from operating freely. To attend to a work of art properly we have to hold the ordinary figure-ground tendency in check. 'In aesthetic contemplation attention is distributed over the whole field of the object. We do not pick out (or allow to jump out) prominent or significant perceptual chunks and let the background sink towards oblivion on the edge of attention.' By analogy (and analogy only) we might say that in aesthetic perception of art we do not attend to an 'apparition' which is a 'figure' against a 'background' of organized material medium. We try to take in the total impact. When, for example, I look at the two marvellous Vermeer pictures in the same room of the Rijksmuseum, Amsterdam—one of 'The Cook', the other of 'A Young Woman, reading a letter'—I see in each, gathered into a concentrated aesthetic focus, a whole world of meaning drawn from their subject matters (which source has not been so far discussed in these pages) organized to a perfection of composition and colour painted in pigments within frames. This total is what I see, gathered into the focus, and not the focal point of a virtual image only.

Speaking generally, I would say that Mrs Langer in her teaching of virtual images has ably drawn attention to what I would call the uniqueness of embodied meaning—which is different, I have argued, from the 'expression' of feeling, or the 'form of feeling'. (Hers is an implicit partial argument for 'embodiment' rather than 'expression'.) But I think she does not do justice to the place of the literal body of the organized medium in its contribution to the whole of aesthetic experience.

I am saying, then, that the 'aesthetic' (and here, of course, I have art particularly in mind) *is* embodiment, *means* embodiment. Wherever the aesthetic is, there is embodiment, wherever embodiment is, there is the aesthetic. The two are identical.

Is this tautology? It depends on what is meant by 'tautology'. If tautology simply means that A is A, that Aesthetic is Aesthetic and Embodiment is Embodiment and Embodiment is merely another (and rather clumsy and superfluous) name for Aesthetic—then the definition of the aesthetic in art as embodiment is not tautology. To say that the aesthetic is embodiment is not to say that A is A, but rather to say that A is XY, uniquely related. The aesthetic in art, certainly, is embodiment, means embodiment.

But here the aesthetic in 'art' is the given, and 'embodiment' is the complex analysis of it. 'Embodiment' stands for the conceptual analysis of the aesthetic of art, affirming that in the aesthetic there is a unique union of content with material form, so that in aesthetic experience content and form are not distinguished, though analytically and intellectually they are distinguishable. And the work of expounding embodiment in detail shows—and I shall develop it further—how the meaning factor is drawn from sources beyond art (including the already aesthetic meaningfulness of perceived forms and materials) and transformed into new emergent meaning aesthetically perceived as *belonging* to what is immediately perceived. All of this analysis, it is claimed, is not just the repeating of synonyms, but helps the understanding of what otherwise is an enigma, how seeing or listening to certain perceptual data in certain ways can come to be of such extraordinary significance and importance.

§5 *A note on expression:* '*a time to speak, and a time to be silent*'

I want to say, in the last part of the present Chapter, that the critical and philosophical language of 'expression' is relevant up to a point at which embodiment, meaning-embodied, occurs. There it has to stop. (So, indeed, also has the *talk* about Embodiment to stop.) Embodiment can receive all that expression has to offer it; then the creative transformation occurs, the *fiat* of embodiment.

It is nowhere being denied that expression enters into the *making* of art, or that in our attempts to *understand* art all round, we often ask, 'What is being expressed in it?'. For critical and appreciative understanding we do this often, and must. We do it much more naturally in the criticism of arts like literature and drama than when, say, we are talking of the very purest of formal music. The great novels, for instance, are about life: sometimes wide experience and subtle understanding are required for their mature appreciation. Sometimes, in reading a novel, we lay the book down in order to muse again on the perennial themes—the interplay of love, hate, good, evil, life, death—returning to the reading with better insight. The same is true of drama, allowing for the differences between the conditions of watching a play and reading a book. None of this is artistically irrelevant; none of it is simply distraction; it is an essential part of the total complex of artistic appreciation and understanding. Great literature and drama express the *gamut* of human experience; suppose the experience away: nothing is left, not even 'pure form': empty form is nothing.

This is one side of literature, the side of its subject matter. But appreciation of literature is not identical with the general reflections upon life; these are conditions of appreciation, not appreciation itself. The subject-matter as embodied in the form of (say) the novel—which as embodied I call its 'content'—is subject matter formed, and transformed, by artistry. In novel reading one is not normally focusing attention upon forms, and in particular upon the use of images and words—though it is the business of the critic at other times to draw our studied attention to these in order that, returning, we may appreciate formed-content in a new way, so enriching our understanding. But in actual reading, the 'form' is that *by* or *through* which, as though through a window glazed with considered distortion, we look out upon the subject-matter, now transformed into content. The form used by the artist is, in its operation, the shaping of the new perspective which is content (though the form, too, is shaped by the content). It is the perspective-content at which we look and which we enjoy, and not, normally, directly at the form which is its necessary condition as well as being an aspect of the whole.

And at *that* point and in that state, where we contemplate formed-content, we do not relevantly ask, 'What is being expressed, expounded? What is the subject-matter? What is it all about? We already possess the only answer possible at that moment—the 'answer' of the presented work. The achievement of creative embodiment and its enjoyment, just means that we are *not* attending to 'form as such', or to 'subject-matter as such', for each are abstractions—and abstractions are not the concern of aesthetic interest (though they may be of aesthetics). We are attending to subject-matter transformed in form and become content. This is the moment of aesthetic achievement in which there is natural, unselfconscious, spontaneous absorption in the fullness of artistic meaning. We are not, painfully, cultivating the state of 'being aesthetic': nor are we talking or thinking about 'expression'. And, although embodiment is in active operation, we are not (thank goodness) talking or thinking about that either. The world, the thought, the subject-matter, what is 'being expressed'—all have been touched with the magic of art. All have suffered

> . . . a sea-change
> Into something rich and strange.

This is the 'time to be silent'.

Each art (with each art's subforms) transforms in its own way: the novel is at one extreme end of the scale where 'subject-matter' looms large. Pure music (e.g. the fugue), which sometimes seems to be *all* 'form' and to have no 'subject-matter' outside music itself (but how scandalous to think of Bach as 'pure mathematics'!) seems to lie at the other end of the scale. Poetry, perhaps, comes somewhere in between. To some of these differences we turn in the next *Part*.

PART III

REPRESENTATIVE, ABSTRACT AND OTHER ARTS

CHAPTER V

REPRESENTATIVE ARTS, EXPRESSION AND EMBODIMENT

CHAPTER V

REPRESENTATIVE ARTS, EXPRESSION AND EMBODIMENT

§1 Introductory

I have been discussing general theory of the aesthetics of art. This has involved a critical examination of the theory of art as expression, and a positive proposal to consider embodiment, not expression, as the key-idea in the aesthetics of art.

One of the great difficulties of general aesthetics *is* that it is general. Works of art on the other hand are not only individual, but there are many different kinds of 'art'. How can any generalization apply equally to everything? Daunted by this, some give up, perhaps defending their action by some *a priori* theory that general aesthetics *must* in the nature of things be impossible. This may be wrong: but the difficulty remains—and it is a partly true allegation of general aesthetics that it has tended historically to base itself too exclusively on this, or that, form of art, on say, painting, *or* drama, *or* music.

The theory that art is 'imitation', for instance, has a good deal of *prima facie* plausibility in its application to some painting and sculpture, perhaps less to the novel, less still to poetry. To pure music it is difficult to apply at all—though it is true that Aristotle had his own view of music as 'mimesis'. The theory of 'expression' may seem appropriate to romanticism (of whatever date) or to post-romantic art in which expression of feeling is emphasized. It is harder (I do not say 'impossible') to apply it to Athenian sculpture of the fifth century BC, or to pure arabesque. Formalism, again, is apt to be anti-romantically biased, and finds it hard to do justice to art in which subject-matter is important or in which human feelings are deeply moved. How, for instance is it pertinent to a drama like *Romeo and Juliet* which makes a universal human appeal to the sentiments of sympathy for frustrated romantic love? It would be absurd, of course, to dismiss important theories of art in single phrases; I am only stressing the difficulty of generalizing in aesthetics. If 'embodiment' is to fare any better than the others as a valid generalization, it has to be *shown* to work out better when applied to the different forms of art—from 'representative' arts like literature and drama and some painting and sculpture at one end of the scale, to 'abstract' arts, visual or auditory, at the other. I shall try to show that it does. Since pure music is one of the most interesting as well as one of the most challenging of the arts for any aesthetic, the discussion of it will take four chapters.

This is not a systematic tome upon the arts, attempting to 'cover' them all. The examples, therefore, which I shall take are bound to be few and to some extent arbitrary. If, for example, there is little reference to such important arts as dance or pottery, or architecture or the novel—this is no sign of disrespect for them as forms of art.

The present Chapter considers 'representative arts', chiefly poetry and painting, with the express intention of looking to see how the theories of expression and embodiment can help us to understand them philosophically.

§2 *Poetry and painting: representation and imitation*

Poetry, and some of the visual arts, are clearly, 'representative' in some sense of that word. The word 'representative' though not perfect, is no worse than any other. A picture on an ancient Greek vase of a maiden gathering flowers, pictures of a dying slave, of Adam and Eve, of the infant Christ, of the birth of the Virgin, of a Haywain, of a Dutch Interior, of a steamer in a thunderstorm, of Tahitian women . . . all these 'represent' their subjects. They do it by some degree of imitation of forms and their relationships, by imitations of aspects of actually perceived or imagined subjects: they do it by means of line and gradation of tone and colour, so that the subject-matter of the painting is recognizable. Sometimes it is recognized very clearly, as in the case of a Dürer drawing or a Dutch Interior, or as when seeing a Rembrandt self-portrait, we look long into the grave eyes of a man of character. Sometimes we see it impressionistically (with small or large 'i'), as in a Turner or Manet. In representing these things, concepts too are represented (but not imitated)—the 'maiden', 'our first parents', the 'infant Christ', 'storminess', the exotic quality of Tahitian women.

In poetry, representation takes place not primarily by imitation of anything but by means of the conventional symbolism of words, grammar, syntax. By means of the words we can 'see' the subject or scene:

> I saw her once
> Hop forty paces through the public street;

> And having lost her breath, she spoke, and panted,
> That she did make defect perfection,
> And breathless, power breathe forth.

As with painting, we 'see' not only the subject or scene; ideas and images are represented. The lines not only give a vivid picture but a striking image ('breathless, power breathe forth'), an abstract concept (making 'defect perfection'). In Hamlet we can dwell upon, and see with new insight, the problems of suicide. Or a 'metaphysical' or religious idea can be presented, full of imagery, but with the focus upon an idea both known and passionately felt:

> He alone
> And none else can
> Bring bone to bone
> And rebuild man;
> And by His all-subduing might
> Make clay ascend more quick than light.

Through the medium of language, literature can present concepts directly as no other art can; it 'represents' concepts by presenting them in the same word-language as that in which they are formed— sometimes with very little change (as in some of Hopkins' poetry), but with the stamp of the imagery of personal involvement upon them.

Realism can be agreeable. But we need not spend time in arguing, negatively, that even if there is an aesthetic element in the enjoyment of imitation (and there may be some) the simple *likeness* of a representation to its subject plays a very small part in the total enjoyment of art. (It may be a misleading part.) Interest in subject-matter may of course contribute much of the final richness of art. The human experience and human interest involved in any real understanding of Hamlet or Macbeth is certainly a *sine qua non* of the aesthetic enjoyment of the plays. (And in the special case of a play about an historical person, there is always the question, 'Is it like him?') The same thing is true in a different way of much historical painting. At the same time, it is not the factor of likeness as such which is of aesthetic importance.

Again, imitation and likeness are of course very partial. Perhaps the nearest thing to full imitation and likeness is to be found in acting. It is interesting, and a little odd, that those who have

D

quoted most often the holding of the 'mirror up to nature' have applied it to the visual arts of painting and sculpture and have forgotten the context of the original image. Hamlet's words, in context, are:

> The purpose of playing, whose end, both at the first and now, was and is, to hold, as 'twere, the mirror up to nature.

It was the purpose of *playing*.

And the first originators—the poet, the playwright—are *interpreters* of life, and not mere imitators or 'realists'. In writing about anything, in using speech at all, there is, inevitably, abstraction and selection; thinking and language are of this nature; the artist picks out and attends to certain aspects and not others.

Moreover, the selection is evaluative: it is selection of what is felt to be significant and important. Even in a slight lyric, where the subject is not of much intrinsic importance, the poet picks out what he feels at that moment to be, in that context, of significance—be it but 'a sweet disorder in the dress'. He is not just describing a banal fact, but (in such an instance as this) something which charms and interests him. Often his interest is deeper, and it is his feeling for what he writes about which is expressed in his writing. George Boas (*Philosophy and Poetry*, p. 9) wrote: 'the ideas in poetry are usually stale and often false and no one older than sixteen would find it worth his while to read poetry merely for what it says'. This may be an overstatement, for poetry can contain profound philosophical insight. But even so, it is not the truth of the philosophical statements (which might sometimes be put better in plain prose) which lends the kind of interest to poetry which it has. It is, in the first instance, that the poet has *felt* these ideas to be significant, and has expressed his feeling in his poetry. He is not imitating, or purveying bald philosophy, but is expressing his felt, poetic reactions.

This is true, as I have just said, 'in the first instance'. But it is only part of the story—that the poets feels things, evaluates them, and that this feeling is expressed and 'gets into' his poetry. The other half of the story, and of central importance, is that in becoming a poem the values and meanings are transformed through their intercourse with the medium (here of words); new embodied meaning is discovered. It is not untrue to say that the poet feels about all sorts of things and expresses his feelings about them—or expresses them-as-felt. But the language of expression is provisional and incomplete, subject to reservation. So, if there happens to be some profound truth in the poem, it is not that bare truth, nor even just the feeling of the poet for that truth communicated to us by his descriptive expression, which we apprehend in the poem, but these things *taken up into* the poem, transformed into embodied meaning. This is a new thing, and it is a new knowledge. 'That life seems meaningless' is a thought which has often been uttered by philosophers of different kinds. But in the familiar lines:

> To-morrow, and to-morrow, and to-morrow,
> Creeps in this petty pace from day to day
> To the last syllable of recorded time,
> And all our yesterdays have lighted fools
> The way to dusty death. Out, out, brief candle!
> Life's but a walking shadow, a poor player
> That struts and frets his hour upon the stage
> And then is heard no more: it is a tale
> Told by an idiot, full of sound and fury,
> Signifying nothing.

there is a new incarnation. It is not simply that it says more than a short paraphrase can give, but that every bit of the quality of the sounding language is a *part* of the felt meaning. Any good critic could show this. The long, dreary, repeated, sounds of 'to-mōrrow . . ., crēēps . . .'; the sound of contempt and disgust in the contrast of the long and the sharp sounds in 'pĕtty'; the compression of 'dusty death'; the passion of 'Out, out . . .'; the despair of 'struts and frets', of 'idiot'; the frustration, by the word 'nŏthing'; the expectation of the long 'signifying' . . . —in all these, and throughout the passage, the 'sound' and the 'sense' are, aesthetically, completely inseparable.

Poetry, then, undoubtedly 'represents', and at all levels. It can be 'realistic' (though not in the strictest sense imitative), but is not merely so. The poet feels for or about the things which interest him; he evaluates them, spontaneously or more deliberately, and his representations are in one sense expressive of his feelings for things or of things as felt. But representation is finally not just expression, but discovery through embodiment in the medium of new meaning, freshly known, untranslatable.

The same things are generally true, *mutatis mutandis*, of the visual arts, for example painting. Painting can, up to a point, imitate nature directly as literature cannot. But not only, as we said, is the aesthetic value of imitation slight, and not only is imitation of the surface of things, rather than of their substance: inevitably and, sometimes by deliberate choice, it is selective. Inevitably so, because however realistic a painting, however near to a *trompe l'oeil* it may be, it is a painting done from a certain point of view and not another; the light, the tone, the colour, the perspective . . . is inescapably a selection of one out of, theoretically, an infinite number of possibilities. And in all cases where extremist realism is not the sole aim, it is deliberate, *evaluative* selection. The painter is interested in and notices certain aspects of the world, both as subject-matter and as visual appearance. The painter cannot directly represent *concepts* (particularly 'metaphysical' ones) as the writer can, so that it may be that subject-matter as such carries less weight in painting than in literature: it would be difficult to argue that any picture can compass such a range of human interest that a great tragic drama can. This is debatable; Giotto's religious piety and his quality as an artist certainly reveals itself in his interest in the subjects of the paintings in the Arena Chapel at Padua as well as in his selective interest in visual appearances.

The painter's interests may vary widely. Masaccio, and, later, Piero della Francesca, are interested in light and shadow and use them to create atmosphere. Botticelli is interested in ancient myths, and his feeling for flowing line and gentle movement deflect him from realistic literalism, to representation of ideal figures in a world far removed from the everyday world. Cezanne was interested in harmony, balance, the representation of three dimensions in colour without line on a flat surface; he arranges his shapes to that end rather than for literal realism. And so on.

In talking about the painter's interests even in subject-matter we are of course inevitably talking at the same time about his sense of the medium and the problem of embodiment. If Masaccio, della Francesca, Botticelli, Cezanne are interested in subject-matter, in *what* they paint, it is as painters in a medium that they are interested; their interest is in terms of paint, as the working poet's interest in ideas is in terms of words. Indeed our way of talking has been artificial, though up to a point necessarily so. The way an artist looks at the external world, we know in a general sort of way, is different from the way in which we casually look at things—at trees and lamp-posts and kerbs when we have to see them only sufficiently for practical needs. But unless we are artists, we don't know exactly how things 'look' to the painter before he paints. Perhaps we don't know exactly how they look even if we are artists—until we paint. Even then, we don't know exactly how they look before they were painted, because the looking, before and after painting, is already affected by thinking and feeling in terms of a medium.

So, although it is certainly right to say that the artist's purpose is not just to imitate, to hold the mirror to 'nature', we are not speaking *accurately* when we talk as if the representative artist were painting nature as he selectively and evaluatively sees it. For his thinking in terms of the medium, and his achievement of embodiment, transforms reflexively everything he does. Some 'likeness' there may be in representative art: of course we recognize what the picture (or the poem) is about: but it is likeness rendered in the medium, transformed there, made intrinsic to it. We value representative painting aesthetically for itself not because it is like something else—though one of the reasons for which we sometimes value it is that it helps us to see the world in a fresh way afterwards. *Why* should resemblance to a supposed 'model' (natural, non-artistic, perhaps a model as Tom, Dick or Harry can see it) be set up as a standard for art at all? The truth is the reverse: good pictorial art itself becomes a new standard of seeing: it sets a standard by which the world can be seen in a new way. Oscar Wilde was, so far, right—though cleverly over-simple —that 'nature imitates art', not art, nature.

If then even representative art must finally be judged, not by reference to its likeness to that which it represents, but by references to its own artistic structure, it suggests at once that the difference between 'representative' arts and those 'abstract' arts which may seem to have no 'life' subject-matter outside themselves is not nearly so great as appears at first sight. Music, and some abstract painting and sculpture, seems to confront us with new, autonomous life. But so, strictly, does *all* art. I shall return to this shortly.[1]

§3 *'Tertiary qualities': their basis, associative and otherwise*
Representative painters are interested in things, or in the appearances of things as they feel for and about them, and this interest

[1] See § 5 below, and Chapter VI–X, *passim*.

and feeling is affected by feeling for the medium. But we know too that things as perceived have aesthetic qualities—independently of any thought of representing them artistically. Visually perceived things have primary qualities (e.g. extension and shape), secondary qualities (e.g. colour, with hue, saturation, etc.) and —what may be conveniently called—'tertiary' qualities[1] (e.g. the 'cheerfulness' or 'sombreness' of colours).

The nature of these tertiary qualities needs some attention. I shall consider them first independently of their relation to art, then in their possible relations to art.

What objective basis have these—extra-artistic—tertiary qualities? We are speaking all the time of course of *phenomenal* objects: it is not being supposed that colours and shapes and sounds can be 'gay' or 'gloomy' apart from all perceiving subjects. Nevertheless is there any reason to suppose that there are trans-subjective, independent causal conditions, determining—at least up to a point—the tertiary qualities we experience? In this I am not for the moment including associational causes and conditions. I am assuming that in any experience of tertiary qualities there is almost certainly some influence of association. But the immediate question is: Are there also causes independently of such associations? For expressionists like Santayana association is *the* ground, the only ground, of expressiveness of perceptual data.

Professor Hospers also argues[2] in the main for an associationist interpretation, but of a 'natural' and 'universal' kind. Colours, for instance, can of course acquire 'expressiveness' through private and personal association; a traumatic experience on seeing violet for instance, can subsequently affect our seeing of violet. Or associations may be culturally conditioned. (This latter he is equivocal about; I shall comment on this below.) But the main cause of expressiveness—still broadly associative—is, for Hospers, 'natural'. 'There is a "natural expressiveness" of certain colours and other sensory items which is invariant from person to person

---

[1] These tertiary qualities—under the heading of 'the expressiveness of sensa and forms'—are discussed, as aesthetic raw material for the arts, in Chapters II, III and IV of my *A Study in Aesthetics*, 1931. Although this book has now been for many years out of print, the bulk of Chapters III and IV are reprinted in *Artistic Expression*, edited by John Hospers, published by Appleton-Century-Crofts, 1967. Hospers also reprints, in *Essays in Aesthetics*, published by Harper and Row, New York, another excerpt from the same book, criticizing Chapter I of Roger Fry's *Transformations*.

[2] *Art and Philosophy*, ed. Sidney Hook, New York University Press, pp. 138 *et seq.*

and culture to culture.' 'Green is the colour of the normal fore-ground of landscapes'; it is harmless and agreeable, and has 'as its affect the feeling of quiet cheerfulness'. Blue is the colour of the sky, 'the source of light and the realm of illumination' and also of the distant hills. There is 'a lack of insistency or aggressiveness about blue'. Red is the colour of blood, the life fluid of organisms, vital to life, belonging to success in the hunt, raid, combat, danger. It is the most dramatic and stirring of colours. On the other hand yellow, the colour of sunshine, is gay, and white has the cold intensity of snow and clouds. Then he adds in the same breath (and in parenthesis) 'The full truth of the matter will probably not be known until neurology has had its say on the subject; I suspect that part of the dramatic character of red lies, not in these universal associations, but in the way in which color itself impinges on the retina of the eye'. He concludes with the usual observations about horizontal lines being expressive of restfulness . . . the horizontal position, etc. If we were not gravitational beings, such expressive-ness would be absent.

(But this last remark, and the remark about neurology, surely would put the thesis on a different footing?)

We may agree—for it is obvious—that some associations are more universal than others, those being based on the associations of the natural world around us being most universal. But even these can-not be assumed to be so universal as Hospers thinks. He is too simple and sweeping. Climatic conditions must surely affect asso-ciations? The 'quiet cheerfulness' of green, 'harmless and agree-able', may apply in temperate climates with good rainfall. But what of the sudden shouting of green in the desert spring? Or, in a northern land of fog, does not the breaking of the clouds and the impingement of blue sky contradict the statement that blue is not an object 'of important reaction'? Again, he under-rates cultural differences. Speaking of the difference between the west, where black is the colour of mourning, and the far east, where white is, he says, 'this in no way shows that the same colour-percepts are expressive of different affects in the two cultures. Rather (the point is not a new one), the Orientals do not share our belief that the symbols connected with a funeral should be such as to express negativity and destructiveness, and despair of death, which black does for us (and presumably for them also); they consider different colours appropriate because they consider a different mood appropriate to such occasions. There seems to be no evidence that culture determines colour-affect, but only that colour evaluations differ in different cultures . . . There is, I would contend, a uniformity of affect . . . which is much greater than the uniformity of evaluation of this affect.'[1]

But there are confusions here. There is the vitiating general assumption that aesthetic affects are easily nameable. There is an inconsistency (with what he writes elsewhere in his article) in his supposition that perceptual data are separable from their 'affective qualities'—which supposition is, in fact, an instance of the fallacious two-term theory discussed in Chapter II above. Hospers is going beyond any evidence in saying that the colour affect (or better, the tertiary quality) of the same colour is the same in different cultures. As we saw above, although we can, on personal comparisons within our own experiences and on general grounds of aesthetics, assert the indivisibility of 'surface' and 'feeling-import', there is no direct way of comparing the aesthetic 'look' of things as between *different* persons and cultures, of showing that the tertiary quality is the same (or different). The only way in which we could test directly would be for one person to live for a considerable time in each of two countries and cultures and to tell us from his multiple experience whether the 'look' of the same colour changed with the migrations. (As it does so, easily, with new associations, is it not most likely that it would?) If, for instance, white is associated, for westerners, with wedding days and for orientals with funerals, then, in certain contexts at least, one would expect white to have a different 'look'. Even if orientals do not associate death with negativity, despair, etc., and the wearing of white seems to them appropriate, nevertheless the irreducible differences between death and weddings would be liable to produce different associations of the colour white, and we should expect the tertiary qualities to be different too.

So much for association. But all 'natural' causes of affective expressiveness (tertiary qualities) are not associative. What about the 'neurology' which Hospers mentions so casually? ('I suspect that part of the dramatic character of red lies, not in these universal associations, but in the way in which color itself impinges on the retina of the eye.') Why, indeed, should not non-associational 'natural' facts be at least part of the condition of there being tertiary qualities? It seems to be shown by experimental use of such instruments as the pneumograph that, as a high or a loud

[1] *Op. cit.*, p. 139.

note is more stimulating than a low or a soft one, so colours at the 'warm' end of the spectrum are more stimulating. If so, one would expect the tertiary quality at the 'warm' end of the spectrum to be, quite naturally, different from one at the 'cold' end, and this distinguishably from the associations the colours might have. The tertiary qualities could not be accurately named (they never can), but 'warm' and 'cold' in themselves are suggestive.

Please note that I am not saying that sensory stimulation is sufficient to determine that a particular tertiary quality be experienced. What a tertiary quality is, is affected also by context and assocation. I am only suggesting that tertiary qualities have some objective and independent ground and are not dependent wholly on associations. (I should think that being a 'gravitational' organism would be an instance of this—but I am not sure. No one as far as I know has yet tested whether the 'look' and 'feel' of vertical and horizontal lines changes for long-term weightless astronauts. And I suspect that this brand of space-research would not be thought to advance national prestige!

The same general principle—of there being an objective, non-associational ground for tertiary qualities—seems also to hold of simple forms like shapes, but requires a slightly different account: it is not that underlying unperceived stimuli are the conditions (as with simple colours and sounds), but the *perceived forms* of the shapes themselves. Are there not tertiary qualities here, distinct from association? If one looks steadily and in a relaxed contemplative way at a simple circle, or oval, or square, is not the enjoyment of their very simple perceived structural characters at the same time the enjoyment of tertiary qualities, unnameable, not simply identifiable with the mathematical definition of the structures, though arising, as I say, directly from enjoyment of the structures? The circle, as we gaze at it, has a quality of symmetrical perfection (it is symmetrical in all directions of a plane, just as a sphere is perfectly symmetrical in three dimensions). The oval is more complex, but its smoothly simplified unity seems to be an appreciable *quality*, immediately emergent from its structure. And the perfect square has 'something' too! (So has an egg, so has a cube.) Of course the tertiary qualities of all these and other shapes can be affected by associations in many ways. And they may have unconscious symbolisms—not only Freudian ones. But they do seem to possess a basis of intrinsic meaning. Although we are not talking of art at the moment, some of the

D*

abstract work of an artist like Kandinsky—his arrangements of perfect coloured circles or spheres—seem to be striving after the intrinsic tertiary qualities of coloured shapes in relation.

Hospers in his paper denies Rudolph Arnheim's view that affective ('tertiary') qualities are intrinsic—e.g. that a colour is 'by its own intrinsic nature expressive of some particular affect'. He agrees that the colour *has* the 'affective quality' (and is in *that* sense 'intrinsic' to it), but holds that it is not intrinsic in the other sense—because the quality is the product of association.

On this count I think he is wrong because, as I have just been saying, there are non-associational grounds of tertiary qualities. I would say that there are, indeed, intrinsic *elements* in tertiary qualities. By this I mean that there is an element intrinsic to the shape or colour, irreducible to association. This statement has however to be guarded against misinterpretation. First—to repeat *ad nauseam*—it is impossible to affirm with certainty that there is ever any experience of tertiary qualities which is not in any way affected by association. (There may be some; I find—like Plato!—looking at circles a very 'pure' experience indeed.) Therefore, because associations may be different, the tertiary qualities may be different for different people. For this reason we cannot affirm a one-to-one correspondence between any objective things or events, and particular tertiary qualities. For another reason—the variation of different people's responses to stimuli, different 'thresholds', variations of health, mood, the effects of drugs (e.g. mescalin), race differences, etc., we could not say that there could be any exact correlation between stimuli and the tertiary qualities of colours. There could be other reasons too—if this discussion had not already gone on so long—for arguing the non-universality of relation between objective factors and tertiary qualities. What I want to say, therefore, is not that there are tertiary qualities 'intrinsic' to given primary and secondary ones in a one-to-one relationship, the same in everyone's experience—but simply that there is, along with other factors, an irreducibly non-associative objective factor in the conditions under which tertiary qualities arise, contributing an intrinsic *element* to the being of tertiary qualities. Tertiary qualities would not, I think, *be* at all if it were not for their emergence from independent colours, sounds and shapes.

The reader may feel that this is all very long-winded—and why bother? What matters for aesthetics, it may be said, is the experience, not its causes and conditions. For an 'expression' theory perhaps it does not matter so much; for an embodiment theory, which insists that the aesthetic emerges through man's psychophysical engagement with an independent world, more than association is needed. The impingement of the world, with its obstinately independent characters, *is* important. If there were not the encounter with the independent world, there would be no foundation for associations to build upon.

§4 *Tertiary qualities and visual art-making: a corrective note*

This talk of the tertiary qualities of simple perceptual data— colours, sounds, shapes—though necessary, is necessarily artificial. The qualities of these data are not, in isolation, of great significance. One *can*, for experimental purposes, spend a great deal of time gazing at areas of colour, or at pure circles and elipses, or listening to single notes of flute or trumpet. But we do not normally experience the world in that way in ordinary or aesthetic experience; we experience things in their various contexts; it is a coloured, shaped, resonant world of the appearance of things-in-relation.

Our talk has given an unreal impression of bittiness. And of course any idea that the visual artist just picks out a lot of units of tertiary qualities and puts them together like bricks in a building, would be absurd. If we speak of perceptual data as 'raw material'— as in a sense they are—the emphasis is upon the 'raw', though even then the analogy is too simple. The perceptual world for the artist is a concrete world of rich but continually shifting aesthetic meaning, and meaning derived not only from sense stimulation, perceived forms or conscious association, but from many other sources—from a vast reservoir of images and ideas, conscious and unconscious.

The representative painter is not only aware of all these things; he uses them, as we said, potentially and actually as an artist working in a medium, *and with tools*. The use of tools in painting, though it is the skilful handling of brush, knife, or other instruments in developing a design, is not only this. It is an involved activity of his whole being. His external behaviour, what he does with his tools, the movements of his arm, the development of the design on the surface—these are united with the meaningfulness of his whole involvement in the activity of painting. Painting is what the *man* is now doing. The work is the living reflection of himself in action.

To understand equally on the one hand the relation of art to life, and on the other art's independence and autonomy, we do need to attend to *both* of two things—appreciation of art as a completed unity, and the complex activity by which art comes into being. Stress on the appreciative side alone can be as misleading as an exclusive stress on origins and making. Because appreciation as such is concerned with the autonomous art-object, it may well tend to isolate art, underestimating the manner in which art is rooted in life and grows out of it, growing at the same time into a process which becomes autonomous. Barbara Hepworth (writing however as a mainly abstract, not a representative artist), describes it vividly:

'Abstract drawing has always been for me a particularly exciting adventure. First there is only one's mood; then the surface takes one's mood in colour and texture; then a line or curve which, made with a pencil on the hard surface of many coats of oil or gouache, has a particular kind of "bite" rather like incising on slate; then one is lost in a new world of a thousand possibilities because the next line in association with the first will have a compulsion about it which will carry one forward into completely unknown territory. The conclusion will be reached only by an awareness of some special law of harmonics induced at the beginning with the second line added to the first. Suddenly before one's eyes is a new form which . . . can be deepened or extended, twisted or flattened . . . as one imbues it with its own special life.'[1]

When one thinks of this kind of thing—art being made, looked at from the inside, discovering meaning, it is plainer than ever how inadequate the language of 'expressing feelings' can sound. Think of this *process* of painting or drawing. Perhaps the first stroke on canvas can be called expressive—maybe of agitation or excitement, partly symptomatic, partly more. (Even here it is embodiment, expression transformed in the paint or charcoal stroke.) But as soon as even the second stroke is made, the language of expression has already become absurdly out of date, for the new line or patch comes to have meaning only in relation to the first; the *picture* has taken charge. As Barbara Hepworth put it, the sur-

[1] Barbara Hepworth, *Carvings and Drawings*, Lund Humphries, 1952. Quoted by Ronald W. Hepburn, *Proceedings of the Aristotelian Society*, 1958-59, p. 207.

face 'takes one's mood in colour and texture'. The new autonomous rule of art is in command. The self-speaking organization or form captures the attention—and it is form not merely of shapes upon the canvas, form abstracted from content, but form charged with meaning, meaning in the context of the whole picture, the form of embodied-content in the picture. It may be harmless, and even up to a point useful, to say that the lines of Picasso's *Child with Dove* express tenderness, or to say Munch's *The Cry* expresses fear, or a Moore sculpture maternal or family feelings. But it also tends to divert the attention to subject matter separable from the embodiment. Moore has often said (in effect), that the meaning of his work is the meaning as 'stone is saying it'.[1]

Generally speaking, it may be that it is more legitimate to speak of 'expressiveness' outside the sphere of art because there the items are simple, more abstracted, more isolated, and associations are more free. *Inside* the complex work they become determined by their context, become individual, far less capable of being even approximately characterized in language. Perhaps this can be illustrated by taking an intermediate case, of something which is not a framed work of art like a picture or a mounted sculpture, but a beautiful object of use. Of a Jenson shallow-bowled spoon with a sinuous handle. I long ago wrote:[2] 'The lines are smooth, easy, liquid, flowing; the handle is deliciously curved, like the tail of a leopard. And strangely, without contradiction, the leopard's tail is finished with little raised nodules like small grapes. It is a queer mixture of a leaf and a leopard. The texture is grey and dull like river mist, with soft lights shining out of it like the moon out of a misty sky. The sheen is like white-grey satin: the bowl is delicately shaped with over-turning fastidiously pointed fronds; it is restrained and shallow, yet large enough to be generous. The lines are fine and sharp with clean edges.' Here, the associations are free, free as the freedom of the common object it is. In that sense, the expressiveness is not controlled as it would be within a formal work of art. Yet it is an art object too. 'If you hold the spoon in your hand, you feel it as a kind of poem which in a strange way unites all these, and many other, values into a single whole.' As a free object, it is expressive in many ways; as an art-object expressiveness in it melts into the wholeness of the individual form which you see and handle. The aesthetic quality of the spoon

---

[1] See below, p. 119.
[2] *A Study in Aesthetics*, pp. 101-2.

is certainly not reducible to, or adequately expressible in the language of the images it calls forth.

§6   *Subject-matter, and the autonomy of representative, and abstract art*

I have been talking about representative arts, which have subject-matter. The analytic understanding of these must include the recognition of the obvious life- or reality-sources, as well as the way in which, through artistic treatment, these become transformed. Aesthetic appreciation, too, implies appreciation of experience of life outside art.

In drama, for instance, there is, as we said, often a very conscious awareness of the life outside art, and an immature and inexperienced person may miss much. On the other hand, although they have subject-matter, the works are also self-contained and autonomous. The relationship of art to reality outside it is not like the truth of propositions, or of photographs, squarely justified by a conformity to something which is not itself. Representative art is an interpretation of life, taking life into itself, authoritatively transforming it, making it part of a total, intenser and more penetrating insight. Whereas on a common-sense view of truth, the truth of the proposition or the picture-photo is subservient to its conformity with fact, being—metaphorically speaking—compelled to pay back equal for equal, representative art, though deriving from experience of the world, is really *borrowing* from it and, in free enterprise, investing what it borrows in the foundation and development of a new construction, a new way of seeing the world, which it offers back to the world. The commonsense view of truth has an analogy with the Old Testament analogy of justice, of 'an eye for an eye and a tooth for a tooth'. But art is not a returning of equal for an equal which was borrowed; it is the repaying of an hundredfold—and in currency which sets a new standard.[1]

It is vitally important to remember this when making the transition from representative to non-representative or abstract arts, because, in view of what has been said, the transition is not nearly so radical as it might have been expected to be. I have tried to show that the study of representative arts leads us on to emphasise what might, superficially, have seemed to be the exclusive property of the abstract arts, namely complete autonomy.

[1] But on truth, see below Chapters XII and XIII.

Abstract arts are commonly supposed to have no subject-matter (whether this is true or not I shall discuss). Their autonomy is therefore little open to question. But neither, now, is the autonomy of representative art. There does not seem to be anything like the division between the two sorts that there is commonly supposed to be—though there are, of course, differences. There does not seem to be, *prima facie*, any need for two different aesthetic theories, one for representative, the other for abstract arts: one differentiated theory should do.

On the other hand it has still to be asked of the abstract arts— such as abstract painting or sculpture or pure music—whether *they* have any relationship, artistically of importance, to the life or reality or experience which is outside them. The main question now is, in fact, the reverse of the question we have been asking about the representative arts. Of them we had to ask, 'If they have any subject-matter outside themselves, how do they come to have autonomy?'

Of the abstract arts, whose autonomy is accepted, the question now is, 'Does this allow of their having any relation to subject-matter or life-experience outside art?' (Clive Bell and others, we remember, denied all such relationships.) If, in fact, they did have none, there would still be a division between the two kinds. This is the question which will have to be discussed. What are the abstract arts really doing? Have they, or have they not, life-sources? Has pure music, for instance, a purely internal life of its own, without life-connections which have any significance within music? In representative art there is transformation of subject-matter in embodiment. But where is the 'subject-matter' (apart from purely musical subject-matter) in the pure music of a fugue? What is the relation of the content to the form of music? Are there some underground connections here with 'life'—or is it an insult to music to say so? These many questions will have to be discussed in the chapters which follow. The visual abstract arts will not, in the light of what has been said, require lengthy treatment. Music is another matter, and will, as I have forecast, take four chapters.

CHAPTER VI

ABSTRACT AND OTHER ARTS

CHAPTER VI

ABSTRACT AND OTHER ARTS

§1   *Abstract art: the complex dialogue*

The following pages are not a history, not even a very potted one, of modern visual art. But it is impossible to understand modern tendencies, modern attitudes towards representation and abstraction, without some allusion to art movements and reactions within, and against, abstraction and representation. Innovators like Matisse, Kandinsky, Picasso . . . are men of their time, notable because of their struggles against what they thought was a deadening tradition and for their attempts to develop new perspectives. And, it should be noted, these movements are not movements of theory divorced from practice. They were practical experiments in art, and the theories which went along with them are related always to these experiments.

It is convenient to distinguish, in these discussions, between two senses of abstract art. There is (*a*) 'abstract' art in the sense in which there is some element of representation of objects in the world, but abstract*ed* in lesser or greater degree from them. And there is (*b*) abstract art in which the representative element strictly speaking disappears altogether; it is sometimes called 'non-objective' or 'non-figurative' art. (This is not to say, however, that all life-influences, associations, suggestions . . . disappear entirely.) Abstracted art (*a*) is seen in Cézanne in one way, in cubism in another, or in the war-shelter drawings of Henry Moore. Kandinsky's first abstract work in 1910, or his later geometrical paintings, are examples of (*b*) non-figurative abstract art: so are some of the works of Mondrian and Ben Nicholson. The movement is one of many vicissitudes, with many swingings backwards and forwards between representation and 'non-figuration'. Life-images keep peeping, or bursting, through.

It is hard to say where abstract art begins—there is some abstraction even in the most realistic art—and there is plenty of abstraction in the primitives. But the nineteenth-century Impressionists are a convenient starting point here. Sometimes, as in certain of Monet's or Pissarro's paintings, there are representations of subjects of traditional or at least post-romantic interest—sunrise, landscapes, houses with red roofs. The treatment is impressionistic, not realistically accurate. The subjects are sometimes interesting in themselves, sometimes not—e.g. a haystack or a swing. But the artist's main interest is in the play of colour and illumination, the surface effects of light and the treatment of it—of which Pointillism is an example. Whatever the subject, the emphasis is upon the surfaces of things, the solid and the massive depicted as shimmering, dancing surfaces of light and colour. The same stress on surfaces and also on the properties of the medium is seen in one way in the later Fauvists, with their concern for the effects of pure colour, or in another way in Whistler's titles—'Nocturne in blue and green'.

But it was Cézanne, in his earlier days a dissatisfied impressionist, who proposes the use of colour no longer as surface decoration, but as the medium for the expression of three-dimensional form. This was not now shown by means of drawing or by use of chiaroscuro, but by the relations of colours and tones. Solidity, depth rather than surface, but solidity and depth in terms of colour. Subjects—landscapes, portraits, still lifes—are still depicted, but as occasions for the experimental use of the medium of paint in building up solid forms, the relations between masses, overlapping planes, an organizing of plastic rhythms into unified patterns. It is a kind of free architecture of nature rendered in two dimensions.

His painterly interpretation of nature 'treated through the cylinder, the sphere and the cone' (a phrase of Cézanne's) is a strong influence in the just-born cubism of Picasso. It is seen in 'Les Demoiselles D'Avignon'. Here a work beginning with a representative impulse is transformed into an abstract design in which the subject-interest is almost, though not entirely, lost in attention to a complex relationship of space directions, movements, of lines, of planes set at an angle to one another, almost like a carving —a fascinating piece of geometrical dynamics. This first beginning of cubism is carried much further in the so-called 'analytical' development of cubism where one still gets representation, but representation not of whole objects as seen in ordinary perception, but of their parts—particularly those parts which are of outstanding interest. These parts are put together in what to the uninitiated might seem a higgledy-piggledy way but are in fact organized into subtle compositions of space and colour relations. Two rather similar examples of this are Braque's 'Homage to J. S. Bach' and a 'Still Life' of Picasso. The subject of both of these pictures is musical objects, particularly the violin, the parts of which are distributed over the picture as the deisgn of the picture seems to demand it. Another example of the same thing, again with the violin as subject (but this time with the whole violin as a part of the picture) is a Still Life of Gris, 'The Album'. One gets here also not only analysed pieces seen simultaneously, but successive views, set down in the single picture. Moreover, there are not only pieces of objects as actually seen from outside; imaginary cross-sections are shown too. The result is a design which can be extremely interesting or even moving. In many familiar Picassos an eye, a breast, a hand, a thigh, may appear anywhere on the canvas, the justification being, perhaps, that these may be seen by the moving eye in any order. But the arrangement is controlled by the composition of the picture as a whole. Here, too, in 'analytical cubism', the superimposed planes set at all angles, is the beginning of *collage*.

The third stage of cubism, called by Gris the 'synthetic' stage, is a curious reversal of the earliest one. Whereas, to begin with, there was representation of whole objects, followed by parts of objects arranged in design, now one gets 'realism', not as the representation of perceived objects, but more, on the analogy of Platonic 'realism', a representation of the abstract forms or essences of things which are *then* made particular on the painted surface. It is, of course only an analogy. The Platonic Forms, Universals, Essences—whatever they are called, are pure conceptions—triangularity, circularity . . . virtue . . . and not just generalized images. The Platonic Forms strictly speaking are not visually representable. But the synthetic cubists got as near to it as they could. Gris claimed that 'from a cylinder I make a bottle'. Picasso, from the most abstract design of rectangles, flowing curved enclosures, elipses with a dot in the middle . . . suggests a human 'Head'. This is a break from representation in the usual sense; it is a construction, first, of abstract general patterns, then there is a return to a suggestion upon the canvas of something in the real world. The movement is from the generalized shape, as analogous as possible with the pure form or essence, to the bottle or the human head, or, as in Brancusi, the passage from the construction of a beautiful shape, to, say, a sculpture entitled 'Bird'. In Kandinsky, the originator of abstract art in the sense of non-objective art, there is a development, out of Impressionism and through Fauvism, to emphasis on the direct impact of colour—and pure form-patterns—without any attempt at representation at all. It is based upon the analogy of pure music. Kandinsky attempted to cut himself off from impressions of the real world in order to create plastic form unadulterated. Associated with Marc and Klée, he turned his back, for a time at any rate, to even the suggestion of the images of real things. Lines, dots, rectangles, coloured spheres . . .; in patterns of virginal purity—these symbolize his feeling of the desire to separate art from nature. On the other hand it is difficult to go on consistently sustaining this separation. In, for instance, some of the later pictures painted within ten years of his death, fantastic figures appear through the abstractions. In (e.g.) 'Balancing Act' (1935) two embryonic forms balance one another.

The return to abstract, charmingly whimsical but undoubtedly life-suggesting forms is seen too in Klée and (though he is perhaps in a different category) Miro. Leger is another who, not intending to represent the reality of perceptual appearance, to give the representation of commonsense wholes, showed abstract human figures suggesting machine-like assemblies or puppets. It is not representation of nature as perceived but rather of schemata of constructed images or ideas. It is, once again, a curious reversal of representation, parallel to what happened in Cubism. Pictures are not now abstractions from perceived objects whose identity may be difficult to detect. Rather they are representations, sometimes very 'realistic' indeed, of queer, often very artificially constructed, abstract images. (One gets this kind of 'realism' too in a Surrealist like Dali.)

Another zig-zag mover is Mondrian. He moved from perceived objects to abstract design, extracting and abstracting coloured forms till they became pure design. He, and Ben Nicholson, who was influenced by him, represent perhaps the most austere geometrical influence of this period. Though these paintings of Mondrian may have been originally derived from perception of the real world, they are as little suggestive of the world of ordinary perception as could be.

A rather different dialogue is represented by Henry Moore and Barbara Hepworth. Moore certainly—as is seen in his wartime studies of night-life in the Underground bomb-shelters (already referred to)—did learn by abstraction from perceptual experience. But in some of his later sculptures there is no direct abstraction from any models. Nor is it even just an abstract representation in stone of an image or concept, say, of a reclining woman or a family. It is not a bodying forth of abstract geometrical forms either—'the cylinder, the sphere, the cone'. The work appears rather to grow out of the very form of the medium, the stone itself. It is 'woman as stone would say it'. Professor Gombrich writes illuminatingly on this. The 'modern artist wants to create things. The stress is on create *and* on things. He wants to feel that he has made something which had no existence before. Not just a copy of a real object, however skilful, not just a piece of decoration, however clever, but something more relevant and lasting than either, something that he feels to be more real than the shoddy objects of our humdrum existence. If we want to understand this frame of mind, we must go back to our own childhood, to a time when we still felt able to make things out of bricks or sand, when we turned a broomstick into a magic wand, and a few stones into an enchanted castle. Sometimes these self-made things acquired an immense significance for us—perhaps as much as the image may have for the primitive. I believe it is this intense feeling for the uniqueness of a thing made by the magic of human hands that the sculptor Henry Moore . . . wants us to have in front of his creations.' (He cites one of his reclining figures, 'Recumbent Figure'.) 'Moore does not start by looking at his model. He starts by looking at his stone. He wants to "make something" out of it. Not by smashing it to bits, but by feeling his way, and by trying to find out what the stone "wants". If it turns into a suggestion of a human figure, well and good. But even in this figure he wants to preserve something of the simplicity and solidity of a rock. He does not try to make a woman of stone but a stone which suggests a woman.'[1]

So, 'abstract art' is not one single thing, but a many-sided conversation in which the artist, nature as he sees it, simplified images in his mind, the demands of the medium, the claims of design, the desire to create a new object in itself with its own absorbing, dominating, sometimes almost magic power—all participate, now one taking the lead, now another.

§2 *Constructivism: Gabo*

A particularly interesting form of abstract art is Constructivism, of which I shall take Naum Gabo's work (done during, after and since the First World War) as a sole example. Whether Sir Herbert Read was right or not in saying that Constructivism 'remains the most revolutionary doctrine of art ever pronounced in the modern

[1] *The Story of Art*, p. 445.

world'[1] it certainly raises particularly interesting questions for Aesthetics.

Gabo's work (largely three-dimensional, but even in the drawings three-dimensional in feeling) is 'abstract' in both senses of the word, sometimes abstracted from models, sometimes entirely non-objective or non-figurative. But it *is* 'objective' in another sense of that word—in that it is a construction of objects in various materials, transparent plastic materials, bronze, etc., wires or threads stretched on frames forming complex three-dimensional structures, or sketches for the construction of these. In his *Realistic Manifesto* (signed also by Antoine Pevsner) Gabo writes: 'The plumb-line in our hand, eyes as precise as a ruler, in a spirit as taut as a compass . . . we construct our work as the universe constructs its own, as the engineer constructs his bridges, as the mathematician his formula of the orbits.'[2] The works are at once abstractions and constructions. Gabo has an engineer's or a mathematician's eye. As a girder or a Tee Beam or a bird's bone shows to informed perception the minimum structure required for strength (*plus* of course a factor of safety), so in Gabo's constructions we see, as it were, *into* the economics of three-dimensional space.

But, though it is engineering, it is not just engineering. The cause of it is not, as with the engineer, the need to make something for practical purposes which will be strong and simple, say, a bridge. The cause of it is the artist's sense of joy in these structures, his feeling for the values of such things. In *this* sense the constructions can be called 'expressive', expressive of the artist's sense of the values of space. On the other hand they are not 'expressive' as some art is expressive—as for instance a curve of Botticelli or a brush stroke of Van Gogh is expressive. There it is the artist's sensitive organism which moves to give the curve or the stroke its calligraphic stamp. But in Gabo's work the shaping of the materials, the stringing of the threads or wires, is done according to a strictly worked-out plan made beforehand which can be methodically carried out by an instructed artisan, given the frame, given the materials, and given exact instructions. The art depends for its existence upon the imaginative conception of a definite construction of space-form out of indefinite possibilities, yet limited by the nature of space. So that though each is laboriously constructed,

[1] *Introduction* to Gabo's Exhibition at the Tate Gallery, Spring, 1966.
[2] Quoted in Read's *Introduction, op. cit.*

mathematically accurate, precise in the highest degree, intellectually very complex, the conceived and finished construction as a
whole is moving as art, and its labour a labour of love. Gabo's
work is a strange fusion of the intellectual and impersonal with
the most sensitive of feeling for form.

Gabo has expressed it thus: '. . . The elements of a visual art such
as lines, colours, shapes, possess their own forces of expression
independent of any association with the external aspects of the
world . . . their life and their action are self-conditioned psychological phenomena rooted in human nature. Those elements
(lines, colours, shapes) are not chosen by convention for any utili-
tarian or other reason as words or figures are; they are not merely
abstract signs but they are immediately and organically bound
up with human emotions.'[1]

Gabo (in his non-figurative work at any rate) does not, as we
said, represent objects in the world—trees, people, still life. . . .
He does not exactly 'represent' the vortices of space either, for
they are constructed first (in imagination and in material) and
then perceived. On the other hand he does seem to be in a sense
bodying forth, articulating, the nature of space in depth. Space,
until constructions are made, appears to us as amorphous; through
the constructions understanding grows. In a sense—though not
exactly the Kantian sense—this constructive understanding (or
Understanding Construction) 'makes nature'. We are shown a
world which is not just the impersonal independent world, and
not a very personal one either: rather, it is a *Zwischending*. Sir
Herbert Read calls his work 'Platonic'. But this cannot be quite
accurate for, as we said earlier, the Platonic Forms cannot be
shown to the senses; only conception can apprehend them. Still,
they are as near to Forms as images or percepts could be—and
there is, incidentally, a stage in the history of Platonic thought in
which percepts are said to 'tend towards' or 'imitate' the Forms.
In Gabo, these constructed objects—in bronze, stone, translucent
media, frames, wires, threads . . . —are made for aesthetic contemplation by intellect, imagination, perception and feeling, all at once.

One thing we have to remind ourselves of in talking about
abstract art is that though the element of representation may disappear, or almost disappear, so that there is no 'subject-matter'
in the ordinary sense of that word, this does not mean that there
is just 'form' without 'content'. The content is there, but it is

---

[1] *The Constructive Idea in Art*, p. 163. Quoted by Read, *op. cit.*

derived from the transforming organization of tertiary qualities as values. Pictures and sculptures have the values of mass, weight, density, volume: colours and tones in infinitely complex relationships contribute their content of value. There is tension, movement, advance, retreat, a dynamic system of interactions which, in a good abstract, can seem to be almost without limit. (Not actually without limit of course: content is *formed*, and form by definition is limitation. But for exploratory aesthetic experience the ranges for exploration stretch far, wide, and deep.) Though an abstract work of art may not represent anything specific, we come to it with all our experiences of tertiary qualities outside art. As Professor Stolnitz has it: 'We could not respond to such art as we do, unless we had already experienced heaviness and lightness, buoyancy and inertia, rapidity and slowness, and all the other, immediately felt properties of our world. If this account is sound, then non-objective art shows us what is at the core of all our experience. "We see what we never saw, and hear what we never heard, and yet, what we see and hear is flesh of our flesh and bone of our bones " (Lavater).'[1] This, as we shall see in Chapters VII–X is most strikingly illustrated by music.

§3   *A Note on Recent Experimental Art*

It is impossible to generalize about the vast complexities of more recent experimental art. Being 'experimental' it is to be expected that some of it should succeed and that much of it should fail. (Even with a great experimentalist like Picasso—all of whose work is interesting because it is Picasso's—it is absurd to assume sycophantically that it is all wonderful and that there are no failures.) Some of it is very serious experiment even if it does not come off: some of it is frivolous: some of it is tricks or fraud, whether the fraud be artistic or commercial, or both. Some is just solemnly, or vulgarly, silly.

What is good or bad is not something called 'modern art' or 'experimental art'—or anything indeed which is merely something because of its label. What—and it should be obvious enough—is bad is this or that work, or this or that artist. In other words, it is good artists and good critics, judging individual works, who can give utterance to competent judgments.

But competence? Here is the trouble with the critics and the artists. We live in a world which is changing from day to day, with

[1] Stolnitz, *op. cit.*, p. 156.

new slogans constantly in the news. It is a world vital and serious in one way, in another it is a world of quick, facile theory stimulated into premature utterance by too many TV interviews or other commercial pressures, and by constant demands for fresh novelties, a consumer market. It is difficult for even the best critic to adjust his ideas so instantly and so often: and if the critic has not got some philosophical balance, he may respond too sensitively to the winds of change, his instability made worse by the fear of making a *gaffe*. Again and again in the past critics have been badly wrong in their judgments of new forms of art. The good critic naturally wants to be open and sympathetic, and sometimes he may fall over backwards in trying to be so, losing judgment in the process. He is not helped either by confusion of art with social comment, or with the word-magic which insists that the whisper of the word 'art' makes art of anything to which it is applied.

Take, for example, the confusions which may arise in the discussion of the work of one man, the late Jackson Pollock. Various questions arise out of Pollock's 'Action Painting'. The achievements hanging on the wall—are they good paintings? If one distinguishes art as strictly an artifact, are conjunction of chance—throwings, drippings, pourings—properly called 'art'? If the final products are largely or wholly accidental, can they be called, as they are called, 'expressions of spontaneity'? Or is there control in the *way* in which they are thrown, dripped, poured? If they are largely, if not wholly, the result of accident, are they properly called 'action' paintings? Is human 'action' not a product of will— or are the squiggles we admire (if we do indeed admire them) the product of the natural forces (with their own natural 'laws') of throwing, etc.? These are all fair enough questions for aesthetics.

But criticism and aesthetics are, as I suggested, very apt to get mixed up with social comment. Harold Rosenberg, for instance (the inventor of the term 'Action Painting'), writes that Abstract Expressionism was 'a major language of social disaffection wherever experimental art was not banned by force'.[1] He is here making a social comment, not talking aesthetics or criticism. Art is sometimes blunderingly misconceived as being nothing but social comment. According to Nigel Gosling[2], writing of the 'Isms' of art: 'Art has always been a method of communication of ideas

---

[1] Quoted in a review of his book *The Anxious* Object, *British Journal of Aesthetics*, Vol. VI, No. 2.   [2] *Observer*, March 27, 1966.

about life by means of marks and signs'. But this is highly superficial; it does not differentiate art at all. The social comment may
be true enough—for example, Harold Rosenberg's. But social
comment not only takes us away from art as art, but may even be
misleading if it encourages us to think of art only as interesting
because it is (e.g.) social satire, a symptom of social reactions. One
bit of pretentious nonsense in so-called 'art' consisted of dripping
the blood of small birds upon people, or smashing pianos with a
hammer ('Destructivist Art'). Another form of 'art' (no doubt
long out of date by the time this is printed) was cutting the clothes
off a young woman in public. No doubt these crazes are the result
of some personal or social degeneracy; it is spurious to claim any
attention for them as art; social comment or such 'expression'
merely masquerade as art. More than this, since anything which
can be displayed in a public place can be *called* 'art', and the public
is invited to view it *as* art, the superstition prevails that, somehow,
it must *be* 'art'. This is again mere word-magic.

Rosenberg goes further than social comment, into morals.
Fanchon Fröhlich quotes him as saying: 'Action Painting has
extracted the element of *decision* inherent in all art in that the work
is not finished at its beginning but has to be carried forward by an
accumulation of the "right" gestures. In a word, Action Painting
is the abstraction of the *moral* element in art; its mark is moral
tension in detachment from moral or aesthetic certainties; and
it judges itself morally in declaring that picture to be worthless
which is not the incorporation of a genuine struggle.' But it is,
surely, sheer muddle to confuse the 'decisions' a painter has to
take at every turn of his work, with the *moral* decisions we have to
take in personal or social life outside art? What is 'right' in the
gesture or stroke of a brush is 'right' in an utterly different sense
from its being 'right' to help you if you are in distress.

Art and social comment overlap but ought to be distinguished.
So again, there is an overlap between works of art as artifacts and
objects which may, or may not, be looked at aesthetically but
which are not art-artifacts. Some of Rauschenberg's works, for
example, present actual objects such as working radios or clocks.
As Rauschenberg himself says (I quote from Fanchon Fröhlich,
already cited): 'I act in the area between art and life'. Another
example of this sort of thing is a particular work of Rauschenberg's
where a picture is joined to a chair which actually projects into
the room.

Many questions arise here, some serious, some artificial and due to muddles between art and the world outside art. A serious question would be: 'How far is an art which presents real objects, or literalistic photographs of them, doing what we do when we put unchanged "found objects" on a stand and look at them?' It would be a misuse of terms, I think, to call this 'art'—except in so far as putting an object on a stand in relation to a background is 'art'. What we are doing is more like setting up conditions for a possible aesthetic experience. An artist might be trying to do just that, to be an artist by minimizing his own activity as an artist. But if he succeeds in entirely eliminating his own part in it, is it still 'art'? Even if the object is not as exciting as a found object we might notice on the seashore and pick up, perhaps anything looked at selectively in a certain way—heaps of junk, twisted metal, and so on—can potentially yield aesthetic experience? This *certainly* can happen. But, one more than suspects, this is not the motive or intention of some contemporary displays. To set up any objects in a gallery, banal pick-ups, clippings from advertisements, any old rubbish off a dump, even Dadaistic try-ons like the display of a urinal—this really cannot pretend, with any honesty, to be 'art' at all. The Dadaists and Neo-Dadaists were more accurate— perhaps more honest in a facile sort of way—in calling it 'Anti-art'. Dadaism is often described as a satire on artistic pretentiousness, and this may be near the truth.

The tendency to fling anything which is 'real' in front of us and call it 'art' is manifest in contemporary 'Pop' art.

To repeat, we are 'led up the garden path' by the mystique of a word. On the one hand, 'art' is wonderful, to be looked at seriously —or at any rate with owl-eyes. On the other hand the word 'art' can be currently applied to anything which can be displayed: and the hypnotism of publicity can persuade us to solemn regard. At the best we get a new aesthetic experience. In the worst cases it can lead to sheer fraud or commercial trickery. Is it not ridiculous, or worse, that we should give so much free publicity through public media to activities (still called 'art') of selling signed-soup-tins to a gullible public?

All this muddle, and the commercial exploitation of muddle, as well as the serious questions raised by contemporary experimental art of a sincere kind, challenge both the critic and the aesthetician to rethink their basic principles.

CHAPTER VII

MUSIC AND HUMAN EXPERIENCE

CHAPTER VII

MUSIC AND HUMAN EXPERIENCE

§1 *Music and life*

One of the most puzzling and interesting instances in the controversy about the relation of art to life, is music. Frank Howes in *The Listener* (March 25, 1965) wrote: 'The fundamental question, which has been debated for over a century and will never be settled, is this: does music mean anything; if so what? if not, what does it signify?' He compares it to the controversy in the visual arts in which Bell and Fry argued that the merits of a picture were purely formal and the subject irrelevant. I do not know whether the problem can be 'settled' or not, in the sense that one can get universal agreement; probably not. Nevertheless the meaning of the question 'Does music mean anything?' and 'If it does, how can it do so?' can be clarified. It needs philosophical analysis: it is this which I propose to offer in these chapters.

The controversy between those who hold that music is in some sense humanly meaningful and those who deny it outright, is of course, very old, though it became more articulate in the middle of the nineteenth century. Until then one may say that the broadly universal assumption was that music is humanly meaningful, though it had not been worked out philosophically. A reaction came in the second part of the nineteenth century, when Hanslick in 1854 and Gurney in 1880 argued for the 'purity' of pure music. The same theme was developed much later in America by Carroll Pratt and many others. Musicians have joined in the controversy; Stravinsky (like Hanslick) has pronounced pure music 'meaningless'.

In what follows, in order to bring into focus what 'meaning' in music may mean, I shall draw from the writings of two out of a number of authors who express one side, who hold that music expresses life-meanings. They are Deryck Cooke, *The Language of Music* (Oxford, 1959) and Donald Ferguson, *Music as Metaphor* (University of Minnesota, 1960). I draw on them just sufficiently to bring out the basic question: 'What is, and what is not, the relation of music and the experience of it, to the experience of life outside music?' Both authors are rather extreme expressionists: fundamentally I think their theories badly wrong: but they do sharpen the issue.

E

Cooke argues that the main characteristic of music is that it expresses and evokes emotion. He contends further that all composers whose music has a tonal basis[1] have used the same, or closely similar melodic phrases, harmonies, and rhythms to express and evoke the same emotions. 'Music is a language, not merely in a vague general sense, but in the detailed sense that we can identify idioms and draw up a list of meanings. There are obvious differences between the language of music and spoken language—music does not convey concepts, only feelings; and its complexity is such that its elements—melodic line, rhythm, and harmony—can combine and modify each other in a multitude of different ways not open to spoken language. But a first attempt has been made here to compile such a dictionary, or at least a phrase-book . . .'[2]

Ferguson believes that music is, fundamentally, an important kind of human experience, that it is 'metaphor', and that musical aesthetics or criticism which treats music as a purely formal exercise in musical syntax leaves out one of its main dimensions. He illustrates this at the beginning of his book (p. 9) by referring to a popular audience's remarkable reaction to an exceptionally fine performance of Bach's Violin Concerto in E (particularly the slow movement) at a Promenade Concert. Many of the audience knew little of formal music; the music undoubtedly gained part of its effects through what was at least in part formal construction, yet, though this, it was far more. How? No words could be commensurate with the idea conveyed by the music; the experience was but dimly understood, yet was gravid with meaning. How? For the audience it was evidently a profound spiritual experience, with a kind of 'truth' about it. How? Ferguson's idea of music as 'metaphor' is broader than Cooke's idea of it as a language; indeed Ferguson criticizes Cooke's view (not unfairly) as 'a portrayal of chemically compounded emotions' (p. 195). (But Ferguson's own developed view, I shall suggest, is very unsatisfactory too.)

---

[1] The restriction to Western music, mostly after 1400, and the exclusion of atonal music, is one of convenience. (See Chapter VI of this book, where Cooke has some very interesting things to say about the expressive limits of atonal music.) The exclusion of atonal music reduces, obviously, the range of examples but not the logic of the argument. The restriction to Western music is more debatable, but again, there is no *necessary* implication that a wider sweep would affect the argument.

[2] This quotation is from the wrapper of Mr Cooke's volume.

§2   *The materials and elements of music and their expressiveness*

In order to understand how music may 'mean' we must look at its materials. Cooke writes: 'Beginning' (p. 35) 'with the basic material —notes of definite pitch— . . . musical works are built out of the *tensions* between such notes. These tensions can be set up in three dimensions: *pitch, time* and *volume*; and the setting-up of such tensions, and the colouring of them by the *characterizing agents* of *tone-colour* and *texture*, constitutes the whole apparatus of musical expression'. Again, 'pitch-tensions can be regarded in two different ways—as *tonal tensions* (what the actual notes of the scale are) and as *intervallic tensions* (in what direction and at what distance the notes are from one another)'.

Each kind of tension, it is held, has its own 'expressiveness' . . . Cooke examines methodically what he believes to be the expressiveness of each of the tensions, between all twelve notes in the scale. Examples are: the *tonic*, which is 'emotionally neutral; context of finality'; the *major third*, 'concord, natural third, joy'; the *minor third*, 'concord, but a depression of natural third; stoic acceptance, tragedy', the *dominant*, 'emotionally neutral; context of flux, intermediacy', the *minor sixth*, 'semitonal tension down to the dominant, in a minor context; active anguish in a context of flux', the *major sixth*, 'as a passing note, emotionally neutral; as a whole tone tension down to the dominant, in a major context, pleasureable longing in a context of flux'. (These, without examples and taken out of the context of this book are bound to seem crude and arbitrary. Even in context they are, I think, often impossibly sweeping.)

The most obvious and familiar examples in Western music, Cooke says, are the contrast between the major third, which 'has established itself naturally as an expression of pleasure and happiness', and the minor third which has a 'depressed' sound; the fact that the minor third does not form part of the basic harmonic series makes it an unnatural depression of the 'naturally happy state of things' (according to Western ideas) (p. 57). 'It is an undeniable fact that composers throughout the centuries, including those medieval churchmen who used the minor key to express a stern, sedate, or sober satisfaction, expressed painful emotion by bringing the minor third into prominence melodically or harmonically' (p. 58). Another example of contrast is the sixth, major and minor; the major being used for pleasure, the minor for pain.

These examples are, of course, chosen for their obviousness, and are recommended with some reservation by Cooke. They are not intended, he hints, to indicate that music is a language in the sense that the same symbols mean *exactly* the same things in different contexts. Actual meaning must always depend upon context and one cannot even say that the minor and the major, though they generally express sadness or joy, must always do so. (I shall ask, a little later, whether this reservation does not vitiate the main thesis.)

So far we have been referring to tone, colour, texture—purely musical facts not shared by anything in life outside music. Now we come to 'the vitalising agents'; these overlap music and life. 'The tonal tensions are the purely musical thing about music; so, in a less fundamental way, are the characterizing agents of tone, colour and texture. The vitalising agents, however, also function in another field—that of speech; and we can get a broad idea of their effect by briefly considering their behaviour in this field. If we think of a group of people talking, it is obvious that the more excited they become, the louder, quicker and higher their voices will get; and the more relaxed they become, the softer, slower and lower they will speak. And the effects of the three different elements can be roughly isolated as follows. The *louder* a person speaks, the more *emphasis* he gives to what he is saying; the quicker he speaks, the more animated he is becoming; the *higher* his voice rises, the more he is asserting himself.'

'The same correspondences exist in the field of physical action; compare the high state of excitement inherent in running uphill, quickly and noisily (by stamping one's feet), with the state of relaxation inherent in walking downhill, slowly and quietly (by stepping gently).

'As regards *volume*, the louder the music gets, the more emphasis is given to what is being expressed, and the softer, generally speaking, the less emphasis.' So again *time* 'functions in music as in life . . . Hence in music it expresses the speed and rhythm of feelings and events, in other words, the state of mental, emotional or physical *animation*' (p. 97).

Finally there is the effect of pitch. In crude tone-painting, pitch corresponds to 'up' and 'down' in the physical world (e.g. the Masses). More subtly the melodic line tends to rise with mounting passion and to fall with depression and despair (e.g. 'Gretchen at the Spinning-wheel'). 'To rise in pitch in the major is normally to express an outgoing feeling of pleasure', whilst to fall in pitch in the major 'is normally to express an incoming feeling of pleasure'. Contrariwise a rise in pitch in the minor normally expresses 'an outgoing feeling of pain', and a fall in pitch in the minor expresses an incoming feeling of pain (examples pp. 105–6). Once again there are reservations. It is all too simple and sweeping as he recognizes; most music mingles rising and falling pitch so subtly that 'no broad expressive intention in the dimension of pitch is immediately discernible' (p. 107). Generally, pitch tends to ebb and flow according to the emotions expressed.

Ferguson's account differs in some respects from Cooke's. He criticizes Cooke at certain points—a technical one is Cooke's distinction between tonal and intervallic tensions, a philosophical one is Cooke's attempt to work out a symbolic 'vocabulary' of music. But he does agree with Cooke's main account of the basic materials of music—tensions with pitch, time and volume, together with the characterizing agents of tone-colour and texture.

Tone and rhythm are basic elements, *tone* appearing either in the guise of melody or harmony, having quality (caused by the mingling of fundamental tones with their partials), often called 'colour'. This metaphor, a visual one, is not the only metaphor that can be used of tones; other sense analogies are used; 'tones or harmonies appear to us as warm or sweet or hard or even fragrant' (*sic*) (p. 13). Tones have three characteristics—pitch, timbre, and intensity, and since the tones forming a pattern must appear in succession, discriminations of time as well as of pitch enter into the image of musical form, of which the principal time factor is *rhythm*, a symmetrical succession of instants or points of alternative stress and non-stress. The rhythmic may be aroused, without other suggestion of stress, merely through the recurrence of similar or striking features of a pattern at the appropriate moment of time; but in music rhythm is mostly made manifest through the *intensity* of tone. *Timbre*, largely incidental to design, illuminates the syntax of music and enriches the rhetorical contrasts of the texture. Pitch and rhythm are the 'bony structure' of musical organization (all *circa* pp. 40–43).

§3 *Does music express life-emotions?*

The two writers, Cooke and Ferguson, give rather differing accounts of a main, agreed, traditional theme—that music is an expression of life and life's emotions. For myself, I do not deny that, as with other arts, expression, in some sense or senses, or human feeling and emotion enters into the total picture somewhere, of music. (How could it be otherwise, since musicians, and we, are human, and music a human artifact?) On the other hand, all *reduction* of artistic—including musical—meaning to the language of life outside art, is, I believe, doomed to failure. Cooke, Ferguson, and those who think like them are, I think, justified in tracing threads of connection between life-experiences and musical forms, but utterly mistaken in imagining that the language of life can ever fit the specificity, the unique individuality, of musical meaning. Our problem now is a very special instance of the one of the main issues of this book: 'How can art spring from life and exist in the context of life—yet be self-contained, autonomous?

Three factors are very relevant to this discussion, two of them matters of fact and the third a debatable claim in aesthetics. There are (*a*) the basic musical characters, unique to music: tensions between notes, tone-colour, texture. There are (*b*) the 'vitalising agents' (volume, tempo or speed, pitch) in which there is a clear overlap between life—the voice, bodily movements—and music. (*c*) And there is the claim that the materials and the elements of music—and music itself—are 'expressive' of the feelings and emotions of life. It is this claim which must be scrutinized. Is it consistent—or how consistent can it be made—with the unique character of meaning-embodied in music?

Consider first the claimed 'expressiveness' of the materials and elements of music, in isolation from the context of actual musical works—in so far as this isolation is possible. There is the 'emotional neutrality' of the tonic, the 'joy' of the major third, the symbolic as well as the physical 'depression' of the minor third, the 'semitonal tension down to the dominant . . . active anguish in a context of flux'. And so on.

I will not say that there is no element of truth in the claims that in these and similar examples there are aesthetic tertiary qualities which can, very roughly, be described in words derived from extra-musical life-experiences, or that they may, in a sense and up to a point express life-feelings to a composer and to us. But here exactly the same kinds of reservation have to be made as those made when we discussed the extra-artistic tertiary qualities of colours and shapes. As embodied they become changed, individualized, and because they are now musical the qualities are strictly indescribable in words derived from other sources. These unique tertiary qualities can only be pointed to in musical experience it-self. The words may give certain indications; then there has to be the 'aesthetic leap': further it is clear that words like 'active anguish' are so inapplicably specific that they become fanciful. The same is true of Ferguson's language—of tones as even 'fragrant'!

The life-language used of the 'vitalising agents' is a quite dif-ferent case, just because the language is literally common to both life and music. Loudness, quickness, emphasis in speech or bodily movement, pitch in speech—these words apply equally to music, with their correlates of excitement or relaxation. Music does not 'express' these: it *has* them. They are not, as named, in themselves aesthetic characters—though they in turn do 'express' feelings and moods, both in music and life. But here again, the important reservation is needed. The loudness, quickness, emphasis, pitch, which occur in life outside music, have their expressive signifi-cance in relation to life-situations, the excitements and relaxations of life. But these 'same' characters, occurring in music, are music-ally embodied, and their meaning is changed into specific musical meaning no longer describable accurately in life-language.

If we now look at the claimed expressiveness of musical ele-ments not in isolation but in the context of actual music, the reservations and objections increase. It is not of course to be denied that 'composers throughout the centuries' have used certain musical tensions, e.g. the minor key, to express certain human feelings, perhaps 'painful emotion'. (Even if they did, it does not follow that they were aesthetically right if they thought that 'stern, sedate, or sober satisfaction' or 'painful emotion' were being literally displayed in the music.) But the exceptions are so many: the minor for instance can be used to show such different moods (e.g. Bach's 'Great' G Minor organ fugue, anything but 'painful' or 'sad'), the generalizations become weak. And, although Cooke makes reservations, saying that actual meaning must depend upon context, he evidently does not see the incompatibility bet-ween this and his claim that we might 'identify idioms and draw up a list of meanings' compiling 'a dictionary or at least a phrase-book'. And if, as he says, 'the meanings of music can only be felt by the musically sensitive and not clearly identified, explained or discussed', how can this possibly square with the 'hope' that one day, after intensive research, it may be possible 'to discover *exactly* what music expresses, and *exactly* how it expresses it', to speak of 'deciphering' the language of music? (And if it *could* be done, why music?) All this completely misses the important truth that, as Mrs Langer says so truly, a work of art is not like a logical argument, a symbolic system of items combined according to certain rules, but is a single unity of indivisible meaning—a 'single symbol', she calls it. Cooke is equally wrong in supposing we could 'assess a composer's work as a report on human experience *just as we do that of a literary artist*' (my italics). What we do *not* do even to a literary work is to assess it as a 'report on human experience'. Of music, Cooke quotes Mendelssohn: 'The thoughts which are expressed to me by a piece of music which I love are not too indefinite to be put into words but on the contrary too definite. And so I find, in every attempt to express such thoughts, that something is right, but at the same time something is unsatisfying in all of them.' If this insistence on the definiteness of musical meaning is to the point, and I think it is, does it not vitiate all attempts at 'translation'?

Ferguson's view of music as 'metaphor' does not fall into exactly the same errors as Cooke's. But he does give, unfortunately, I think, a dualistic account of 'form' and 'expression'. 'The objective of the artist . . . is to arouse two types of awareness: the one, *im*mediate—the direct response to the art-work as a fact of substance and form; the other, mediate—the indirect response to suggestions of experience not, in themselves, necessarily related to those offered by the form of the art-work as such. We may conveniently call these two values, respectively, form and expression, the word expression being understood in the sense of utterance or communication . . . The word content is also acceptable as equivalent to expression' (p. 23). He goes on: 'The beautiful object, however, indisputably offers more to the mind than the mere additive sum of these two values. That excess, in any adequate definition of beauty, must be accounted for . . . We must therefore attribute this excess of value to the fusion of the two.'

Several things have to be said here. Ferguson is undoubtedly striving after something true, namely that music is influenced by and draws from ranges, sometimes depths and heights, of human experience outside music, that it springs from roots in the soil of common experience. The trouble is his theory—that life-meanings somehow enter into music by being 'fused' into it. This is a special form of the 'two-term' fallacy (Santayana, the early Arnaud Reid and others) criticized in Chapter II. There are, Ferguson is

saying, the 'forms' of music (one thing), and suggestions of—
extra-musical—life-experience, the 'expression' side (the other
thing). These two are not just added together, but 'fuse'—and the
fusion, it is said, is more than the sum of the parts.

The dualism and the 'fusion' are wrong. Ferguson speaks often
as though the 'pure' *musicianly* interest in music was in musical
form and 'syntax'. This interest is (rightly) not enough for him;
he thinks we must fill it in by affirming the 'expressive' elements,
the expression of meaning. But this, for him, is *extra*-musical
meaning, and miscalled 'content'. Meaning in music, however, is
not extra-musical meaning fused in. It is *musical* meaning. And
this musical meaning, though, by an effort, we can distinguish
it *conceptually* from form and syntax, is as we saw not thus distinguishable within actual experience of music itself. We do not,
musically, apprehend form and syntax *and* meanings fused into
them. The form and syntax of music in musical operation and
musical experience is the form and syntax of a total thing, music;
the form and syntax is the form of musical content; the form and
syntax, in operation in musical experience, is in itself musically
content-full, meaningful. And to say this is by no means to deny
that the human musician, in constructing meaningful musical
form and syntax, is influenced by his experience and knowledge
of life-meanings outside music. But the influence is subtle, underground, not direct. To the question of how it does in fact work,
we shall return.

There is, of course, the study of musical 'form' and 'syntax', a
separate study, familiar to all students of music and to musico-
logists, an essential part of their training and education. The
mistake in the understanding of musical meaning arises only when
this legitimately abstracted aspect of music becomes hypostasized,
conceived as a separate entity instead of an aspect. It is then falsely
supposed to exist inside music alongside an equally hypostasized
'content', 'expression', 'meaning' (on Ferguson's view coming
straight from 'life' outside music): the two then have to be united,
or 'fused'. This is a tortuous exercise, wholly artificial, wholly
misconceived. Aspects which are experientially indivisible are torn
apart, then, impossibly, stuck together again. There is utter confusion between a legitimate, conceptual, leisurely examination of
abstractions, and what happens in the living experience of music,
where form is meaningful, meaning is musical, the meaning *in*
the music.

E*

§4   *Further questions*

I suggested much earlier (Chapter III) in a discussion of Mrs Langer, that since feelings (and the 'form of feelings') are specific, inseparable from their content, art cannot strictly be said to express the feelings (or the forms of the feelings) of life outside art: the 'form of the feeling' in a work of art can only be the form of the feeling *of* that work of art. But the discussion of feeling in Chapter III was only preliminary. In order to understand better the untranslatable individuality and specificity of feelings, it is necessary to investigate further the nature of feeling: it will take up most of the next chapter.

This, and all that has been said in this chapter about the impossibility of 'deciphering' music, is one side. Musical meaning cannot be translated into life meaning—and that is firm. On the other hand it has never been denied that life feelings and meanings, in which a composer as a human being must share, must in some way, perhaps indirectly, affect the music which he writes—or that our experiences of hearing music are in some way affected by extra-musical feelings. And the fact that we do use ordinary life-words, not accurately but at least with some point, of musical characters, suggests that the connection between life-feelings and musical ones is not *just* negative. We speak of music as sad, solemn, gay, agitated, passionate, tender, pastoral, flamboyant, elated. . . . When we do use such words we are not just talking nonsense; there must, it would seem, be *some* modicum of applicability. Mendelssohn's words may be recalled. In attempts to express in words the 'thoughts' of music, 'something is unsatisfying'. Yet, also, 'something is right', How can this be so?

The next chapter (VIII) will be almost entirely about feeling and emotion. The following one (IX) will explore the obscure processes by which life-feelings become expressed and transformed in art into embodied meaning, how life-feelings are up to a point like, and yet also unlike, art-feelings. I shall attempt to show this with the aid of a general hypothesis, worked out in some detail in the specially difficult case of music. The chapter following that (Chapter X) will test this out by taking some examples of different types of music.

CHAPTER VIII

FEELING, EMOTION AND MUSIC

CHAPTER VIII

FEELING, EMOTION AND MUSIC

§1 *Feeling and Emotion*

It is common to talk, very loosely, about feelings and emotions (in life or music) as though they were much the same thing. I have followed this usage so far because it is current: yet it is misleading: it is time to pause and consider. The word 'emotion' is often said or written when what is meant is something much less dramatic, or melodramatic, namely a feeling of some kind. If art in any sense expresses feelings, there are many feelings expressed which are not emotions, or emotional. Emotional feelings, I shall argue, occur when, for one reason or another, we are moved or stirred up in some marked degree—and this is only sometimes. It gets our problem wholly out of proportion to state it as though it were one mainly of the relations between the *emotions* of life and those of art. Feeling is a basic mental concept, emotion a derived one, and to talk of the derived before the basic is to put things in the wrong order.

§2 *Feeling: older views—and an alternative*

If feeling is a basic mental concept it is a difficult one: anything said here can only be a sketch.

For the older psychologists 'feeling' was a thin and abstracted thing, usually identified with hedonic-tone, pleasure-unpleasure. For Ward it was a 'strictly subjective state varying continuously in intensity and passing from time to time from its positive phase (pleasure) to its opposite phase (pain) or vice-versa'.[1] Stout says: 'The affective attitude consists in being pleased or displeased with something, in liking or disliking it.'[2] Others say much the same. Hedonic tone, identified with feeling, was supposed to be a positive or negative quality which varied in intensity, sharply distinguished from the concrete character of the mental states of which it was the hedonic quality.

Again, feeling when (sometimes) used less exclusively in this hedonic sense (as when one says 'I feel tired, lazy, hungry . . .') was denied to be *transitive*. 'The word "feel" is commonly used as a transitive verb, equivalent to "perceive" . . . This usage is apt

---

[1] Ward, *Psychological Principles*, p. 45.
[2] *Manual of Psychology*, 4th Edition, p. 107.

to create confusion . . . As a verb "feel" should be used only in the intransitive sense, as when we say "I feel tired, etc." ' . . . And because of this it was argued that feeling 'is not *cognitive*: it is not "knowing something", even about your subjective condition; it is simply "the way you feel".'[1]

Let me make a preliminary comment on the three points italicized.

(1) It is, I think, far too limiting to *identify* feeling with hedonic tone. The subjective state, affect, feeling, may be characterized (sometimes, not necessarily always) by hedonic tone, may be pleasant or unpleasant. But when we speak of 'feeling' we do not, surely, mean simply the abstracted quality, pleasure or unpleasure? It seems nearer the mark to say that feeling states have, or may have, the *characteristic* of being pleasant or unpleasant. It is true that by usage 'affect' has come to mean feeling-tone. I shall try to show that a wider use is far more fruitful in trying to understand the life and function of feeling.

(2) We must agree that 'feeling' (or 'to feel') is not a transitive verb in the primary sense of 'feeling'—immediate experience of our own states, though 'feeling' can have the extended use, as when I say 'I feel the shape'. But if 'feeling' in its primary sense has not, grammatically speaking, an *object*, it does, I shall argue, always have a *content*, distinguishable though never separate from the feeling of it.

(3) Feeling is being affected by something—by whatever it is that affects us. This is the content of feeling, what it is feeling *of*. In this sense, and in this sense only, I want to say that feeling in its primary sense is *cognitive* of its content, immediately cognitive of a content of which there is awareness, without any intermediary or third term—as there must be in all other cognition, namely relation to some concept. I am not saying that cognitive feeling of content without any third item, the concept, usually or more than rarely occurs. It may do so in very borderline cases, as may occur when we are halfway between consciousness and unconsciousness, e.g., when waking from deep sleep or from an anaesthetic. Or if I receive a sudden unexpected blow from behind I may feel something before there is time to raise the question 'What's that?'. Normally, when one feels something, it is interpreted, by means of a concept, *as*, say, 'toothache', 'tiredness',

---

[1] Woodworth, *Psychology: a Study of Mental Life*, p. 172.

'anxiety', 'joy'—and this of course happens when we are not thinking of the words or the concepts as such. Nevertheless, whether immediate feeling of content without any concept actually occurs or not, the very use of a concept which is meaningful and relevant presupposes an immediately cognized datum or content of feeling.

Many philosophers would thoroughly disapprove of the idea of primary feeling as a unique two-term form of cognition. My defence of it is that we do talk of feeling as immediate awareness of something, and that this is far more illuminating than the older view of feeling as identical with hedonic tone and as being non-cognitive.

§3 *Feeling as cognitive*

Feeling—according to Susanne Langer the mark of mentality[1]— emerges at a certain state of evolution. A neuro-physiological process can be said to 'break through to feeling'.[2] The phenomenon usually described as a feeling is really that the organism feels something, i.e., something is felt. Being felt, Mrs Langer holds, is a phase of the process itself—and a phase is a mode of appearance, not an added factor.[3] There is an analogy, but only an analogy, of feeling with the incandescence of a piece of iron at a high temperature. Feeling is living process becoming aware of itself.

At the human level, feeling is so inseparable from what is felt that in *experience* itself it is impossible to distinguish between them. In the experience of acute toothache how can we distinguish between feel*ing* and *what* is felt? The unfelt ache is inconceivable (though of course an unfelt state of the disturbed organism which causes it is not). Yet, as so often happens with things existentially inseparable, it is possible and necessary to make a conceptual distinction; and here one may and must distinguish between something which is not so much a mental activity as a mental happening, that of feel*ing*, and the content of this feeling, *what* is felt. Since the word 'feeling' is so highly ambiguous, sliding from one of these meanings into the other, it may be convenient to give each a technical label to avoid confusion. The word 'awareness' is useful. When we are aware, it is true that we are always aware of something; but the word 'awareness' can be and sometimes is used in a more general, open, less specific way than is

---

[1] *Mind: an Essay on Human Feeling*, p. 4.   [2] *ibid.*, p. 9.
[3] *ibid.*, p. 21.

possible with 'feeling'. This use is vague; but it does happen. 'To be aware' is more open and less specific than 'to feel'; 'awareness' is more exclusively subjective and less ambiguous than feeling, and may therefore be borrowed to distinguish technically between the subjective, cognitive aspect of feeling, and its content. Feel*ing* is an immediate awareness. I shall therefore, when relevant, distinguish between Feeling (IE) (= immediate awareness) and Feeling (C) (= content).

Feeling (IE) is primarily of our own processes and states, bodily and mental, psycho-physical. It is cognitive in the sense that we immediately and indubitably know the content of feeling—in one sense of the word 'know'. In that sense, too, feeling (IE) shares the character of all cognition of having content, knowing, feeling, *something*. Indeed this is saying just the same thing in a different way.

But although it is true that the something which we feel is primarily our own psycho-physical organic states, it is a truth which would be wholly misleading if we stopped there. For the psycho-physical organism of course lives in a world external to itself, a world in which, as mind, it is interested, a world which it comes to know bit by bit and with some discrimination, to which it responds actively as well as reactively. The life of the psycho-physical organism is its life in the world (in the case of human beings, the whole of the human world) and to attend to the inner life of feeling of the organism by itself is to perform an artificial if necessary abstraction. Moreover, if this is true, and if feeling is cognitive and (though purely as feeling not grammatically transitive) shares the transitiveness of all cognition, there must be a sense in which feeling participates in our total psycho-physical intercourse with the world we live in. Some forty to forty-five years ago, I suggested some of the implications of this in three published papers.[1] I would not now want to express in the same way everything that was said there; but one main theme I still think true, namely that feeling does share in the objectively directed character of our cognitive-conative relationships with the world. Cognition and conation are in different ways focusing, grasping, acting and

[1] (1) 'Instinct Emotion and the Higher Life', *British Journal of Psychology*, Vol. 14, July 1923.

(2) 'Towards Realistic Psychology', *Journal of Philosophy*, Vol. 21, August 1924.

(3) 'Immediate Experience; its Nature and Content', *Mind*, Vol. 31, April 1931.

reacting functions in relation to the world; and feeling includes feeling *of all that*. We feel the whole transitive cognitive-conative process, outwardly directed, directed towards the world. Feeling is the feeling of oneself, dwelling within the psycho-physical organism, in total cognitive-conative relation to the world. In *this* sense, feeling is not only cognitive of immediate content: as sharing in cognition and conation it is cognitive of *objects* in the world.

The account of what we feel has, so far, stressed two things: (1) the intra-psycho-physical content as such (the content of my feeling when I try to attend, with some artificial concentration, on what is going on within my organism). The other, (2), is what I feel, not just as with inmyself, but as functioning in cognitive-conative relationship with the independent world. I feel myself-living-in-the-world. This is the more normal and less artificial state, though the sense of it fades into the background when I am concentrating hard on what I am doing or thinking.

There is, nevertheless, an important question whether, fading or not, my feeling of participating in my life in the world has not a very important part to play in my knowing and acting and responding, and in its efficiency. If the feeling is there all the time (and though we may not be thinking of it, there is always the accompanying feeling of being alive), it would be surprising if it only remained passively in the sidelines, so to speak, and had no retroactive effect upon our knowing and acting. Feeling may be compared to incandescence at its elementary and primitive stages, but it may take on a more positively active function of its own in highly intelligent conscious and self-conscious life.

There may, in fact, be said to be a sense in which we feel, not simply our own private states, not simply the participation in our life in the world, but feel, cognitively, something of the characters of the world itself; in which we increase, or illuminate, knowledge through the infiltration of feeling. We 'size up' a situation; we take a decision, moral or otherwise; we 'balance things up'. In all this, of course (it may be taken for granted without argument here), all the mechanisms of perceptual and conceptual thinking are involved. (Feeling (IE) by itself is a non-entity.) We feel (IE) (or we can feel) ourselves as active in these ways in our coming to terms with the world. But is not our feeling more—or may it not be more—than the mental 'incandescence' of all the rest that is happening? If feeling shares in, is inseparable from, cognition and conation, can it not intimately affect their active enterprise too? May not sensitive feeling be a positive asset in knowing or otherwise coming to terms with the world? It does certainly seem to be so in our knowledge of the arts at least—music or painting or poetry—though it is not confined to them. There does seem to be a sense in which to 'feel' the structures of things and their values is a way in which we positively come to know more of them.

This may seem strange language to a philosopher—though it is commonly enough used in ordinary speech. We speak of 'feeling' the sense of the argument; we say 'he has a nose for the important things': 'Being sensitive to the atmosphere, he was much more understanding than some of the other, cleverer, people'. But is such language strictly justified?

§4   *Feeling: the 'proximal' and the 'distal'*

It can be clarified, I think, by referring to a distinction frequently made use of by Professor Polanyi in his discussions of 'tacit' knowledge. In a paper 'Science and Man's Place in the Universe'[1] he cites two experiments, one by Lazarus and McCleary, and the other by Ericksen and Kuethe. In the one case a person was presented with a number of nonsense syllables and, after being shown certain of the syllables, was given an electric shock. Soon the subject showed symptoms of anticipating the shock at the sight of the 'shock syllables'; yet on questioning could not identify these syllables. In the other case a person was exposed to shock whenever he happened to utter associations to certain 'shock words'. Presently he learned to forestall the shock by avoiding the utterance of the associations, yet on questioning did not know that he was doing this. In both cases, the subject must be assumed to have in some sense (i.e. 'tacitly') *known* more than he could 'tell'.

This 'tacit' knowledge has two terms. In the examples cited, the shock-syllables and the shock-associations formed the first term, and the electric shock the second term. The connection between the two remained tacit, because the subject was riveting his attention on the electric shock, relying on his awareness of the shock-producing particulars only for the purpose of attending to the shock. Tacit knowledge combines two kinds of knowing. The subject knows the electric shock forming the second term by attending to it, and hence its knowledge is specifiable. He knows

---

[1] In *Science as a Cultural Force* (Johns Hopkins), ed. Harry Woolf. All the quotations which follow are from this paper.

the shock-producing syllables only by relying on his awareness of them for attending to something else, namely the shock, hence his knowledge of them remains tacit. Polanyi speaks of 'attending *from*' something '*to*' something else, namely from the first term *to* the second term of the tacit relation. 'In many ways the first term of this relation will prove to be nearer to us, the second term farther away from us. Using the language of anatomy, I shall call the first term *proximal*, and the second term *distal*.'

Further, in the above cases since the sight of certain syllables led to the expectation of the electric shock, they may be said to *signify* the approach of a shock: this is their *meaning*. 'It is their meaning to which our attention is directed. It is in terms of their meaning that they enter into the appearance of that *to* which we are attending *from* them.' An interesting extension of this idea is the account (to be found in several of Polanyi's works) of the use of a stick as a probe. If we use a probe for the first time we can feel its impact against fingers and palm. But as we learn to use the probe, our awareness of its impact on our hand is transformed into a sense of its point touching the objects we are exploring. Thus 'meaningless' feelings are transposed into meaningful ones and our interpretation places these at a distance. We become aware of the feelings in our hand in terms of their meaning located at the tip of the probe, to which we are attending. Meaning tends to be displaced away from ourselves.

This can be directly applied to our account of feeling. We may attend at will to various aspects of the total content of feeling—as purely private, as participating in our life in the world, and as 'feeling', cognitively, the very characters of the world. It is upon the last—rather strange-sounding claim—that the distinction, and relationship, between 'proximate' and 'distal' throws light. If we consider the illustration of the probe, or even of ordinary perception of the characters of things at a distance from the body, we know that by means of constructions based upon bodily experiences we become aware of the characters of the world outside the body— e.g., of shapes in space at a distance. Through exploratory movements, registered in immediate experience as kinaesthetic and other sensations, we learn from babyhood to locate coloured objects at a distance, and to distinguish them from the immediate body image. Shapes, recorded by means of inverted binocular images, are perceived as 'out there'; colours, sounds, temperatures, etc., though (with one kind of attention) sensed (and felt) within the organism, are located as coming from sources outside the body. Through and by means of the proximate we apprehend the distal, and the 'meaning' (in Polanyi's sense) is there, outside. And although we are not always aware of the proximal, as when our attention is fully directed outwards, we can at any time become aware of it by shifting attention. Light, heat, sound, coming from 'outside' sources can, if their intensity is increased, be uncomfortably sensed within the body—though the recognition that they originate from outside still remains.

Feeling, as the immediate experience of everything that occurs in conscious psycho-physical life, shares in all this. We can feel our inner private states as such, or our total participation in the world of things and people, and we can even, in a comprehensible sense, be said to 'feel' the world outside us, the total world of human experience.

Ordinarily, although the feeling of being alive and involved is never absent, the fact that in our practical knowledge of the world or in our thinking abstractly, the presence of feeling is not particularly noticeable, may mislead us into thinking it absent, or superfluous. We are attending to clues for action or to the structure of things or of thought. But feeling is certainly present, and moreover not simply present but (I believe) often actively auxiliary in what we do and think. We notice clues sufficiently for efficient action, but in acting by means of them we are constantly 'feeling' our way. We walk along the street in a directed way, guided partly by feeling. We avoid lamp-posts and other pedestrians not just by locating them coldly as discrete objects but by feeling as well as perceiving the total gestalt, and by feeling our way along. (This becomes very much more obvious when walking along a very dark road, when the awareness of proximal feelings becomes more prominent.) In driving a car through a narrow passage, or in reversing, we know largely what to do by feeling towards the distal from the proximal. The totality and concreteness of massive feeling is indeed an indispensable condition of success. If the particular bits of the situation remain as discrete bits, and the feeling of the whole gestalt is lost, everything goes wrong; either, like the over-intellectual centipede, we are paralysed for action, or, we crash into the gatepost. Success is the result of a fine balance between the proximal and the distal, and the balance is known by feeling.

Much could be said too about the presence and function of feeling in the experience of abstract or any other discursive thinking: this however would take us too far from our main theme, which is art-experience.

§5 *Feeling and the knowledge of art*

From what has gone before, we may assume that the sophisticated and mature knowledge of an art-structure presupposes the vastly complex processes—conceptual, perceptual, symbolic and the rest —involved in the understanding of any structure. Taking all that for granted, the question now is of the function and place of feeling in the understanding and knowledge of an art—of which music is an example.

Art is embodiment of meaning, and the experience of art is a personally-embodied experience of meaning in an artifact. As a personally-embodied experience it is a felt one, and feeling participates in all three emphases of attention—to the intra-organic, to the participation in the work as objective, and to the feeling (illuminated by the proximal-distal concept) *of* the work itself. The attention to any of the three aspects is legitimate—but on different occasions and with different purposes in mind.

As philosophers experiencing art we are entitled to attend to all three, and to any of them we please, as suits our purpose. We may notice the intra-organic, e.g. the feelings of the psychophysical manifestations of our experience of listening to music, or to these as directed more focally towards the music; or we may be fully absorbed in cognitively 'feeling' the music itself and be aware of subjective aspects only by an effort, and retrospectively. The artificiality—necessary as it may be for philosophical-analytic purposes—of attention to our own feelings is most clearly seen in this last: we cannot properly attend to the music and to our own feelings strictly at the same moment. Full aesthetic attention must be to the music itself, the distal aspect, the 'meaning', and that meaning is not to be identified with our own subjective feelings. On the other hand, the musical meaning is apprehended through and *along with* our own feelings, and if in a sense they are always tacitly there and function tacitly, there is no reason why we should not become aware of them provided they are intrinsic to our attention to the music. And this awareness of our own feelings as we intensely attend to and intensely enjoy the music is certainly a fact of much of our experience. In listening (or playing) we are not only very much alive in our attention to the 'life' of the music, but we feel alive too. Absorption in what we hear is not only not incompatible with acute subconscious awareness of the enjoyment of it; it is a part of it, and as a part of it is even necessary to full discriminating understanding. We can, by sympathy and empathy, see it happening as we watch a master performer at work. If he did not 'feel the music', feel his way through it with his whole being—which must include awareness of feeling it with his organism—he could not make it speak. Feeling is here cognitive in an important sense. Likewise we 'feel' the forms of space in sculpture, or the weight and rhythm of the sounding meaningful words in poetry.

§6 *Emotion*

'Emotion' may now be briefly considered in the light of what has been said about feeling.

As feeling, being feeling-of, is dependent for its content upon that which is not feeling, so emotional feeling, a kind of markedly stirred up feeling, is dependent for its character upon distinguishable factors, which are not, as such, feeling (IE). These factors, the content of emotional feeling, are stirrings-up (in varying degrees) of our normally objectively directed cognitive-conative relationships with the world. Errol Bedford,[1] in an effort to establish that emotion has a cognitive content, denies that emotion is 'any sort of feeling or mental process'. This is a bad overstatement. Certainly emotion in a full sense cannot be *identified* with feeling (IE) in the sense of immediate experience, nor just with feeling of internal subjective states. But emotions—I am not speaking of emotional dispositions—are certainly felt, and what are felt are excitations of some kind, normally bound up with our relations to the world. Actual emotion unfelt is a contradiction in terms. We may certainly 'be angry' without acutely feeling it all the time: but unless we are feeling it pretty acutely we would not naturally speak of having an (occurrent) *emotion* of anger. It is convenient to distinguish between the aspect of emotional *feeling* (IE) and its content (C) and to call the *total*, emotional-feeling-of-its-content, by the name 'emotion'.

C. A. Mace[2] in a happy metaphor, describes an emotional state as 'a kind of subjective weather'. He attempts a general description of an emotional state as follows. 'An emotional state is a complex upheaval of bodily and mental processes, affecting most, if not all, of the functions of body and mind, generally (if not always)

[1] *Proceedings of the Aristotelian Society*, 1956–57.   [2] *ibid.*, 1961–62.

instigated by relatively sudden changes in the circumstances, the fortunes or welfare of the individual, and issuing in bodily and mental responses some of which adversely affect and others of which facilitate appropriate action in the changed situation'. He agrees with the general view that emotions involve, in a wide sense, reference to an object, or to an objective state of affairs, though this is not peculiar to emotions. But 'object', or 'objective state of affairs' must be interpreted liberally, for it may be complex. 'A young woman, for example, can be all churned up, angry *with* her children, angry *about* their breaking a cherished piece of china, but angry with the children *about* the breaking of the china *by* her husband's surly complaint about the dried-up bacon served to him for breakfast.' And there are the 'objectless' emotions—states of being 'het up', states of floating anxiety, sheer *joie de vivre*, nameless fears and acute depressions.

It can be seen from this that emotions can be very complex, and not only complex but very individual. There is no single name (except a vague one like 'churned up') for the woman's state just described. *Some* general names there are—like 'fear', 'anger', 'sexual excitement'—and they are sometimes useful, for psychological or social purposes, giving clues as to how practically to approach and deal with people. They are useful enough in some life-situations. But general names for emotions can be positively mischievous when we try strictly to apply them to an art like pure music, because in music, the concreteness and individuality of the feeling or emotion is aesthetically *all*-important. A musical feeling or emotion, bound up with utterly individual musical embodiment of meaning, is strictly subject to no *precise* general name—though, as we shall see, it is still necessary to account for the quite reasonable language we talk when we say that music is 'sombre', tender', 'agitated'.

Mace also suggests, I am sure rightly, as against those who think that emotions cloud judgment or confuse or frustrate action, that emotions are functional as well as dysfunctional, that they can facilitate as well as frustrate. We know that under strong emotion a man or animal can run or perform other physical feats not ordinarily possible (though emotion can paralyse too), or can interfere with delicate skilled movements, such as threading a needle when all het up or when a homicidal maniac is holding a revolver at your head. This has a bearing on what we think about the influence of emotion on the making or appreciation of art.

CHAPTER IX

MUSIC: THE TRANSFORMATION OF FEELING

CHAPTER IX

MUSIC: THE TRANSFORMATION OF FEELING

§1 *Feeling: expression and discrimination*

The purpose of this apparent digression on the nature of feeling and emotion has been to try to achieve a better understanding of these in order to throw light on their place in art, and particularly music. One of the main questions was whether, or how far, life-feelings and emotions can be expressed in art. Another question, suggested by the last paragraph of the previous chapter, is, What place do feeling and emotion have in the discriminating experience of art? It has been argued in the past that experience of art is an 'emotion', or sometimes, that feeling and emotion get in the way. Perhaps our account of feeling as cognitive might suggest a different formulation of the questions, and a different answer?

There is another problem which, although closely related to these, is distinct from them—and very difficult to formulate in a sentence or two. It is, broadly, How does the account of feeling bear on the understanding of the transformation of life-feelings into aesthetically embodied ones? How do a poet's . . . a musician's feelings about and responses to experience of the world outside art influence the construction of artistic forms? The muscan writing pure music does not have a life-subject-matter as the word-using poet has, yet the tensions and dynamics of music do seem up to a point (the point of transformation) and sometimes, to express life-tensions and dynamics. How is this to be understood compatibly with the purity and autonomy of music? In the present chapter I shall say something about this, suggesting a general hypothesis which might account for it. In the next chapter we shall test the hypothesis by considering some examples and types of music.

The discussion of feeling and emotion has strongly reinforced one part of the main thesis of this book—that the aesthetic in art does not, *in any simple and straightforward way*, indeed cannot, express exactly the feelings of life: the aesthetic in art is not to be identified with 'expression', however much expression may be involved in the total process of art-making. Since the content (C) of feeling (IE), including emotion-feeling, i.e. *what* we feel, is always particular and different in each individual case, the concrete feeling, the feeling-of, is what it is, and cannot be exactly reproduced, except by identical repetition, which is impossible in the case of an individual, personal, historical event. If, to take an extreme case, the feeling is an utterly private one—say of some 'objectless' elation or depression, then, as we saw earlier, *you* would have to be *me* in order to know it fully as it is. I could of course talk to you about it, and you, possibly out of your similar experiences and temperament, could imagine my state and echo it in your own. If, on the other hand, the feeling or emotion is one arising from our ordinarily outward-directed relationship to the life of the world outside the psychophysical organism, its content—what it is of—cannot be exactly reproduced either. If it is (say) an emotion of love, then a representation of a *somewhat* similar emotion (not the same emotion) may be evoked in you if I write a novel or a poem about it. But the love of the character in the novel or poem (or his personal 'objectless' depression or elation for that matter) is concretely quite different from a life-emotion outside art. It is concretely embodied in the medium of the novel or poem, and the content of what is embodied is an entirely different individual (though of course there may be resemblances) from the individual content of the life-emotion. And, if all this is true of representative arts, like literature, it is *a fortiori* true of an art like pure music. Pure music does not use ordinary representative symbols like literature: it presents a unique object, a unique objective musical situation, and the feelings and emotions that may arise on perceiving it aesthetically are individually and concretely so different from life-feelings and emotions that it is far too simple just to say that music 'expresses' them. Music, in Mendelssohn's words, is not too 'indefinite' but too 'definite' to express life-feelings exactly.

Then there is the question of the place of feeling and emotion in the discriminating experience of art. Some have held that in the apprehension of art there must be emotion—sometimes called 'aesthetic emotion'. I have argued for the distinction between 'feeling' and 'emotion'. I see no reason to think that in every experience of a work of art our feelings are so stirred up that they can be clearly labelled 'emotional'. They may sometimes be so; but they need not be. As for 'the aesthetic emotion', it should be clear by now that there is not one sort of entity, such as Clive Bell seemed to suppose, which can be labelled 'the aesthetic emotion'. When aesthetic emotion does occur, as it certainly sometimes does, it will be specific to this or that experience of art, and any general description of 'aesthetic emotion', if such were possible, would have to be a general description of works of art and our total experience of them: I imagine that any attempt at such general description would produce, if it could produce anything at all, something pretty vague or thin.

On the other hand, cognitive *feeling* there must be. And the whole answer to the question whether feeling and emotion facilitate, or frustrate and confuse, discriminative aesthetic perception, depends upon whether the feeling and emotion are relevant to aesthetic understanding. This is a circular statement (though not a vicious one) and inevitably so. 'Facilitation' *means* here aesthetic facilitation, facilitation for better aesthetic apprehension, 'frustration' and 'confusion' are their opposites. Sensitive feeling (via the organism) for the right word, right weight, pause, stress . . . for the proportion of the part in relation to the whole . . . sensitive feeling keeps the proper balance between the proximal and the distal, the proper concern for objective aesthetic meaning, so that the proximal is instrumental to the meaning and does not obtrude itself. If this is *not* so, the proximal may get in the way; feeling (and sometimes emotion) instead of being directed and relevant to artistic meaning, obtrudes irrelevantly its own subjective stirrings-up. Instead of disciplined feeling and emotion instrumental to finer aesthetic perception we may get an indulgent wallowing in feeling, an emotionalism.

§2 *Life-feelings into poetry*

I have dealt at great—perhaps too much—length with one side of the coin, the autonomy of art, the irreducibility of aesthetic meaning in art and music to life-meanings. All that stands, and, I hope, need not be weakened in any way. But there is the other side, that in the process of art-making (and in a different way, the process of coming to appreciate art) expression, expression of life-meanings, indubitably does have an important part to play. This is most obviously evident in literary and dramatic arts and least so in pure music, though it is subtly present there also. I want now to consider this side carefully, and with particular reference to music. I want to examine how a musician's experiences of and responses to life situations outside music can affect his music making, how they are up to a point expressed in the process so that we can, without utter inappropriateness, use life-language in speaking of music—*yet* these experiences and responses are transformed and become unique when musical embodiment has been achieved.

Since pure music has no overt life-'subject-matter', it will be easier if we approach the difficult question of the transformation of feeling in musical embodiment through an intermediate stage, and first look for a moment at how the transformation of feeling in embodiment takes place in poetry.

Art, in so far as it expresses life, expresses it as *felt*. (In a later chapter I shall suggest that it is *values*, not facts, which art expresses.) Suppose, now that a poet is expressing his feelings about a life-situation. They are *his* feelings in the first place. It may be true—it is true—that the poet is not merely having his own private feelings and giving vent to them symptomatically: but feelings, feelings-of, feelings about life he must have in the first place. We may safely conjecture, for instance, that preceding the time that Milton wrote a certain passage in *Samson*, he was thinking, pondering, feeling much about blindness, his own experience inevitably related to his image of Samson. A biographer could tell us, in fairly neutral prose if he made an effort to, the facts of his circumstances and some of his likely reflections. The full inner story we could never know: only Milton could know it: but it would certainly have to be a story of feelings reverberating through Milton's psychophysical organism, the feelings of inner vibrant processes, organic, cognitive and conative, responding to the dominating idea of a man overcome by blindness. But Milton does not rest there. He is a man whose genius includes profound feeling for the expressiveness, the weight and rhythm of sounding words. The natural outlet for his inner feelings, and in unbroken continuity with them, is the utterance of words the pattern of whose sounds and rhythm is consonant with the inner feelings and how he expresses them. In the passage:

> Oh dark, dark, dark amid the blaze of noon
> Irrecoverably dark, total eclipse
> Without all hope of day

the pace and rhythm and tone, the long and the short, the breathing and the withholding, the sharp and sibilant contrasted with long sounds . . . all these, as intensely felt, are constituent of the aesthetic meaning embodied in the poem. And since Milton's life-feelings are expressed, though transformed in the poem, as we read the poem aloud with full intelligence, we know, through the feelings of our psychophysical organisms, not just the bare fact, but something of the very quality of the tragedy of Samson's blindness. (Samson's blindness, not just Milton's.) Feeling carries the imagination to the point of identity with the tragic life realization as it flows relentlessly along. The words do not just picture, or tell us about, Samson's agony: in living through them we participate in it. The word 'dark', repeated, contrasted with the different long word 'blaze', the breath-exhausting despair of the words 'irrecoverably', 'total' . . . the utter dejection of the sound-and-sense of the phrase 'all hope of day'—all these as spoken with feeling are inseparably a part of the meaning of the poem. Both 'proximal' and 'distal' feelings are at work and feed one another in the poet's and our experience. The focus of attention is upon the meaning—in this case of a piece of representative art, including the transformed life-meaning of Samson's blindness—but this 'distal' emphasis in the poem is inseparable from the 'proximal' feelings, the organic psychophysical feelings of the reverberation of the meaning. The meaning of the poetry is felt in the close co-operation of these two sides, the direction of the emphasis being outwards towards the meaning. By reason of our own felt responses to the meaningful words, we are able to share in some measure the feelings and responses of the poet to the total aesthetic meaning. This last statement is of course a general statement, and is speculative not empirical: we have no direct means of knowing what Milton felt—and this is not in fact the direct concern of art-experience at all. But it is quite certain that we know the poignancy of the situation Milton is depicting through our participating feelings as we could not know it by detached intellectual cognition alone.

§3 Life-feelings into music

It is awkward to jump from poetry—the words of which, uttered with poetic understanding, express not only the felt tensions of life-experiences (e.g. of blindness), but because they are referential symbols can describe them—to pure music which uses no words, and is not, as such, expressing specific, describable feelings about life. It is therefore convenient, and it may be illuminating, to consider the transitional case of music which has a 'programme' of some kind—using the term 'programme' descriptively, not pejoratively. I have in mind such examples as music with a life-reference in its title or description (e.g. feelings on 'the death of a hero'), or the music of opera or song. Schubert, Wagner, Brahms, Wolf . . . all wrote music highly expressive of a wide range of life-feelings, in which the sounds, tensions, patterns of the music are universally recognized as fitting to the sentiments expressed in words.

There can be no doubt about this acknowledged fact of aesthetic experience. If so, it is the strongest evidence, not only of the affinity between the tensions and feelings of the psycho-physical responses to certain life situations on the one hand, and the psycho-physical responses and feelings of music on the other, but of a continuity between them. It is the same psycho-physical organism which feels the tensions—say—of love frustrated (or the image of it), which feels the musical tensions that musically express the meaning of the words describing it, and which intuitively recognizes them as intimately related. What happens here is the same in kind as what we see happening when we apprehend the intimacy of the relation between the psycho-physical reverberations of Milton's being when he contemplated the horror of blindness, and the reverberations which occurred as the poignant sounding words of the poem spelled themselves out. Vibrant feelings about life, vibrant feelings for the statics and dynamics of the tremendous meaningful words as the poem takes shape— the two are continuous, and, though the feeling for the created poem is different from the life-feelings, a new thing, it is not just a separate form of words which we apprehend, or an aesthetic unity which has no relation to life, but the terrible poetry of life.

Music written on a life-theme is certainly an interim case. It is not 'pure' music, which has no explicit life-theme, and no words. But if an interim case, it is a transitional one too. For, although pure music has no words and is not written on a life-theme, the *stuff* of pure music is exactly the same as the stuff of good music which is written with words. And if in the latter case, music can express and transform explicit life-meanings, there is no reason for denying that in pure music it can express and transform implicit (not defined or described) life-meanings. The music of song is done into musical tensions; it is not *reduced* to anything else. And if pure music can express life-feelings, it transforms them none the less in musical embodiment; it is not reduced to less than music. It has never been suggested in this book that in embodiment expression is annulled—only that expression is not the key criterion of the aesthetic.

It is usually assumed—and I have so far been rather assuming—that pure music because not specifically written on a life theme, simply starts from music itself, bits of tunes, harmonies, fragments of counterpoint that come into the composer's head and are used as materials and elements for a musical composition. No doubt it does often happen in this way. If so, given the composition, we have, if as philosophers we are interested in the expressiveness of music, to work back from the given music to speculations about life-suggestions. We have amply seen how dangerous this is, particularly if the suggestions are made very specific. I have argued strongly that there can be no inferences backwards from music to life. The speculation is not so dangerous if it is not too specific, though it is always chancy. Moreover, in the light of what we have just been saying about the continuity between life and music, speculation can make out quite a good *prima facie* case. There is a general similarity between the psycho-physical feelings of the statics and dynamics of some life-situations, and the feelings of the statics and dynamics of some music. Consider, for example, the first few bars of the 'Hammerklavier' sonata slow movement. If one hears, or plays it, with feeling, there is a sense of a rather heavy lifting movement from a stable, even inert position (the minor chord in the tonic) to which one is gravitationally pulled back to the tonic. It is rather *like* the weary, heavy, lifting-movement-feeling which we experience when, rather tired, perhaps slightly depressed, we rise with an effort to take up some interesting task to which at the moment we hardly feel equal. I hasten to add that I do not imagine, even for a moment, that this subjective description is of something which the music *means*. What I do suggest is that there is a relationship between the feeling of the statics and dynamics of some music and the feeling of the statics and dynamics of some life-situations, and that it is in the psycho-physical feeling of statics and dynamics in the human organism that the relating element between life and music is to be found. Thus is a hint of the 'hypothesis' that I mentioned earlier.

Without pinning things down too much, and without assuming that a pure musician consciously sets out to express anything particular of life or life-feelings, it seems not only likely, but I think, certain, that the feelings of the statics and dynamics of responses to life-situations can influence the music that he writes. It is impossible in the case of pure music (as distinct from music with some life-subject-theme) to know, except in the rarest cases, what

F

particular life-feelings might be related in subtle underground ways
to particular pieces of music. But one ought, on the other hand,
to be careful not to deny possible correlations because of what
looks like negative biographical evidence. We know that Mozart
wrote some of his most lively music at a time when he was ground
down by poverty and depression, and it is sometimes said (for
instance by Professor Hospers) that the existence of 'gay' music
does not imply that the composer was gay when he wrote it:
then comes the biographical information just alluded to. True
enough. But as everyone knows, depression may quickly alternate
with cheerfulness, sometimes manic cheerfulness. In the case of
Mozart we simply do not know enough. I am not, of course, arguing that the various moods of music correspond merely to private
and personal feelings, that music is just symptomatic expression.
The thesis is a general one—that there is some important relation
between the statics and dynamics of life-feelings and those of
music. I am arguing that there is no more of a jump from the
feelings of life-tensions to the feelings of musical tensions than
there is a jump from Milton's life-feelings about blindness to his
feeling for the expressive tensions of words as they are used in
poetry.

§4   *An hypothesis*

I shall now try to state the hypothesis which I think can help to
explain why it is that musical meaning, the content of the cognitive feeling of music, is *both* concretely different from all life-feelings and meanings, *and* is related to life-feelings and meanings,
sometimes suggesting and echoing them, though never reproduc-
ing them.

The hypothesis derives from the rather obvious fact that it is
the human psycho-physical organism, a sort of power house (with
powers so complex and remarkable that it is doubtful whether they
could ever be completely enumerated), which is the common centre
from which we deal with the ordinary world on the one hand, and
the world of music on the other. The organism is 'designed by
nature' in the first instance to live in and to come to terms with
the world of ordinary experience, physical, perceptually meaningful, biologically, socially, personally meaningful, and so on. I
will not take space in attempting to enumerate its functions and
ways of functioning, biochemical, glandular, equipped with a
vastly complex brain and nervous system, possessing innate in-

stinctual drives with their accompanying feelings and emotions, building up human sentiments and other dispositions, coming to know and to respond to the world physically, conceptually, imaginatively, emotionally—it is, as I have just said, a vast sort of power house, storing potential energies of many kinds, deploying them in responsive adjustments to its world on the one hand, coming to *make* a characteristically human 'world' on the other.

The active psycho-physical organism is *directed*, orientated to the world, and, in particular, to whatever life-situations are relevant to the organism at the time. We, living inside the organism, have our interests directed (under normal circumstances), our attention fixed, on the objects and situations which have to be actively met—a sexual encounter, a dangerous situation, an aggression-evoking challenge . . ., a personal, social, political, intellectual, moral . . . problem to be solved. We are, as inside it, involved in it all: cognitively we feel it; and (under normal circumstances) the feeling is for the self-transcending meaning, the distal.

We *can*, however, by a somewhat artificial diversion of attention, an act of introspection, become aware in feeling of something of the complex dynamics of our own responses to the objective situation, i.e., of proximal feeling-content. Even without this deliberate attention we are, as I pointed out in the last chapter, to some extent aware of the proximal—or we sometimes are. Even in outwardly directed activities we feel alive, we feel ourselves as actively involved. Of *everything* that is involved in our responses we cannot be aware—the chemistry of the blood, the functioning of the ductless glands, the operation of the nervous system. These, however, are the causes and partial conditions of our more conscious responses and other activities; our ignorance of them does not affect the main point, the feeling of our own dynamics.

Since the dynamics are outwardly directed towards life-situations and are, as experienced in feeling, felt *along with* their objective meanings, it is difficult to describe them without seeming to make them into separate self-existing entities; if we talk of them at all, as we must, it has to be remembered that they are being abstracted from their living context. But with this precaution, it is possible to give many examples of these dynamic elements and the feelings of them. I shall, rather arbitrarily, select only a few, and those which might be relevant to our main discussion, which is of music. (Some dynamic-feelings, for instance, of sexual desire, or terror, or anger, are so life-bound, so extra-artistically human in content, that they are almost too humanly-definite to be relevant to any discussion of music. This may be an overstatement: anyhow, I shall leave them out.)

Here, then, are a few examples of dynamic elements and the feelings of them, involved in responses and reactions to life-situations. There is Attack (on people, problems, enterprises), active Elation (in success, love, challenge . . .), the Rhythms of effort—periodic, quick, slow, suspended, reinforcement alternating with relaxation . . . (involved universally in every human activity), Weariness, Depression, sense of Defeat (present in very varying circumstances, characterized by drooping, sagging, slow, heavy demeanour, movements, posture . . .), Dissonance and Strain, Consonance and Peace (in personal relations, conversations, arguments . . .). And there is Loudness, Softness (of voice or movement), Rising (to meet a guest or challenge), Sinking (in acceptance or acquiescence). Of course the list is crudely stated, artificial, overlapping, vague, incomplete. This does not greatly matter; they are merely indications of dynamic elements torn from their context.

What does matter, what indeed is the point of this whole exercise, is that the dynamics of human response are a very large part of the very materials out of which music builds its constructions. Or better—since this language might suggest that music merely takes the materials of human dynamics as they stand and compiles them into music—music takes up this raw material of dynamic-feeling, by itself and as abstracted, meaningless, and by using it creatively in the context of constructed music, gives it entirely new concrete meaning. Music as such is not interested in the purely human, extra-musical *objectives* of attack, elation, depression, 'dissonance' 'consonance' (in human non-musical context), pace, volume . . . But it does employ essentially dynamic *materials* as aesthetically felt, turning them into music.

Two observations are needed here. (1) I said in the last paragraph that human dynamics are 'a very large part' of musical material. They would include of course what Cooke calls the 'vitalising agencies', high-to-low pitch, soft-to-loud volume, quick-to-slow pace. These belong to music and life alike. The purely musical tonal and intervallic tensions seem to be in another category; it may be said that they are unique to music. In a way they are. The scale of tones is not to be found, as it stands, outside music. On the other hand tones and scales are a construction out of extra-musical sounds, high and low, and depend on them—and these extra-musical sounds and noises, and relations of them, have at least potential human and perhaps aesthetic expressiveness. Some present-day music indeed is using these extra-musical sounds and noises, from nature or electronic machines, as part of musical material—in somewhat the same way as visual artists are using almost any material for building up collage. So, even *tonal* tensions are not so completely isolated from life experience outside music.

(2) I spoke of 'entirely new concrete meaning' in music. In the sense in which I have so far argued it, emphatically yes. Musical meaning is not life-meaning. But since dynamic tensions belong to life as well as to music, and since the feeling of the life-tensions is concretely fulfilled only in relation to life-situations, and since the musician cannot escape from his human skin, it would be surprising if traces, echoes, flavours of life-meanings did not penetrate into and become fused with purely musical meaning. In fact they can do so—and this is made use of in music-with-words or other music associated with a life-theme. We would not be aware of these fused echoes from life-feelings as such in pure musical experience because they would be transformed in music. But assimilation and transformation does not mean annulment or elimination. Music is a new creature, certainly; but it in expressive content can be a contribution to the new emergent. In the alchemy of music the artist takes up the vital dynamic stuff of quite ordinary human encounters and transmutes it into the pulses of new autonomous life.

We may return now to the main hypothesis, illustrating it by means of a simple diagram. The hypothesis claims to help us both to understand the autonomy of music, musical meaning, and musical language, *and* to justify the—limited and somewhat metaphorical—use of the language of life in speaking of music.

Not all life-language is naturally applied to music. We *do* sometimes talk of 'sad' music, but as we have seen, 'sadness' is rather too specifically relevant to life (bereavement, loneliness, etc.) to be very aptly applied to music—though it *is* often applied. 'Angry' is less applicable still, '*sexually* passionate' almost beyond the limit. But we do talk of the 'excitement', 'elation', 'suspense', 'attack' of music, or of its 'quietness' and 'peace': and these words are applicable to life-situations too. On the other hand of course every one of those applicable words has a concretely different meaning in a life- or in a musical, situation. The concrete differences of content depend upon their particular objectives, life-situations or the forms of a particular piece of music. A word like 'triumphant' would illustrate this (in a battle, game, argument— musical flourish . . .).

At the common base of these different experiences is the psycho-physical organism, producing dynamic responses appropriate to the life-situations or the forms of music. The potentiality in the organism for dynamic responses, is common to both: the operation of the responses is specifically different. All the same, although specifically different, there are some similarities between the two sorts of dynamic response in music and life—e.g. responses to 'pastoral' music or a pastoral scene, or excitement in music or in life. Moreover there are (as was mentioned) associations in the musician between tensions with life-contents and tensions with musical ones. Generally speaking there are traces of similarity here and there: but it is the differences that are outstanding.

A diagram may help to illustrate the positive and negative relations.

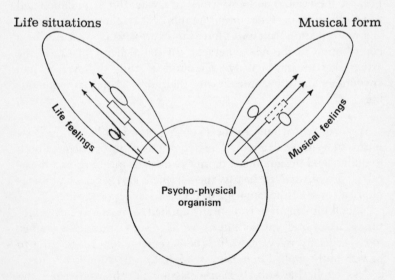

Comments. The psycho-physical organism is the common source of all dynamic responses.

Arrows represent different dynamic patterns of response in different life-situations, and in different pieces of music.

The different shapes on each set of three arrowed lines symbolize differences of dynamic pattern. The approximate, but not exact correspondence between these shapes in the life- and music-situation respectively, symbolize some, but not exact, resemblances between the patterns of dynamic response in life and music, and in the feelings of these.

The elipse-like shapes represent the total concrete feelings in life- and musical-situations respectively.

Direct comparisons between life-feelings, meanings . . . in life-situations and in music are mistaken.

The next chapter will test out these reflections by taking some examples of different kinds of music.

CHAPTER X

MUSIC AND LIFE-MEANINGS: DIFFERENT TYPES OF MUSIC

F*

CHAPTER X

MUSIC AND LIFE-MEANINGS: DIFFERENT TYPES OF MUSIC

§1 *Introduction: three types of music*

What I have been saying has necessarily been general. I shall now try to test the validity of the hypothesis sketched by taking some examples—not, as before, of the materials or elements of music, but from actual musical compositions. The problem is still the relations—positive and negative—between musical, and life-meanings.

We shall work under three headings. The first is (1) pure music, where we have nothing but the music before us; one of the best examples is the fugue. The second (2) is music where, as well as having the music before us, we have some extra-musical information about the music. It may be biographical information about the conditions under which the music was composed, or it may be information derived from some programme which it is known the composer had in mind. Or it may be suggested by a title, such as 'Funeral March'. The third (3) is music which is one factor in what I call a 'compound art'[1]—an art exemplified in opera, where music and drama and words all play a part in a compound whole, or more simply, in songs of the *Lieder* type.

§2 *'Inferences' between life and pure music*

(1) Ferguson gives a very full and fine musical analysis of Bach's great fugue in C sharp minor from the first book of the 'Forty-Eight' beginning

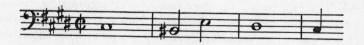

He speaks of this first subject as having a 'motion . . . intrinsically impeded', dragging 'its slow length along' 'with neither any sensible rhythmic propulsion nor any apparent aim for its motive

[1] 'Compound arts' were discussed in my *A Study in Aesthetics*, in the Chapter entitled 'The competition of interests in the Work of Art'.

effort'. If we assume that the initial C♯ is the tonic, its 'length and its low register, as well as the certainly implied *pianissimo* of its utterance, give it weight, solemnity, even mystery'. 'The long C♯ moves at last downward to B♯ (in itself a hint of weight in the C♯) which note, for the same reason, still moves slowly although its activity as leading-tone is manifest. But this B♯ now rises to E; and the interval of a diminished fourth *makes active* this E, which is normally a rest tone.' The whole fugue is analysed in comparable language, in an analytic presentation of the musical structure of the fugue. But, he says, there is 'more in this design than a feat of structure'. If we 'ask what, in our own store of emotional experience corresponds to the suggestions here given, we shall probably agree that such motion implies a heavy spiritual burden; that the tone-stresses are like those of perplexity and doubt; and that together they shadow forth a state of groping anxiety, pervasive and deep-seated, not concerned with trivial things' (pp. 115–16). Again (p. 117) 'We found in the themes suggestions of depression, animation, and confidence—or at any rate of spiritual states which, for lack of more precise and vivid verbal symbols, we call by such names as depression, animation, and confidence. These words serve merely to symbolize these states in their gross aspect. The themes define them (and hence define the words also) with much of that discrimination for their intrinsic character and intensity with which we observe the states themselves as we undergo them.'

Notice the cautionary language here. To be fair to him, Ferguson is often aware of the dangers and limitations of ordinary language when talking about music: he speaks scornfully of the 'unwarrantable plots' which writers on music sometimes read into music. But he often falls into the trap himself.

What he might have realized, were he working with the sort of hypothesis which I have been suggesting, is that when we have nothing before us but the pure music—and, legitimately, refuse to regard it as mere form abstracted from everything else—the life-language which we naturally and up to a point quite allowably use, gets such validity as it possesses from some similarity between the basic *dynamics* of the musical, and the life-situations, and not between the completed *concrete* feelings, life- or musical. In the absence of such an hypothesis there is inevitably a confusion; musical experiences are described as if they were life-experiences— 'yet not-quite'. I cannot find 'sadness', 'heavy spiritual burdens', 'perplexity', 'doubt', 'groping anxiety' in the music as heard.

Such minimum justification as there is for any language of this sort comes from basic similarity of dynamics. To put it too simply: they have similar *movement*. The 'movements' in the life-situations might be the dynamic aspects of sadness, anxiety, perplexity— these words describing the *whole* life-experience quite correctly. The 'movements' in the musical situations would be the dynamic aspects of the whole, concrete, always individual musical experiences which would not be accurately described by any 'life' words (for 'the music defines the words'). The common-dynamic-basis theory explains why the similarity and why the difference.

Ferguson makes similarly detailed analyses of a Beethoven sonata (in A, op. 101), and of two sonatas of Mozart (in F—K332, and in C minor—K475). Of the Mozart in F he thinks that although it is formally perfect, 'the threshold of expression is less easy to locate' (p. 128). He says 'It is inconceivable that such contrasts of character and such general looseness of design as this movement exhibits could have been the product of any sharply defined expressive purpose . . . the music lies only occasionally above the threshold of expressive interest' (p. 130). In a footnote he suggests that therefore the music is of relatively little value: 'profound thought *is* more significant than triviality'.

Waiving the point that it seems inconsistent to speak both of 'formal perfection' and 'looseness of design', and agreeing that this particular sonata though charming is not profound, *why* need a piece of music, to be of high value have a 'sharply defined expressive purpose'? Surely we decide the importance of any piece of music by studying its form—its form in the full concrete sense, embodying meaning, not just form and syntax abstracted—and not by looking for defined expressive purposes? The C minor sonata, in contrast, he thinks 'could not have been written without some coherent and governing purpose in mind' (p. 137). This, he cautions us, cannot be verbalized, but 'non-musical experience —too comprehensive to be "typed" by any specific event—was the prime generator of the music' (p. 137). But again, why? It may very well be true in fact that Mozart had some coherent non-musical governing purpose; his biography might show this. It may sometimes happen in this way, as we shall see. And it may be true more generally that profound human experience may give rise to profound music. But where we have the music before us alone (and this is the case we are first considering), it would seem that only 'purpose' which we can with musical competence dis-

coverer is *musical* purpose. The profundity of the Bach fugue or
of the Mozart in C minor is the profundity embodied in the very
forms of the music—in direct contact with which it seems irrelevant to talk of extra-musical 'purposes'.

The same kind of thing can be said of Ferguson's comments
on part of Beethoven 101—made as usual after fine detailed musical analysis of the first six bars of the tremendous Adagio begin-
ing

Langsam und sehnsuchtsvoll

Of the 'expressiveness' of the first bar he says, 'Propelled by the
initial harmonic unrest, the long E, attaining concord (on "three")
reveals its momentum in a preliminary turn and an easy upward
leap. In the dissonance there is no harshness, yet its gentle propulsion is irresistible; and in the upward leap, from the attained
concord, there is neither effort nor the excitement of action, but
only a high awareness of spiritual quietude. But this quietude is
a kind of ecstasy . . . This is no love music (unlike a previous
example, of not dissimilar pattern, depicting the ecstasy of Brunnhilde). Here is no breathless expectancy, no anticipatory, passionate warmth, no self-centred delight. Rather, there is the understanding bred of fruitful retrospection—an extraverted gentleness
profound even to ecstasy' (p. 145).

What is one to say of this? I make these quotations not with any
intention of captious criticism, but rather to illustrate the hair-line
between appropriate talk about music and what is just-over-the-
line of inappropriateness. I find the language appropriate and
sensitive up to about the last twenty words of the quotation,
appropriate because the language directs us to the meaningful
structure of the music itself, and appropriate because the life-
language is general enough to allow itself to be complemented by

the thought of the music. Though not confessedly, he is in fact talking of the dynamic basis of the music. Towards the end the language becomes too specifically life-language, reading an interpretation into the music which cannot be found there.

The real root of the trouble is that Ferguson assumes 'expression' to be the key-idea in the aesthetics of music. If you harp too much on expression, forgetting the transformation in embodiment, you will *always*, at some stage, walk into the trap of supposing that *what* the art 'expresses' is some life-content which is not contained in the art itself.

One more critical comment, on 'pure' music and its relation to 'expressiveness'. Ferguson puts forth a difficult theory of the 'truth' of feeling (pp. 147 *et seq*.). Not only (he thinks) must music have some truth relation to life and life feelings, but those life feelings in turn can be 'true' or 'false'—and music should represent true and not false life feelings. As an example of an expression in music of 'false' life feelings Ferguson takes the Liszt Sonata in B minor. Analysing the music, though not in detail, he says that it is 'a composition whose experiential basis is essentially fantastic, and whose whole conveyance of meaning is similarly unrelated to genuine experience'. Again he speaks of 'the surface of a trumped-up experience' and of 'the futile agitation' of one of the themes.

Here the language seems to be very much on the *wrong* side of the hairline. The sonata *may* be a formal exercise in thematic transformation, and it may not be a significant work. But if so, is it not, once again, so judged from its *musical* structure or lack of structure, its bittiness, irrelevancies, fireworks, lack of musical coherence, depth? Ferguson does of course criticize the form and basically makes his judgment on the form. If so, isn't the judgment of *musical* fatuousness enough? Liszt's shallowness of life-experience may possibly be a fact but there is no *inference* from the music to this, and Ferguson seems to be talking out of turn when he brings in 'false' life experience.

§3 *Music and extra-musical information*

(2) The second and third cases (p. 171 above) which have to be examined, though different, have this in common that they both presuppose some attention to extra-musical knowledge, coming either from biographical information or from the titles of pieces of music (e.g. 'Funeral March'), or on the other hand from words

to which the music is set. They need not be illustrated in detail, since it is the same problem, the type of inference involved, which is in question.

Ferguson gives a musical analysis of two contrasting funeral marches—Beethoven's from the *Eroica*, and the March from Chopin's sonata in B flat minor. The musical analyses are, as usual, excellent with the occasional inevitable lapse into pure life-language (e.g. 'sense of weakness and defeat'). Of the Beethoven, which he rightly regards as the profounder, he writes—referring to the first eight or nine bars—of the importance of rhythmic propulsion. The first six bars begin with notes of identical and impressive length, so that their weight is extraordinary. 'But that force is all but exhausted in the one rhythmic thrust, so that the third and fourth beats (counting the time as 4–8, not 2–4) must themselves gather momentum to reach the next strong beat . . . The whole sense of forward progression in the musical substance (to which the tone-stresses will contribute greatly) is extremely retarded. Its motion is dragged and weighted, heavy-footed and slow; yet the sense of underlying energy is abundant, so that there is no rhythmic sense of weakness or defeat.' (And so it goes on, in great detail: pp. 106–109.)

Although Ferguson affirms that 'the artistry with which the two musical concepts are realized is at least nearly equal', Chopin gets a thorough slating on the ground that what the music expresses, the attitude to life and death, is, in Chopin's as opposed to Beethoven's, case, poor and defeatist, seeing 'death as a mere misery of extinction' or (in another vein) 'almost maniacal' (p. 112). And 'if the Beethoven march be accounted the greater it is not because of his superior skill as musician, but because of his ability to reflect, through the medium of music, experience that is in itself neither musical nor in any immediate way aesthetic.'

In all this Ferguson, in spite of the validity of his main insistence of some relation between music and life, is inconsistent. In spite of his insistence that the two pieces are musically almost on a par, the musical analysis of Chopin strongly suggests that Chopin's *musical* richness is inferior to Beethoven's. (It is very difficult to prove this point without long quotations impossible here. Little extracts out of context may give an unfair impression. But a fragment like the following may indicate what I mean. 'The laborious melodic ascent of the minor third which we noticed in the Beethoven march appears here also; but its sense is notably different. For that ascent now occurs, wearily, at the fourth beat of the measure, so that the normal rhythmic strength of the following first beat is weakened by the already half-accomplished descent. This weaker C then falls to a succession of B flats whose dwindling vitality suffers complete exhaustion at the third beat of the bar. The superficial motion-impression . . . here suggests, even more than in the Beethoven, the physical reality of slow, measured treading; but the implication of energy is vastly different. The lack of rhythmic variety is greatly enhanced by the even greater monotony of the harmony . . .' (pp. 109–10). Unless I am wrong, he is inconsistent both because, in spite of what he says about the artistry of the two musicians being 'nearly equal', he does seem to think Chopin to be musically inferior in this piece, and inconsistent too because the argument should be from *that* fact (supposing that it is a musical fact) and not from extraneous judgments concerning Chopin's and Beethoven's attitudes to life and death.

We might agree that it is, possibly, independently true that Beethoven had greater 'stature' in his attitude to life and death than Chopin. Possibly: a defence of this would have to be long and elaborate, and it would be largely about biography and not music. What we ought not to agree to is to accept *inferences* from the quality of music to the quality of life-attitudes, or *vice versa*, which is what, in spite of his provisos, Ferguson expects us to do. A speculation is not an inference. It might be true in fact that greater 'depth' in music is correlated with capacity for 'depth' in extra-musical experience. But that is another matter.

The influence of biographical *information* about the conditions behind the composition of music—or of the suggestive titles of pieces—is debatable. Some find such information helpful, others an irritating obstacle to concentrated listening. We know, for instance, that Beethoven's Fifth Symphony was composed during the unhappy period when he was coming to realize that his deafness was incurable and was resolved to acceptance. And it can be said that if (and only if) one knows the biographical facts can one recognize a certain community between the dynamic tensions of the music and the dynamic patterns which are at least part of the basis of attitudes to life—'invincible determination to overcome affliction and adversity, serenity and triumph, the rise from darkness to periods of light (compare the *Andante*), the gathering of momentum rising out of despair to triumph (compare the *Finale*).'

What are we to think of this? It is difficult to generalize about the effects of extra-musical information upon different people's listening. One obvious truth stands out. It is that if the *Fifth Symphony* is being played and one's mind is straying into speculations about Beethoven's life (as some programme notes miseducate people into doing)—the information is distracting attention from the music. Some musical people therefore either refuse to read musical biography or if they have unfortunately done so, thrust it out of their minds, with understandable impatience. So let us agree to condemn (musical) *sin*! On the other hand it is not impossible, the fulsome details being forgotten, that assimilated knowledge about Beethoven's life *might* help. Talk, in musical contexts, about *total* detailed life-feelings and sentiments is misleading and false. But, against this, we have seen that there are some similarities—though not identities—between the feelings of certain basic dynamic tensions in life and music, and not only that, but echoes, suggestions, of some of the life-contents which complete the concrete feelings. And it may just be possible (*a*) that assimilated biographical knowledge sometimes reinforces attention to meaningful musical dynamics, and (*b*) brings to it *nuances* of fused life-content-feeling which without any extra-musical knowledge it would not have. I feel very uncertain about all this: but it seems dangerous to deny outright that extra-musical understanding coupled with mature experience of life's tensions and meanings *could* enrich one's total and yet essentially musical understanding.

Music with a definite programme, on a definite life-theme, is a rather different case. Here, the musician's intention is quite specific. In a television interview (June 1, 1967) Maurice Gendron, discussing Debussy's 'cello sonata, pointed out how necessary it is for the player of this—highly programmatic—sonata, to be aware of the story of the Verlaine poem on which it is based. 'Pierrot is angry at the moon.' There are scenes, musically 'represented', in which trees stand out against the background of dim light, the moon coming out, the sound of laughter, depicted on falling notes, moods of love-longing and despair. . . . If Gendron is right—and I think we must accept what he says—then what applies to the player should apply to the listener too; we understand better if we know the story—and it is, after all, as I have remarked, a deliberately descriptive piece.

The point however is that if we know the story and scenes,

related point by point to the music, our knowledge must be assimilated aesthetically to the music, which is properly the dominant focus of our attention. Conceptions and images may in a sense be there, but not by themselves, in detail crudely, and as such. They must not get in the way; they are there as background to give atmospheric significance to what is central, the sequence of the music. There is always the danger that the listener may have the detailed story too much in the forefront, trying to translate the music back and so missing its quality as music. For the devoted player, on the other hand, such conflict hardly exists, if at all; he is, in playing, freshly discovering embodied *musical* meaning. Whatever he knows outside the music, his attention to the music is single-minded.

So far I have been talking in the main about 'pure' music, where extra-musical meanings are taken up into music and transubstantiated, so that there is no inference back to life.

§4   *Compound art: music-with-words*

(3) But there is the third class of case, of music with words. It may seem to be an exception at first sight to what has just been said. For where you have music with words (or action) as in opera and song, it seems that not only do you have 'life'—what can be suggested by words and actions, with their extra-musically understood meanings—and music together, but that in this compound art of music-with-words, the *music* itself is deliberately designed to express a life-meaning. For simplicity's sake, I shall concentrate on music-with-words. (There are of course many other interesting examples—e.g. music in the film.)

Music-with-words *does* express life feelings, and expresses their *nuances* often in a very remarkable way: earlier I mentioned Schumann, Wolf and others. Ferguson quotes Hugo Leichentritt[1] who points out how Bach and Handel made a sharp distinction between their vocal and their instrumental music, the vocal music being full of picturesque symbolic touches, while the instrumental music relies almost exclusively on purely musical constructive features. We might accept the 'picturesque symbolic touches' with reservation. If these are really just *added*, and are not integrated musically with the musical form, it could be argued that, as extraneous, they are inartistic. This however would beg the present question which, as we shall see, is how *words*, which are also

---

[1] *Music, History and Ideas*, p. 148, Harvard, 1948.

'extraneous' to music, can become part of a larger artistic whole of words-with-music. Whether this can really happen we shall have to discuss: but if it can, why should not the 'symbolic touches', symbolic in the straightforward sense of indicating or even pointing to what is outside music, become integrated into the larger compound whole too?

That, however, is to anticipate. I was pointing out that vocal music does, and requires, what pure music does not. It expresses, and it sometimes presupposes a background, both of which might be irrelevant (as merely biographical) when considering pure music. The background—and the total work itself—of Bach's B minor Mass is Lutheran; it could not be Catholic. Again, his choral preludes are profound expressions of his personal religion— the title of the last one which he wrote: *Before Thy Throne, My God, I Stand* being a particularly poignant example. The religious meaning becomes explicitly united with the music in a larger compound whole as it would not be accurate to say that religious meaning is 'united' to pure music. In music-with-words the life-meaning may be said to be 'fused' with the other, musical, factor in the compound. 'Fusion' is not an illegitimate word here, since the meaningful *words* are one part of the content of feeling or emotion, whilst the musical forms are the other. For this reason I believe that, other things being equal, it is probable that the person who is thoroughly cognizant of and sympathetic to the religion of which the music in the compound is the expression, is able to be more competently appreciative of the compound than one who is neither, though he may be equally musically gifted. This is a very controversial matter; and there are, of course, many degrees of cognizance and sympathy, from the fullest understanding and the firmest faith to the generous concession of the sympathetic outsider. I very much doubt whether the total unbeliever, who has 'no use' for religion, can, however musical he is, get more than a limited amount from the *total* compounds of the *Masses* or the *Passions*. I must stress the word 'total'. He may, of course, be understandingly appreciative of the musical aspect, both as abstracted form and as embodiment of meaning; but the rest of the assimilated meaning is outside him. Here again of course there are degrees; the formal theology implied in the *Credo* of the *B Minor* may be more difficult for some people to swallow than some of the universally human elements in, say, the Matthew *Passion*. These are matters, to repeat, of opinion. I should guess that more musical people in the past got more out of religious music than equally musical people do now, because of the decline in the influence of Christian theology and Christian religion.

It is not of course only in religious music that human cognizance and sympathy seem to be required to appreciate the compound of music-with-words. Another sort of example can be taken, from Brahms. We know from biographical information quite a lot about Brahms' habits as a recluse and his deep inhibitions over making contacts with other people in friendship and love. We know that his struggles against these inhibitions were particularly acute about the time when he wrote the *Alto Rhapsody*. His internal conflicts, the desire for love and the inability to accept it, the seeking of relief and comfort from the divine, are articulated poignantly in Goethe's poem which is the verbal component of the *Rhapsody*

> Who doth stand there apart? In the brake he loseth his path;
> Close behind the branches twine about him,
> The grass springs up again, the desert surrounds him.
>
> Who will heal his affliction?
> For to him balm is poison,
> Naught but hate of men findeth he in the cup of love;
> Once despised, now a despiser,
> Secretly he wastes all the good he hath
> In a vain self-communing.
>
> Father, ever loving, send from the Psalt'ry
> One tone that may breathe o'er his being,
> Let it quicken his heart.
> Open then his clouded eyes,
> Show him then the thousand fountains,
> Springing for parched souls in the desert.[1]

The affective 'dynamics' of the feeling of these ideas are marvellously suggested in the music-with-words of the *Rhapsody*. The ideas-felt could not be discovered from the music alone since music, unlike words, has no means of conveying directly the ideas contained in the verbal account of Brahms' life, or the ideas expressed in the poem. In this case, of music-with-words, we do

[1] Translation by W. G. Rothery.

know, by the combination of chance information about Brahms' life with the poem, something of what it seems to have been Brahms' intention to 'express'.

Ferguson gives a detailed musical analysis of the Brunnhilde music as a 'portrayal of nervous tension' (93 *et seq.*) but of course as deliberately and purposefully expressive of life-ideas. The music is—and Wagner means it to be—expressive of love. But not any love. 'Love is tender; but have we here the languishing tenderness of Tristan and Isolde in the garden? Love is eager and expectant; but have we in the hesitant, wondering expectancy of this music any hint of the insatiable eagerness of Isolde as she quenches the torch? Love is ecstatic; but is this the piteous, self-forgetting ecstasy of Isolde as she sings her life out in the *Liebestod*? We know at once, *from the music itself*, that the passion here portrayed burns in the heart of quite another character than Isolde. Yet we find, in that same portrayal, something strange to our own experience. This love is too simple in essence, too lacking in physicality, and above all *too young* to be quite credible as the experience of one living on the ordinary plane of passion. Still, to think of this love as young, in the sense of immature and callow, is also impossible. This is no childish dream. It bears an unmistakeable stamp of mature reality. The creature who loves thus, we must infer, is someone not quite human. We can test this inference. We are supposed to have heard the earlier dramas of the *Ring* cycle . . . Our understanding . . . however comes from knowledge of events that are neither portrayed nor directly implied in the music' (pp. 98–9).

This epitomizes our problem. Music-with-words *is* deliberately expressive of life-experiences with their feelings, and it seems indubitable that the subtleties and complexities of the music in music-with-words as heard are in some way able to refine and develop our cognizance of the life of feeling. The life of feeling here is not *just* a development of life ideas and feelings (though it involves it), nor is it *just* a development of pure music. It is a complex which unites and fuses life and musical experience and is transformed into a whole which is more than an addition of two parts.

Ferguson says 'We know at once, *from the music itself*, that the passion here portrayed burns in the heart of quite another character than Isolde' (etc.) Is he right in insisting on the phrase italicized? Yes and No: No and Yes. If he is thinking of the music itself just as music, the answer must of course be No. We could not possibly know, simply from music, all that he says in the sentences which follow the quotation (see above). And he himself is bound to say also—though inconsistently—that we know it, *not* from the music itself, but from our previous knowledge of the dramas of the Ring cycle. He says explicitly (p. 99) 'Our understanding of that scene . . . comes from knowledge of events that are neither portrayed nor directly implied in this music'. But he also talks, in a muddled way, of 'testing and inference' of the complicated love-meanings alleged to be in 'the music itself'—testing by referring to the other parts of the Ring cycle. But in the first place, as we have been repeatedly saying, there is no 'inference' from the music itself. And in the second place, it is not 'testing' at all, since, as he admits, the very information about the complexities of love are all the time derived not from the music, but from the already mentioned knowledge of the Ring cycle.

But if Ferguson is wrong (as well as inconsistent) in saying that we can infer the literary and life meanings 'from the music *itself*', it would not be wrong to say that the music *which is part of the compound art which is The Ring* expresses and contains literary and life elements. This may look, at first sight, like a plain contradiction of all that we have been saying—that music cannot contain these extra-musical elements. But it is no contradiction, because it is not 'pure' music which contains them, nor (as was said) is the compound a compound of pure or 'absolute' music *plus* verbal knowledge, literary information. It is a new creation, in which, if it is successful, the two elements are fused, each flowing into the other in a new aesthetic embodiment; it is not a co-existence of separate elements. It is in an aesthetic transformation that the life-words and ideas enter into the meaning of the music itself ('music itself' here meaning not 'pure music' but the music which is an integral part of the compound as the words and their meanings are another part of it). The assertion of the undiscoverability of explicit life meanings in music is not contradicted, for here it is the literary elements, which can be independently known but which are fused and transformed in the music—which give us the clue. And because they are fused and transformed in the new compound art, we experience life-ideas, feelings, values embodied in a new way which in its turn can never be translated back literally into the life-language from which it came. The *nuances* of aesthetic meaning have to be, as always, experienced to be known, and cannot be conveyed except through the embodiment.

This is necessarily rather ideal language. Compound arts like song, opera, oratorio, dance, composed as they are of different parts, sometimes of different arts, are difficult to unify, both in the making and the appreciation. Considering the appreciative side of one art only, that of song, one may be attending more to the musical aspect than to the words, or *vice versa*, or there may be a rapid alternation of attention. Perhaps this alternation is necessary in coming to learn a particular song; perhaps it is difficult ever quite to overcome it and achieve the perfect embodiment of the fusion. Ideally, one should know, and have assimilated, each aspect so completely that in the mature aesthetic experience itself of the art which we have been calling 'compound', it is no longer 'compound' but single, and in aesthetic experience indivisible, the 'parts' or even the 'aspects' indistinguishable. In speaking about these things we have to remember the difference between the meta-musical *talk* which is artistic analysis, or criticism, or philosophical aesthetics, and the experience itself. The talk must always analyse, abstract and divide; the experience unifies a complex so that it seems that there is one rich, single, indivisible quality. As Pope, writing of poetry, says:

> 'Tis not enough no harshness gives offence,
> The sound must seem an echo to the sense.

I am saying that in the 'compound' arts, this is particularly difficult to achieve. I think that this may be the reason why Susanne Langer, in her *Feeling and Form*,[1] suggests that bad poetry may make a better component of song than good poetry. She may not be right: but it may be easier to appreciate song as a form of music if the form of the words of the song does not tend too much to distract the attention to itself as poetry. The fusion of words-with-music may be easier to achieve.

There are other complications too. If one knows a poem first, then comes across it as set to music, the words may monopolize the attention. (Or even the opposite might happen: taking the poem for granted, one *might* devote too much attention to the music as pure music.) There may be a difference too between the situations when the music and the words are written together by

[1] pp. 153, *et seq.*

the same person, where music is written to words, or where (less common) words are written to music. That is to say, there can be a 'competition' of interests as between the different components of a compound art. (See the chapter, 'The competition of interests in the work of art' in my *A Study in Aesthetics*.)

PART IV

AESTHETIC MEANING, KNOWLEDGE, TRUTH

CHAPTER XI

MEANING, FEELING, VALUE,
SYMBOLISM AND THE ARTS

MEANING, FEELING, VALUE, SYMBOLISM AND THE ARTS

§1 *Introductory*

Throughout this book we have been centrally concerned with the idea of aesthetic *meaning* in the arts, and the conception of 'meaning' has been provisionally discussed, sometimes implicitly, sometimes explicitly, in many places. In Chapters II and V, for instance, we discussed the 'meanings' of perceptual data, of 'aesthetic surface', the tertiary value-qualities which are aesthetically apprehended. We have considered at length senses in which music has 'meaning'. And, since 'meaning' and 'symbol' are, at least in many cases, closely connected, we have provisionally discussed in Chapter III, §§3 and 4, and in Chapter IV, §5, the place of *symbols* in art.

The time has now come for a more general, if brief, reconsideration of aesthetic meaning. In part it must sum up, or restate, what has already been said, taking it a little further. In particular, we shall have to look again at the claim that art expresses and 'objectifies' feeling, and at the relation between feeling and what is embodied. Is it really 'feelings' which are 'objectified' and embodied? And, since 'meaning' and 'symbol' are so closely related, and art is aesthetically 'meaningful', we must look again at the still half-open question whether a work of art can be called a 'symbol'.

§2 *Sources of meaning in the arts*

I begin by a brief recapitulation. Generally speaking meaning arises, in the making of art, from three sources—out of life subject-matters, from the materials of the arts, and from both of these as transformed within the work into a new systematic emergent artistic unity. (1) The subject-matter of poetry, for instance, includes what it is about—ideas of mortality, love, religion, nature . . . as well as the feelings, thoughts, desires, emotions, moods, etc., of the poet's inner life, these last being the more obvious subject matter of lyrical poetry. The words of poetry can in the ordinary sense symbolize all these, as well as 'express' them in other ways. Meanings in representative painting and sculpture again, arise from their appropriate subject-matters. The 'life' subject-matter of music (and other 'abstract' arts) raises, as we have seen, far more difficult questions, but it can be plausibly said that sometimes at least music has some sort of life theme; in music with words this is most obviously true. (2) Meanings are derived from the *materials* of the arts. The materials which become elements in the arts already possess perceived characters with aesthetic meaning, as we have seen: colours, textures, shapes, sounds, sound sequences, rhythms . . . already possess various meanings—often called 'affective' meanings—before they enter into a composition and become assimilated into it. (3) The work of art, as an aesthetic *system*, drawing from these two sources and transforming them, comes, through the agency of the artist, to possess a new, wholly internal aesthetically systematical meaning, a meaning which is *sui generis*. It is this which is presented to us for appreciation.

§3 *Art, Feeling and Value*

This meaning is often referred to as 'affective meaning', or as 'objectified feeling'. As we know, these are awkward notions. Why is the word 'feeling' so much used?

On the one hand because feelings seem to be experienced—varying much with persons and circumstances—in the creation and appreciation of art. In spite of what some writers say, feelings of excitement in the making of art are probably normal—whether or not one wants to go on to say that these feelings are expressed *in* the art. In appreciation too, we feel. We are moved in different ways by music, poetry, painting, sculpture, architecture, drama, the dance. On the other hand there is the objective emphasis. The characters of art as appreciated are said to possess what are called 'felt' or affective qualities—of melancholy, plaintiveness, boisterousness, and so on. There is the 'sweetness in the very words'. Feelings are claimed to be part of the content.

The reasons why feeling-words are used, with some metaphorical appropriateness, as well as the difficulties of speaking of feelings felt by no one, have been discussed, and need not be repeated. Talk about art indeed uses a very mixed-up language, often swinging between the subjective and the objective, with a criss-cross swing between the descriptive and the evaluative. The handiest language available often seems to be a sort of transferred language of feeling. But the idea of 'feeling-objectified' remains awkward. Can this awkwardness be avoided? I believe it can, and by employing the idea of value.

It seems better to say that it is *value* which is embodied, not feeling. Accepting—not necessarily in all its detail, Perry's well-known account of the matter (in his *A General Theory of Value*), value is interest-in-object, or, alternately, object-as-interesting—which would include object-as-felt-about.

This is of course a very general account indeed of 'value'. Value in this general sense might be described, on its subjective side, as a function of psycho-physical *valency*. (This could be positive or negative: 'interest' can show itself in attraction and pleasure or in revulsion and unpleasure: in this sense things-for-me can be 'good' or 'bad'. For present purposes we need consider the positive side only.) The question whether what-is-felt-as-valuable is 'truly' valuable or not, is another and a further question, in part at least a question for ethics. This is not our concern here.

Value in the general sense is, then, a bi-polar idea. So when I call a work or a part of a work, for want of better words, 'plaintive' or 'joyous', I am referring to the objective pole of a subjective-objective relationship. This objective use is as natural and common as could be, when speaking of values. In realms outside art I quite naturally apply the terms 'good', 'valuable', 'efficient', 'convenient' (the latter two instrumental in meaning) to objects, motor cars, instruments, houses, food. In brackets or parenthesis I know of course that they are, or have, values *for me* or other people, but this does not prevent me from attributing value ordinarily to the object, or from sometimes saying 'they are valuable' or even 'they are "values"'. I can also say that situations which are going well or badly are 'good' or 'bad'. In C. I. Lewis's language, values 'inhere' in objects. Value, then, is a subjective-objective word rather than a subjective, or purely objective one. We can as naturally focus upon the objective as upon the subjective side of it.

And it is much more natural, as I said, to speak of values than of feelings being embodied in art, since our attention is normally directed outwards. Values, although dependent upon a subjective factor, are often spoken of as though they belong to the objective world as feelings do not. So, in listening to music, for example, it is natural to think of values as being actually made (or made again as we listen) as the work progresses, and much more natural than to think of music embodying or containing or making objective 'feelings'. It is not so much that feelings are objectified in art as

G

that feelings have unique objectives in our experience of art-struc-tures; and the situation 'feeling-in-relation-to-objective' is a value-situation. If I apprehend a 'serene' piece of music, the aesthetic quality of the musical structure as apprehended, is the objective of my experience, the objective pole of a subjective–objective relationship. We can say the same thing in two ways: we can say that the phenomenal structure-as-felt-aesthetically possesses value, or that the aesthetic feeling of and for the structure is the feeling of its value as art.

This view does, I think, help to avoid the several disadvantages of the objectified-feeling view—that subjective states are pro-jected, that something is being 'expressed' which is other than what is before us, and that this other is something general like feeling, or the 'morphology' of feeling. In fact what we know and feel is new individualized objective aesthetic value.

§5   *Symbols: conceptual thinking and art*

In Chapter III (§4) there was a preliminary discussion of the question whether art can be called a 'symbol'. The development of this discussion was postponed until the idea of embodiment could be worked out and tested more fully: it is now time to return to the problem of symbols.

It is plain that symbolic expression is one essential way in which we human beings come to terms with the world we live in, come to understand it more clearly, learn to adjust ourselves to it practically. The words of ordinary language are the commonest examples of symbols, symbols without which mature, civilized, intelligent life would be impossible. There is, of course a pre-symbolic life of awareness before speech develops in human beings —and we must suppose that animals are acutely aware of *their* world in their own ways without any developed language in the human sense: the cat stalking a mouse is not without 'knowledge' of a kind! But human knowledge in any of its developed forms involves conceptual thinking, and it is by means of symbolic language that concepts are formed, fixed, and applied to particular things. We do not know clearly what particular things *are*—horses, cows, trees, desks . . . —without having concepts of them, and it is the word-symbols for concepts which enable us to express and fix the concepts and to recognize the particular objects which are instances of them. We come to understand the world in terms of concepts expressed symbolically. In learning the meaning of the words 'tree' and 'horse', we learn to pick out trees and horses. The concepts of 'tree' and 'horse' are the meanings of these terms, and the concepts enable us to isolate the references. We are assuming, of course, that there *is* an independent world, of trees, horses and many other things: but this world we only *know* through having concepts expressed in the symbols of language. An independent world impinges upon us, but the characterization of that world is apprehended in terms of symbolized concepts.

This is not the place to give a general account of symbolism and meaning. But of ordinary speech use it may be said that 'symbol' and 'meaning' are correlative. One of the things which an ordinary symbol does is to refer to a meaning—connotative or denotative—distinguishable from itself, which may be called its 'referent'. Another thing a symbol does is to *articulate* meanings together. The symbol-sentence 'the pen is on the table' articulates the meanings of the words, with their syntactical order, into the meaning of the sentence as a whole. Susanne Langer (partly following Cassirer) develops this, and stresses that it is the articulatory or *formulative* function of symbols which enables us to apprehend our world as ordered. 'This formulative function is common to all symbols, though in some it is very elementary. Any sign—for instance, the little noise that a word physically is—by being conventionally *assigned* to any object, event, quality, relation, or what not that it is to signify, bestows a conceptual identity on that designated item. Symbolization gives it form.' (One would here include in 'conceptual identity', propositional identity.) She continues, 'The perception of form arises, I think, from the process of symbolization, and the perception of form is abstraction.' And she suggests tentatively that 'Any device whereby we make an abstraction is a symbolic element, and all abstraction involves symbolization.'

How does all this bear upon the question of art as a symbol?

If we distinguish between the 'symbol in art' and the possible 'art symbol' it is clear that symbols *in* art, being ordinary symbols, have 'reference'. The words of *The Charge of the Light Brigade* are symbols having final reference to an historical event. A descriptive title in Beethoven's Third Symphony has an implied reference to Napoleon: certain motifs in Bach's *Passions* to events in the life of Christ. *Hamlet* has no very plausible connection with historical events: but, although the play is not 'true' in the sense that it corresponds as a whole to facts, the content of the play has indirect reference.

But admitting all this—that 'symbols in art' have reference to what is distinct from the symbols, it is not simply true that art, *qua* aesthetic embodiment, the aesthetic in art as such, is a symbol in the ordinary referential sense. That some art (representative art) contains referential symbols in the ordinary sense, we have been repeating. Blake's

> Tyger! Tyger! burning bright
> In the forests of the night,
> What immortal hand or eye
> Could frame thy fearful symmetry?

contains symbolism, with intensity, depth, and range of referential meaning. But the poetic meaning, though it employs the ordinary symbolism and syntax of language, *is* not, is not identical with, the meaning of that ordinary language, connotative or denotative.

As organized embodiment the meaning is self-contained. The poem assimilates and transforms meaning into itself in new, presented, indivisible embodied unity. The same is true of a representative painting or sculpture. The self-containedness, the absoluteness, of pure music is more obvious still.

Art *qua* aesthetic, then, though sometimes containing, and assimilating ordinary referential symbolic meanings, connotative and denotative, into itself, is not referentially symbolic in the ordinary sense. The unified embodiment of art is not at all like the use of ordinary words, which have conventionally recognized general meanings.

What of the *formulative* function of symbols as related to art? If it is the formulative function of symbols which enables us to apprehend our world as ordered, does this apply to the 'world' of art.

Art does in some sense, 'formulate' experience; and the forms and formulations of art are abstractions in the sense of being highly selective and specific constructions. Every work of art is a unique formal construction. Sometimes, as in representative arts, it is a construction abstracted (in various degrees) from 'life', from nature or human form. Sometimes the construction (which being specific could still be called 'abstract') stands on its own, as in pure music.

Art is abstractive formulation of experience in various media. But I find it difficult to agree with (perhaps to understand) Mrs Langer's insistence that it is a *conception* which is abstracted. Art is presentational, as Mrs Langer herself insists, and what is presented is individual rather than general, as a concept is. Of course all mature perception is saturated with concepts. We do not perceive a tree *as* a tree without the concept of tree, or a Moore sculpture *as* a sculpture of reclining woman-cum-mountain-cum-stone without concepts of these, plus many more. Some art-forms have markedly conceptual structure—e.g. *Oedipus* or *Lear*. But as we have already seen, whilst concepts symbolized in words enable us to recognize particular things sufficiently well for practical purposes, the forms of the word-symbols are *instrumental* to this purpose and have no intrinsic interest as such. But the forms of the abstractive formulations of art are primarily and essentially presentations, and it is they, not disembodied general conceptions, which are of intrinsic aesthetic interest. We may talk about Shakespeare's—or Moore's—'conceptions' (and of course there are conceptions), but we are thinking of these 'conceptions' as embodied meanings and as presented before our bodies-and-minds for contemplation.

It is very difficult to find exact, clear, unambiguous language in which to define the sense in which art can be a 'symbol'—if indeed it can at all. And even stated clearly, there is a major certainty of continuing to be misunderstood by philosophers not expert in aesthetics, because 'symbol' for them has an established use not applicable straightforwardly to aesthetics, and the habit of mind engendered by this use tends to close their minds to any other interpretation of 'symbol'. (We saw how this compelled Mrs Langer to be uncertain about the use of the word, and to abandon 'meaning' for 'import'.) In spite of this, we must continue to try—even at the cost of recapitulation, some of it elementary.

Conceptually speaking, the ordinary distinction, and correlation, between symbol and meaning is basic, and definitional. A symbol *means* (refers to, articulates, etc.), and *what* it means, its meaning, in a broad sense its referent, is always conceptually distinguishable from the symbol itself, which is—ordinarily anyhow—a perceptuum with a form of some kind. Examples are, words and sentences, in any language, or mathematical symbols (e.g. $(x + y)(x + y) = x^2 + 2xy + y^2$). Here the symbolic formulation is necessary for clear understanding of the concepts and propositions which the symbols express, and the concepts and propositions are distinguishable from the symbolic formulation.

The symbolic formulation is necessary for clear understanding of the ideas involved. But note that though necessary, the *particular* perceived symbols used are only some of a number possible, and are instrumental only to the expression of meaning. Some other perceptua would do equally well as symbols, so long as the form in which they are arranged expresses the structure of the ideas. One can say, indifferently, 'The book is on the table' or 'Le livre est sur la table'. Any language will do: so long as the pattern of sounds and shapes expresses the distinguishable concept or proposition which is the single meaning of all comparable words or sentences in any language, the symbolic instrument does its work. Similarly, the meaning would be the same if one substituted any other letters for x and y, above: $(a + b) (a + b) = a^2 + 2ab + b^2$ means the same as when 'x' and 'y' are used. (I mention this here because, as we shall see, it is in sharp contrast to the 'aesthetic symbol'.)

If we are going to talk of *aesthetic* 'symbols' at all, we shall have to accept the same basic conceptual distinction between the perceptuum which is the symbol, and what it means, its meaning. We shall have to say that perceptua such as colours or sounds or shapes or patterns of them are (conceptually) distinguishable from what, aesthetically, they mean. In *this* sense and context, we have to say that the perceptuum symbolizes, or is a symbol, for its unique aesthetic meaning, distinct from the perceptuum.

Yet, although this analysis is basic, and definitional, for both 'ordinary' and (supposed) 'aesthetic' symbols, if we stop there we get a wholly misleading account of such a supposed aesthetic 'symbol' as it actually functions in aesthetic experience itself. If we consult this actual aesthetic experience, we find the foregoing language unnatural, artificial, misleading. The perceptuum does not 'symbolize', or 'mean' something *else* which is, *aesthetically and in aesthetic experience, distinct* from itself: aesthetic meaning is embodied. The perceptuum is not just instrumental to, and expressive of, meanings distinct from itself, as 'ordinary' symbols (e.g. words) are. The aesthetic perceptuum, aesthetically experienced—e.g. the pattern of sounds or shapes—is indivisibly and uniquely united with its meaning so that (though it sounds strange), we may be moved to say that the aesthetically perceived pattern *is* or is part of, its aesthetic meaning. The meaning of the aesthetic symbol is ingredient in the symbol.

Is it a contradiction of the very idea of symbol to say that the form of the aesthetic perceptuum, the form of the aesthetic 'symbol', aesthetically perceived, is *part* of aesthetic meaning? In a way it is: in another, perhaps, it is defensible. Certainly, if we were to say of ordinary symbols—words, sentences, mathematical formulae . . . that their perceived shape or form *was* 'part' of their meaning, we should undoubtedly be wrong, because here the particular symbols used (which, we remember, can be in different languages) are not only distinct, but *separate*, from their meanings. The words, the sentences, the formulae, are one thing—symbols, noises, marks. The concepts and propositions which they mean, are another. They are clearly separate, because, as we know, there can (on the one hand) be many sets of symbol-perceptua for one single conceptual or propositional meaning: and on the other hand, the perceptuum is separate from the conceptual or propositional meaning because it is a different sort of thing from it. But of the *aesthetic* symbol these things are not true. Philosophically or conceptually speaking, the aesthetic perceptuum can, and for logical purposes must, be distinguished from *what* it means, its meaning. In one sense it is the patterns of shape, sound, etc. (the perceptua, in one sense the 'symbols') which *have* meaning, distinguishable from them. 'In one sense': that is the sense in which the aesthetic symbol is a species of the genus 'symbol', sharing the nature of all symbols. Yet, although this common distinction between symbol and meaning must be sustained in the case of the aesthetic symbol, and has just been applied to it, it leaves out the 'something more' which is an essential characteristic of the aesthetic symbol, and so fails to differentiate it.

I said that, 'philosophically or conceptually speaking' the 'aesthetic perceptuum', the 'symbol', must be distinguished from *what* it means. This is a necessary and proper carry-over from general language about symbols. But it is inaccurate and misleading language too. For if it is strictly the *aesthetic* symbol, the perceptuum *aesthetically* apprehended, which is meant, there is *no* distinction (in aesthetic experience) between the aesthetic perceptuum and its aesthetic meaning, and certainly no separation. It is this kind of thing which is hinted at when we say that the *aesthetically* perceived pattern is, or is 'part' of, its meaning, or that meaning is ingredient in the symbol. At least it is not a downright mistake (as we saw that it is a mistake if applied to ordinary symbols, which are not only distinct from but separate from their meanings). But it is language full of difficulty and obscurity. Why?

If we talk, in aesthetics, about the aesthetic symbol and aesthetic meaning, we are talking a meta-language which is continuous with talk about symbols in general. In this language, as has been made clear, 'symbol' and 'meaning' are distinct, and correlative. If we are applying this language to aesthetics, we can distinguish between the form or 'shape' of the perceptuum as perceived aesthetically (the 'symbol') and its aesthetic meaning. In *this* kind of language it would be nonsense to say things like 'the symbol means itself', or, 'the symbol is part of its own meaning'. It is nonsense because a symbol cannot mean 'itself' (the symbol) or part of itself.

But we can also talk another kind of language—perhaps it might be called a 'first order' language—a language which attempts to describe what actually happens in aesthetic experience itself. Aesthetic experience has to be known at first hand if we are to attempt to begin to understand it, for it is a unique kind of experience. Supposing we have such experience, we know very well that, when we begin to try to describe it, we are forced into the language of metaphor and analogy, a language which can suggest and point, but which requires what I earlier called the 'aesthetic leap' to be fully understood. Suppose, then, that we are trying to talk this language. We should not, I think, use at all *naturally* the language of 'symbol' and 'meaning' as distinguishable ideas—for this language belongs to a more general philosophy of symbolism. We should talk naturally, not of 'perceptua-symbols' 'meaning' things but of the forms of a picture or sculpture or dance or piece of music as 'just full of meaning', or 'meaning*ful*'. We should naturally be talking (whether we use the word or not) of embodiment, of meaning-embodied.

Suppose, however, that a perfectly respectable philosophical conscience urges us to try to relate the idea of aesthetic meaning to the more general theory of symbols and meaning. We may then be thrown into a deeply disturbing—though conscientious—conflict, between loyalty to the aesthetic facts, which cannot be 'done' into straight philosophical terminology, and desire to be clear whether in fact the concept of symbol and meaning can be applied to aesthetic experience—and if so how. In such a dilemma, half-unwillingly forcing ourselves to use the ordinary language of symbol and meaning (designed not at all for aesthetics, but for other, general, use), and yet, on the other hand, desperately loyal to the linguistically indescribable facts of aesthetic experience, we may find ourselves using just that obscure and difficult language mentioned—about a symbol 'meaning itself or part of itself'—which in other contexts certainly (and perhaps even in this) is strictly speaking nonsense.

We have seen, very early in this book, that neither the language of criticism nor of aesthetics are strictly designative, but often can only point suggestively, using metaphor and analogy. But some metaphorical and analogical language is better than others. To ejaculate after (say) listening to music, 'But the symbols mean *themselves*!' may be naturally expressive to one who is half-loyal to philosophy (because he uses the artificial word 'symbol'), unnatural to a *musician* (talking about music but loyal to the word-spurning significance of music too). It is not, however, good philosophical language. It is not good to say that 'the symbol means itself', or 'the symbol is part of its own meaning', since logically symbol and meaning are distinct. It is better to say that the aesthetic meaning (distinguishable logically from the perceptua, the pattern of sounds, logically the 'symbol') is, aesthetically, completely 'bound up with', 'inseparable from', the musical form. It is meaning-embodied. As the perceptuum is an individual, so is the meaning. In *aesthetic* experience itself one makes no distinction whatever between 'symbol' and 'meaning' (though logically in another context of discourse the distinction holds): we enjoy, aesthetically, the meaningful, *given*, individual.

Further, philosophical reflection afterwards, recapitulating, can show, using the technical language of symbolism, how the unique aesthetic symbol is different from other symbols. Ordinary symbols, we saw, are *instrumental* only to the clear apprehension of meaning quite distinct from themselves. The instrument is necessary, but the symbol *is* instrumental, a means to an end—the grasp of conceptual or propositional meaning. And the meaning (denotative or connotative) is not only always clearly distinguishable from the symbol, but separable from it. (The sentence, e.g. is separable from the proposition.) The *aesthetic* 'symbol', on the other hand, though it is instrumental, is not so only but is (as we have said) bound up with, aesthetically inseparable from, its meaning. Because of this, because the *very form and shape* of the perceptuum, *this* individual perceptuum, is necessary to and inseparable from

G*

the meaning, the meaning too is utterly and uniquely individual, not denotative or connotative, like the ordinary symbol. Further, the individual symbol, being so internally related to the individual meaning, is unlike the ordinary symbol, where alternative symbols, in different languages, will do their instrumental work just as well.

If, then, we are to use the term 'aesthetic symbol' which—in spite of the dangers of being misunderstood—I think we must, it will be a unique kind of symbol, in being the aesthetic embodiment of its own meaning. For that reason I will call it the *embodiment-symbol*.

§6 *Jungian symbols, and the 'embodiment-symbol'*

This discussion so far has turned on the comparison between the use of 'symbol' by logicians and philosophers and its different use in aesthetics. On the other hand 'symbol' has a much wider cultural context than this, and it may further illuminate the concept of the 'embodiment-symbol' if we look at the employment of 'symbol' in depth-psychology.

Both Jung and Freud speak much of symbols. I have no intention here of trying to expound in any detail Jung's—or Freud's— theory of art. They are discussed quite fully in a book by Morris Philipson,[1] to which I am indebted. I shall only refer to these theories in so far as they bear upon the meaning of 'symbol'.

Freud's view, roughly speaking, is that art is a sign or a symptom of the individual's unconscious. For Jung, on the other hand, 'the true symbol differs essentially from [symptoms], and should be understood as the expression of an intuitive perception which can as yet neither be apprehended better, not expressed differently.'[2] For Jung, symbols represent or (in some sense of the word) embody an excess which is over and above what is necessary for ordinary, natural life. And whilst, for Freud, symptoms represent blockages in the natural system, symbols, for Jung, have the function of extending culture rather than furthering the purely natural life. Further, the function of the symbol is to express a complex fact which is 'not yet' clearly grasped by consciousness. As Philipson puts it, 'the symbol is a representation which is not logically equivalent to that which it represents, and the reference

[1] Morris Philipson, *Outline of a Jungian Aesthetics*, Northwestern University Press, 1963.
[2] *Contributions to Analytical Psychology*, 1928, pp. 231–2.

is not known except through the medium of some natural or artificial representation; it is not known directly.'[1]

Jung distinguishes between two types of (literary) art which to some extent overlap. (1) In the first mode, which he calls the 'psychological' mode, the subject-matter is drawn from the realm of human consciousness, the lessons of life with their emotional shocks, the experience of passion, the crises of human destiny, all of which go to make up the conscious life of man. This is illustrated in many works dealing with love, the environment, the family, crime and society, as well as in didactic poetry, and in drama both tragic and comic. Here the subject matter comes from the 'foreground' of life. About this class of art he says, 'there is nothing that the psychologist can add to it that the poet has not already said in better words'.[2]

(2) In the second mode of art, which he calls 'Visionary', the subject-matter is no longer the familiar one of common experience but of a strange something which derives its existence from the hinterland of man's mind—that suggests the abyss of time separating us from pre-human ages, or evokes a superhuman world of contrasting light and darkness. It is a primordial experience, which surpasses man's understanding. It arises from the timeless depths. It is foreign and cold, many-sided, demonic, and grotesque. In this kind of art, Jung says, the work positively imposes itself upon the author who is, as it were, seized, his pen writing things which his mind perceives with amazement. Nothing here is self-explanatory. Jung has in mind such examples as the second part of Goethe's *Faust*, Dante's *Commedia*, Wagner's *Niebelungering*, Blake's writings, *Moby Dick*, *The Shepherd of Hermas*.

I shall not comment on this twofold distinction except to say that, although it is useful and important and does illuminate two different types of art, the distinction, in spite of Jung's safeguards, is rather too sharp. The important point for us here is that, for Jung, the term 'symbol' refers to the 'Visionary' type of art rather than to the 'Psychological', the 'something' which is expressed being derived from the 'Collective Unconscious', the realm of the 'Archetypes'.

Jung's symbols do not simply 'point' to something, as signs do, nor do they refer to a concept, as symbols do on Cassirer's or Susanne Langer's interpretation—though they certainly do 'articu-

---

[1] Morris Philipson, *op. cit.*, p. 26.
[2] Jung, *Modern Man in Search of a Soul*, p. 10.

late' something which comes from the Collective Unconscious. The Jungian symbol is the symbol of a strictly untranslatable or unsayable meaning. As Jung says, 'It is impossible to say what they refer to'.[1] The evidence which we have of the Collective Unconscious, which he calls 'a universal and homogeneous substratum' is a 'world-wide identity of similarity of myths and fairy tales'. These, however, are developed and given individual conscious expression in the diversity of individual psyches. The contents of the Collective Unconscious are residues both of archaic but specifically human modes of functioning, and of residues of functions from man's animal ancestry. He sometimes calls these 'precipitates', 'mnemic deposits', 'engrams' (after Semon). They are condensations of 'innumerable, similar processes'.[2] Jung says that 'in itself the collective unconscious cannot be said to exist at all; that is to say, it is nothing but a possibility, that possibility which in fact from primordial time has been handed down to us in the definite form of mnemic images, or expressed in anatomical functions in the very structure of the brain'.[3] The Collective Unconscious seems, then, to provide the conditions for imaginative thought in the individual psyche, conditions which have to be individuated, either immediately and naïvely, as in dreams, or consciously and sophisticatedly as at the high levels of religion, art, and science. They are, of course, at this stage no longer unconscious, but conscious.

Jung's account of symbols is sharply different from Freud's. For Jung, the meaning of the archetypal symbol is unknown. (There are passages, which I shall refer to below, in which Jung seems to hint at a possible future scientific understanding of archetypal meaning: but for the present at any rate we only have the symbols of which the full meaning is unknown.) It is unstatable, except in symbolic terms. For Freud, on the other hand, the meaning of symbols (which are symptoms of repressed conflict) can become known exactly—e.g. through analysis. The stick-like shape, or knife, or hollow object can become recognizable as symbols of definitely known objects, sexual organs, the recognition of which was repressed and disguised in consciousness. The symbol stands as a substitute for some knowable object, which is its 'meaning'. If these symbols occur in art (as they do) and their 'meaning' in

[1] Jung, *Essays on a Science of Mythology*, p. 104.
[2] Jung, *Psychological Types*, p. 556.
[3] Jung, *Contributions to Analytical Psychology*, p. 246.

art were to be interpreted in this way, this would be a *reductive* interpretation of art, art not embodying its meaning, but indicating meaning outside art. No one denies that Freudian symbols can be (in Langer's term) 'symbols *in* art'—but that is another matter. If they are to become, organically, part of art, they must be embodied, and irreducible. In Jung, *if* the meaning of archetypal symbols could be scientifically stated, there could be reductiveness too. But in his main thesis Jung is saved from this by his contention that the meaning of the archetypal symbols is *not* known, and that they do *not* stand (as with Freud) for actual objects of common experience.

How far does the idea of the Jungian symbol illuminate art as symbol?

Jung, as we have seen, does not say that archetypal symbols are, as such, art. He distinguishes the conscious objectivications of religion, art and science, from the more immediate, non-artistic manifestations in dreams and visions and fairy-tales. What he does say is that archetypal symbols enter into one type of art, the Visionary type. In other words the archetypal symbol as such has not necessarily any characters of artistic form; artistic form is something over and above. To this we can agree, and we can say that of the 'over and above', one of the characters is embodiment.

The interest of the comparison is this. On the one hand, the archetypal symbol is an expression or an articulation of something that cannot be expressed or articulated otherwise at all. I have urged, and shall continue to urge, that meaning in aesthetic embodiment is never translatable back, that you cannot say in other words what art is saying in its own way. In this respect art is like the Jungian symbol. In Jung's own words 'it is *impossible* to say' (of contents of an archetypal character) '*what* they refer to'.[1] In the same passage he says, 'what an archetypal content is always expressing is first and foremost a figure of speech'. (As we saw, 'Every interpretation necessarily remains an "as-if" '). 'If it speaks of the sun and identifies it with the lion, the king, the hoard of gold guarded by the dragon, or the force which makes for the life and health of man, it is neither the one thing nor the other, but the unknown third thing that finds more or less adequate expression in all these similes, yet—to the perpetual vexation of the intellect—remains unknown and not to be fitted into a formula.'[2]

[1] Jung, *Essays on a Science of Mythology*, p. 104.
[2] *ibid.*

This is one side. Like artistic embodiment, the Jungian symbol presents meaning which cannot otherwise be stated. But, note, it is the peculiarity of the essentially *unconscious* nature of the archetype which makes it impossible. In the forms of *art*, on the other hand, although it is always impossible to state content exactly in other words, the reason is different. There may be a special, additional 'Jungian' reason for untranslatability in the case of the art which Jung calls 'Visionary', but there is a more fundamental, and aesthetic, reason for artistic untranslatability which applies equally to both 'types' of art. It is, simply, the transforming nature of artistic embodiment, which creates new, untranslatable uniquely aesthetic meaning. Untranslatability is not dependent upon the character of the subject matter (e.g. as derived from the Collective Unconscious), but upon the nature of aesthetic embodiment.

This is one essential difference between the Jungian symbol and aesthetic embodiment. But it at once points to another difference, which is the opposite side of the same coin. It is that, however impossible it may be to say what the content of an archetypal symbol precisely refers to, there is, nevertheless, always an idea of reference to something else in the symbol, even though what is referred to cannot be stated. Though the symbol cannot exactly express what it refers to, an ineffable 'other', yet it *is* nevertheless striving to express it, though not succeeding. And—as I have already hinted in passing—in spite of Jung's affirmation that the archetypes in the Collective Unconscious can never be known, he does, in some of his writings, seem to be hankering after a translation of them into conceptual terms. There is, on the one hand, the emphasis we have seen, emphasis upon some reference of the symbol to an unconscious 'core' of meaning—which was never conscious and never will be. On the other hand, he also says that the archetypes, the mythological forms, 'are in themselves themes of creative fantasy *that still await their translation* into conceptual language, of which there exists as yet only laborious beginnings'. (My italics.) 'These concepts, for the most part still to be created, could provide an abstract scientific understanding of the unconscious processes that are the roots of primordial images.'[1] So, although the presented archetypal image does not and cannot refer to anything, in any comprehensible sense of the word, known, yet it does also refer to and articulate imperfectly, in an *as-if*

[1] Jung, *Contributions to Analytical Psychology*, p. 246.

form, this 'third thing', which has already been mentioned, which is unknown, and 'for which there is no formula'.

In this referring aspect the Jungian symbol seems to differ from what we have called 'embodiment' of meaning, which makes it seem doubtfully wise to call the work of art a 'symbol' even in this more generous Jungian sense. The work of art is not trying, like the Jungian symbol to express, in an *as-if* fashion, what *cannot* be expressed because it is unknowable. It is not trying, and failing, to do the impossible; it is not, *essentially*, *in*adequate to fulfil its task. Works of art do draw into themselves, especially in the 'visionary' mode, and absorb, from vast storehouses of human (possibly pre-human) experiences, conscious and unconscious. But they do *absorb*, and transform, this material, so that there comes into being a new creation, with its own kind of perfection. They do not try, and fail, to say it all. The work of art, as such, is not a faulty and imperfect mere *instrument* of conveyance. It is an *intrinsic* and self-sufficient entity, existing in its own right and with its own autonomy. The Jungian archetypal image has an inadequacy or imperfection built into it, because it refers to what it itself cannot completely say. The work of art has no such built-in inadequacy. It is an individual, to be evaluated completely within its own structure and not by reference to anything outside it.

I have just said that Jung's symbol—or better, the idea of Jung's symbol—has inadequacy built into it. This, however, is a bit one-sided. In one way, the symbol may be inadequate; but it may also *feel* 'right'. The archetypal dream, for instance, may feel marvellously, and intrinsically, important, its form and meaning seeming to be one. It is something like an *objet trouvé*, or even more than that, almost a work of art which is automatically *given* to us, with perfection of form better than we could ever, we feel, have made consciously. (The given 'art' of the dream can be staggering: we could, we feel, never have 'done' it so well.)

But this very fact really brings out the point of the *difference* between the work of art, and the symbol with its inevitable reference element. The archetypal symbol is not always shown in a work of art, though it can be. But even if it is not, there can be aesthetic experience of it as something self-contained and complete, as the *objet trouvé*, or as the *quasi* art object, say of the dream. In *this* case, there seems to be no 'inadequacy'. But this is just *because* it is being taken aesthetically, as embodiment symbol and not just as Jungian symbol. It is when it is taken as a symbol, symbolizing something *else* which Jung says (or usually says) cannot possibly be stated conceptually, that the symbol is, as such, here inadequate. A Jungian symbol has the instrumental function—of referring to, of expressing, of articulating, or suggesting in an *as-if* form, something which is distinct from itself (although it may be continuous with it, as in the etymological analogy of the half-token). In the case of the archetypal symbol it can, admittedly, only do this imperfectly. If it is regarded aesthetically as an art, or *quasi*-art, object, there is no 'imperfection' 'built into' it. When Jung is writing of 'Visionary' works of art, and saying that they are puzzling, baffling, impossible to interpret adequately, he is thinking of them as symbols of an indecipherable subject-matter rather than as works of art strictly, form and content one. And this brings out very clearly the *difference* between the work of art and the symbol proper.

I conclude, therefore, that the idea of the Jungian symbol, though it has interesting bearings on the symbolism of art, does not in itself measure up to the uniqueness of the 'embodiment-symbol'.

CHAPTER XII

ART, KNOWLEDGE AND TRUTH

ART, KNOWLEDGE AND TRUTH

§1 *Knowledge and Propositions*

It is clear that some arts at any rate presuppose and assimilate 'knowledge' in a quite ordinary sense—knowledge in senses in which the word can be used outside art. Drama and poetry may be about life, death, love, tragedy; the story of the novel is a story of imagined life happenings, and our ordinary knowledge of these things is a condition of appreciation of the arts which use them as subject matter. And we saw that even in the 'abstract' art of Kandinsky and Klee life-suggestions keep coming in: again, there is music-with-a-programme, or music with words. All this 'outside' knowledge is assimilated and transformed in embodiment, becoming aesthetic knowledge. It seems hardly disputable that knowledge of art is a kind knowledge.

But even so, there is the familiar danger that if we call aesthetic apprehension of art 'knowledge', we shall be expected to state in words *what* this knowledge is, or what it is 'about', or why it is true. So much important knowledge—of commonsense, science, history, philosophy—is propositional and discursive that there is still, in spite of recent writings, a strong tendency among philosophers and others to assume that if anything is knowledge it must in the end be statable propositionally.

But this is too simple. It is, of course impossible to eliminate the influence and implicit presence, in the knowledge of adult human beings, of knowledge-that, or knowledge-about. Our minds are loaded with it from childhood onwards. On the other hand there are elements, or aspects, of *all* knowledge which are not, as such, propositional, and there seems to be at least one kind of knowledge which is not in itself propositional at all (though propositions may indirectly contribute to the understanding of its meaning); I mean the knowledge of art. Let us first look at non-artistic knowledge.

In ordinary sense-perception there are given, presentational elements which are not propositional. As I look round the room a changing pattern is *given* to me and given as a whole. It is a complex whole, its specific complexity dependent on past-analysis; and it can at any time be analysed further, in an analysis which may, but, need not, employ words. (I can, e.g. perceive the

desk against its background immediately, without using words.)
Our use of words is in the background all the time, but their relevant use is dependent upon impacts immediately apprehended.
The same is true of involuntary images (e.g. memory images)
and of intellectual intuitions of simple or complex relations within
a whole. I can 'see' a very simple mathematical proof. Again, there
is the impact of the face-to-face *given* of other persons, or of the
qualities of moral good or evil. We can, and do, say things about
conceptual relations, other people, moral good and evil—but saying depends upon different kinds of 'givens' which are not sayings.

Another side of the same thing is that in all knowledge whatever
there is an experiencing, indwelling element which in itself has
to be lived through and cannot be stated. This indwelling is not
just a condition or ground of knowledge; it is a part of it. There is
an essential aspect of knowledge which is know*ing* by a mind and
which, as such, is unsayable because it is something else, an
experience, known from inside the intuitive gestalt-knowledge
which we must have as the condition of sensibly saying true things.
(And here let me say that I am not using 'intuition' as the name of
any magical, occult, or infallible faculty, but simply as what must
be present when we apprehend a gestalt.)

We have seen how Professor Polanyi in his various writings[1]
has laid great stress on the implicit or *tacit* element in knowledge.
All knowledge is either tacit or rooted in tacit knowledge; wholly
explicit knowledge is unthinkable. Many sorts of examples illustrate this. If one looks at things through a pinhole, excluding the
normal setting for the perception of objects, the different appearance (e.g. difference of apparent size) of things shows vividly how
dependent we are upon unnoticed background in the perception of
focal objects. Or we immediately recognize, 'know' a face among
ten thousand without any idea of how we know it. We do not have,
or give, reasons. We read complex sentences, or follow complex
arguments with intuitive grasp, and do it with a speed almost
infinitely greater than when making explicit inferences between
propositions. And of course we know perfectly well *how* to do
things like balancing a bicycle without knowing explicitly *what*
we are doing. And so on. As for scientific discovery (and scientific
knowledge), it 'cannot be achieved by explicit inference, nor can
its true claims be explicitly stated. Discovery must be arrived at

---

[1] Michael Polanyi, *Science, Faith, and Society, Personal Knowledge*, and a
recent article in *Philosophy*, Vol. 41, No. 155, 'The Logic of Tacit Inference'.

by the tacit powers of the mind, and its content, in so far as it is indeterminate, can only be tacitly known.'[1]

§2 'Knowledge by Acquaintance' and Knowledge of Art

I have been speaking of non-propositional 'elements' or 'aspects' in all knowledge. But one can put it more strongly. One can claim that there are some *kinds* or *forms*, of knowledge which are in themselves not propositional, though propositional knowledge may be presupposed. One candidate for this claim is 'Knowledge by Acquaintance'. Since knowledge of art would seem *prima facie* to be a form of knowledge by acquaintance, it is necessary to see whether the idea of such knowledge is tenable, and whether it can be applied to knowledge of art.

Long ago, in *Problems of Philosophy*, Bertrand Russell distinguished between 'knowledge by acquaintance' and 'knowledge by description', or 'knowledge about'. He was pointing out, very profitably, the difference between the acquaintance with simple colours and sounds, which he thought was a kind of knowledge, and what we can say about them. Critics admitted the distinction between acquaintance and description but denied that 'acquaintance' is 'knowledge'. One of these critics, Moritz Schlick, called it a 'most terrible' mistake . . . '*the* most fundamental mistake of the philosophy of all times'.[2] Since Russell was talking about simple sensations (or sensa), and it has always been disputed whether we ever *know* these in their purity without the influence of any other knowledge (such as: 'this is a "colour" ', 'it is red', 'it is in such and such a place on the spectrum band'), a less exaggerated condemnation than Schlick's may be right.

But John Hospers, who quotes Schlick, and who at that time was writing before Logical Positivism had finished doing its final posthumous reflex jerks, makes use of the criticism to argue that experience of art is not knowledge. This criticism, I think, is confused and invalid.

Hospers writes of knowledge and acquaintance:[3] 'The one is knowledge about things, the other is immediate acquaintance with them; the one is given *par excellence* by science, the other by art. When we hear music, we have deeper, richer acquaintance, not knowledge—it is not the function of music to give us that.' But

---

[1] *Philosophy, op. cit.*   [2] Moritz Schlick, *Gesammelte Aufsätze*, p. 190.
[3] John Hospers, *Meaning and Truth in the Arts*, University of North Carolina Press, 1946, pp. 235 *et seq.*

if it is a mistake, as it may be, to call acquaintance with bare sensa, 'knowledge', it is a far worse mistake not to distinguish sharply between these, debatable, border-line cases of acquaintance, and the acquaintance we have of the most complex objects of art, and to assume that an argument against *knowledge* by acquaintance of sense data has any validity in the more complex case. If it is true (as it is) that 'we have deeper, richer acquaintance in the experience of music, *why* are we not to be allowed to call this 'knowledge'? If bare sensational acquaintance exists at all (as I think we might allow it does, though it may not be 'knowledge'), it is, by definition, free of all importation from 'knowledge-about'. But my acquaintance with a piece of music—or, for that matter, my ordinary acquaintance with this room I am now in—is nothing of this sort, and to suppose that it is, is simply to be misled by the use of one word, 'acquaintance', for two very different things, one artificially simple (Russell's) the other very complex. If my experience of music, or the room I am in, is 'enriched' experience, why is it not enriched acquaintance-*knowledge?* My acquaintance with the music or the room presupposes a wealth of knowledge-that. It is elementary (as I have said) that the whole of my past, from infancy onwards—and from post-infancy transformed by the influence of language—contributes to the discriminated content of my present acquaintance in perception. This is true also of my 'enriched' acquaintance with art. I know *that* it is a symphony I am listening to, *that* it is the second, slow movement, *that* the opening passage has been repeated in inversion . . . etc., etc. I am not, of course, *saying* all these things all the time. Nor am I saying that enrichment is a function merely of propositional knowledge, or that acquaintance-knowledge of music is a sum of all that could be said truly. But without any knowledge-that—and in fact there is an indefinitely large accumulation of knowledge-that—it would certainly not be an acquaintance of any discernment or 'richness'.

My contention then is that this 'enriched' acquaintance *is* a form of *knowledge*. It may be called (to distinguish it from Russell's use) 'acquaintance-knowledge' (not knowledge by acquaintance). To call it 'enriched acquaintance' only, denying it to be knowledge, is only a verbal operation, a concession to a far-too-limited conception of knowledge, dominated by one form of it, the propositional. And the operation fails. For how does the 'enrichment' of the aesthetic apprehension of the parts of a fugue, in relation to one another and the whole, grow from vagueness into the clarity of understanding, if there is no growth of *knowledge* of the fugue (which is certainly not identical with the things I can say about it)? If this is not increase of knowledge, if I do not know the fugue better, and so have more knowledge of it (and not merely about it) what is it? Is not the experience of the emergent aesthetic meaning, an increase of knowledge?

§3   Know-how—and 'talk' in science and art

In citing Professor Polanyi, I referred to 'knowledge-how' to balance a bicycle. We learn how to ride a bicycle without necessarily learning any propositions about it. This 'knowing how', in an extended sense, has a close bearing on the special kind of acquaintance-knowledge which art is.

Knowing how to ride a bicycle, or how to hit a golf ball effectively, is practical knowledge of a useful, or pleasurable, but obviously of a rather limited kind. Aristotle speaks of 'practical' knowledge in a wider, i.e. moral sense, and one which has a closer relation to knowledge of art. Aristotle, indeed, thinks of the practical judgment of the morally wise man in particular situations as being guided by a kind of artistic or aesthetic intuition. You can't decide how to act merely by 'reasoning'; it can only be discovered by 'perception' or 'intuition'.[1] To have properly balanced moral feelings, one must not be affected too much or too little; one must be affected by the 'mean' or 'moderate' amount 'at the right times, and on the right occasions, and towards the right persons, and with the right object, and in the right fashion'.[2]

'Knowing how' in making or appreciating art is not 'practical' knowledge in Aristotle's special sense of the word, but there are close analogies. The artist's work is a very special kind of practical work. He has to know (in painting or poetry or anything else) 'the right amount'. There must not be 'too much' here or 'too little' there; he must know the right time and occasion for this word or patch of colour, and he must know how to put it in the right way. None of it is adequately done by knowing truths; what to do must be known by the peculiar thing we—with Aristotle—call aesthetic 'intuition'.

On the side of discriminating appreciation, the same kind of thing is true, *mutatis mutandis*. We have to learn how, when, and where to look and listen; we have to learn to detect 'excess' or

---

[1] Aristotle, '*Καὶ ἐν τῇ αἰσθήσει ἡ κρίσις*', *Nic. Eth.*, Bk. 2, Chap. 9.
[2] *ibid.*, Chap. 6.

'defects' of different kinds. And we do it not by learning 'truths about' art, but 'on the job', by being involved in the art. We learn true sense of values in art by learning to feel them with cognitive discrimination which is not essentially propositional at all. The values of art can never be known in the detachment of propositional thinking. There is a detachment proper to aesthetic judgment. But the contemplative detachment towards art is also one in which we are very much involved. We contemplate the *structures* of art, but we know these structures aesthetically because we cognitively *feel* them. Our feelings are not boilings-up of irrelevant emotions which would get in the way, but relevant, and essential, to artistic understanding.

Of course we talk a lot *about* art, and when we talk we use propositions. Some talk about art, critical talk, can be (as we saw in Chapter I) an important auxiliary to the appreciation of art; it can enhance and illuminate our knowledge of art. But it does so by enabling us to re-experience more effectively; though critical talk is propositional, the re-experience is not. Propositional knowledge is presupposed, but knowledge of art is not constituted by propositional knowledge: it is a fresh intuition, enriched by and assimilating what we relevantly know in other ways.

In this, knowledge of art is in sharp contrast to knowledge of science. Scientific knowledge, as we have seen, has its implicit or 'tacit' aspects, and a scientist, to be a scientist, must have *his* special sort of involvement with science; he has intuitions which, because they *are* intuitions of relationships within a systematic whole, are never completely reducible to propositional form. On the other hand, propositional knowledge is intrinsic to science as it is not to art. Propositions are a necessary part of science; science *has* to make explicit propositions to be itself; there could be no science without scientific statements, as there can be art without statements.

It might be argued that, as talk about art is auxiliary to the indwelling knowledge of art, so talk about science is auxiliary to an (already admitted) indwelling scientific knowledge. Scientific knowledge, it can be fairly said, does not *consist* of the true propositions which the scientist knows; scientific knowledge is the scientist's intuitive grasp of scientific systems. This is true enough. Nevertheless scientific propositions are not 'auxiliary' to scientific understanding in at all the same sense as propositions about art may be auxiliary to the understanding of art. For the scientist's grasp of science is grasp of wholes which are, as we said, *essentially* propositional in nature. Aesthetic grasp of art is of wholes which are essentially non-propositional. Talk about art is radically different from the talk of science, being (in the sense described) extrinsic to it; the talk of science is intrinsic to it. There is necessarily propositional talk in science as a part of it. There is, necessarily, no propositional talk in art as a part of it. In other words, scientific propositional talk is not talk *about* science, but the talk *of* science. Critical and other propositional talk about art is talk *about* it, not the talk *of* art. There is no talk *of* art as such. Knowledge of art is a knowing which intrinsically contains no talking, no propositions in any sense in which we have been using this word.

§4 *'Adequacy' of artistic knowledge*

So far, I have argued that we have knowledge of art, that it is intuitive apprehension, and that it is not, as such, propositional.

But 'knowledge' is a very demanding word; in the strictest sense it suggests the fulfilment of a norm. I have not, however, been using it in this strict sense; our discussions of science and art have allowed for the correction and progression of knowledge; in some quite understandable sense, surely, there may be degrees of knowledge? But if so, it becomes important to be able to distinguish between these degrees, to discover the difference between more, and less, adequate knowledge. Suppose that a number of people are looking at some established work of art, say a Rembrandt portrait, or listening to a Brahms concerto. There will be many degrees of the understanding knowledge of either of these works. So much is (or at least seems) self-evident and to need no argument: what is difficult is to define the criteria and tests of adequacy and understanding. What is meant by saying 'he really *knows* that Rembrandt (or Brahms)'?

One might say that it means that he knows the truth about it (and can give good reasons). Yet in view of what has already been said, this can be misleading and constricting. ('Reasons' in art-criticism, we early saw, are odd things.) The word 'truth' is more naturally and appropriately applied to propositions than to knowledge; and the making of true propositons is, as we have seen, only one part, though a vitally important part, of knowledge. 'Knowledge' is a wider, richer notion than the truth which belongs

to propositions; conversely, the truth which belongs to proposi-
sitions is a much more definite and constricted concept than the
knowledge of which it is the manifestation and expression. If we
say that someone—say a scientist or statesman—has a wide or
profound 'knowledge' of his own field, we include, of course, his
ability to make an indefinite number of propositional statements
which are true. But we mean much more than that. If we say he
has profound knowledge we mean that he has understanding, not
just of the meaning and truth of the particular propositions he
makes, but of their relationship to one another and to the whole
field. The man has perspective; he sees the situation as a whole
in a way which, because it is intuition of a gestalt, is never (as we
saw) adequately statable. He has the flexibility of the master mind;
he can pass from any point to any other point, and he can see,
as the less knowledgeable person cannot, when it is necessary so to
pass, and exactly where it is relevant. If action is called for, he
knows how, when, where . . . to act. He has what is called 'grasp'
of the situation—and this is, incidentally, a telling metaphor.

It seems, therefore, better to speak of (more or less) 'adequate'
rather than 'true' knowledge.

Mutatis mutandis, and without at the moment going into detail,
one might say that adequacy of knowledge of art would be judged
in something of the same way. The knowledgeable critic makes
true statements about the work of art. Some of them are 'true'
in the straightforward sense. 'It belongs to this period and style,
the artist was influenced in manner and technique by such and
such influences, it is of this "form" rather than that . . .' The critic
also makes statements which are 'true' in the peculiar critical
sense which we discussed in Chapter I, statements which are
relevant to more discriminating re-experience of the work. But
what he says, and the truth of it, is (as before) a manifestation
and expression of knowledge possessed by him which goes far
beyond anything he says or can say. He too (like the scientist or
statesman, though differently) has understanding, perspective,
flexibility, the intuition of the complex whole. He has aesthetic
insight and 'grasp', and something of this, by his special language,
he tries to convey to us too.

The condition of his saying sensible things about art is this
aesthetic insight. Conversely, if we also have some insight we can
recognize that the critic has knowledge by the kind of things which
he says. We know that he is competent because he talks relevant

and illuminating sense. Although there is always an irreducibly subjective *element* in criticism, this does not mean that criticism is merely subjective: there can be intelligible communication, appraisement, mutual understanding. If we ourselves are sufficiently competent, we can often safely say, 'He knows what he is talking about'.

There is, sometimes, another way of telling whether a person has understanding knowledge of a work of art—and one more effective than judging by his statements. It occurs in the 'performing' arts. By the way in which a poem is read, or a piece of music played, we can sometimes tell (if we are competent) how much understanding knowledge of it there is. The test is not valid in all directions. We recognize, if the poem is superbly well read, or the piece superbly played, that the artist-performer has adequate understanding of what he is rendering. On the other hand, if the reading or the performance of the music is not good, it does not follow that understanding is lacking. What might be lacking could be skill, practical competence. Fine control of the voice or fingers is needed if performance is to *show* understanding. But when it does come off, artistic performance is the best test there is—and a much more certain and complete one than the talk of the critic. But it is of course only more certain and complete because it is another art, the performing art. It is more certain and complete because (no doubt in a somewhat paradoxical sense) the only adequate language of the elucidation of art is the language of art itself.

To the reader, much of all this may seem to be circular talk. Possibly it is: whether talk about knowledge of art must be circular and if so whether it is invalid—these questions can be decided only after much more consideration.

§5   *Art and truth: general*

The discussion so far has been of the adequacy of understanding knowledge of works of art which have been assumed to be 'good'; we made the safe choices of Rembrandt and Brahms. But the work, given to us as completed, assumed 'good', is itself an artifact made by a human being in a more, or less, successful effort. It is a striving after something which may, or may not quite 'come off'.

In discussing appreciative knowledge of art, I have been saying that it may be better policy to speak of the 'adequacy', rather than the 'truth' of knowledge. But the artifact which is the work of art, though not propositional, is objective, 'out there' (at least in one sense). Though not a proposition it might be thought to be true or false: it might be said that the externalization which is the artifact could be 'true' or 'false' in some special sense. Of course the artifact, like the proposition, has no meaning except in relation to an interpreting mind, so that in speaking about the truth of either we are thinking of the truth as (at least potentially) apprehended by a mind.

It is, perhaps, particularly important to keep this last in the back of our minds when thinking of the possible 'truth' of art. The knowledge of art, and of any 'truth' of art, is essentially knowledge of an indwelling kind; it can be known only in that way. Though a full understanding of, say, a scientific or historical truth, requires indwelling scientific knowledge too, scientific and historical truths can be stated independently and in impersonal language which can at least up to a point be understood without any or much personal insight into science or history. Any normal half-educated person can understand the truth of the propositions 'William the Conqueror landed in 1066' or that 'if you double the pressure you halve the volume'. The truth of such propositions is relatively isolated and simple, and therefore can be independently recognized and understood. But (as we saw at the beginning) there are no simple isolated impersonal designative truths about art. So, if it is possible to speak sensibly of the 'truth' of art, we must expect it to be 'truth' of a kind which is more intimately and essentially bound with indwelling knowledge—here aesthetic knowledge—than truth in the more ordinary sense.

But is it appropriate to apply the term 'truth' to art? If it is, in what sense or senses?

§6 *'Truth' and 'standards' in art: canons and categories*

In what senses might the term 'truth' be applied to art?

There are two senses in which truth and art may be related, but which are insufficient in themselves for understanding any possible truth *of* art. In the light of what we have already said (in Chapter V) a few words should be enough to make this clear.

Art—or at least representative art—may contain, assimilate, and transform 'truths' in two quite ordinary senses. These are (*a*) the truths of propositions and (*b*) the truths of likeness or imitation. (*a*) A poem, like Milton's on the massacre of Piedmont, may contain sentences which express what is true in fact. Sentences in a play like *A Man for all Seasons* may represent what was on some occasion actually said, and express propositions true to fact. Or it may be true that the lover has illusions, and 'Sees Helen's beauty in a brow of Egypt'. (*b*) Representative pictures, such as Dutch Interiors, may be 'true' in that they may closely resemble an original scene.

All this is quite straightforward. But from what has been said, we know that although these truths may occur *in* art, they are not sufficient to account for the (possible) truth *of* art. Embodied in art, they acquire new unique embodied aesthetic meaning and, perhaps, participate in a new kind of artistic truth. It is not truth to the facts (of either kind) that we value in art but something else. This is 'the impact of a total experience which may contain affirmation of truth but is much more, and which is enjoyed only in so far as we are actually entering into the life of the poem as uttered or the drama as acted. The truth of a statement (or of an imitation) is, on the commonsense account of truth, its quite impersonal relationship to the independent real; what we enjoy in the poem (or realistic picture) is not the recording of an abstract relationship, but a total participation, felt and understood throughout a single experience, in a fresh insight. A truth, as such, once recorded, can be docketed and assumed; it does not need to be rediscovered unless it has been lost; once is enough. The insights of a poem, on the other hand, are in a sense discovered in a fresh enjoyment each time: once is not enough. Furthermore, whilst a truth of fact can be stated in a number of ways, or in different languages, and it does not matter so long as it is clearly indicated, what the poem or the drama is saying can only be said exactly in the language of that poem or that drama'.[1] Whatever the 'truth' of art may be, it cannot be its impersonal conformity to something other than art, or other than the artistic.

If not to '*other* than the artistic', what is left? 'The artistic.' Could the 'truth' of art be said to be conformity to 'the artistic'? This suggestion (the only possibility left) may be profitable: I think it is. But as it stands, it is very obscure. It needs careful analysis. It raises the question of 'standards' in art.

We are, I think, bound to assume that there must be standards of some sort in art: no one really believes that anything is as 'good'

[1] Louis Arnaud Reid, 'Art ,Truth and Reality', *British Journal of Aesthetics*, Vol. 4, No. 4, October 1964.

as anything else. There must in some sense be 'good', 'better', 'worse'. This inevitably suggests criteria or standards of assessment, and if there are such, they must be *artistic* standards. But what could this possibly mean?

The very notion of a 'standard' as ordinarily conceived implies something at least distinct from that which is measured against the standard, and often separable from it. The term 'yardstick' (often used as a metaphor for 'standard') is a good illustration of both. In the Weights and Measures Office in London there is a rod, carefully compensated against expansion and contraction, which is the standard measure for all other rods claiming (as it were!) to be a yard long. Any 'yardstick' could be measured against that one. But of course a standard need not be of a weight or measure; it could be of a function or structure. A knife is 'up to standard' if it fulfils a simple function for a reasonably long time; a gramophone is up to standard if it fulfils a very complex one, defined by various requirements. A 'sonata' of a given period conforms to a fairly flexibly defined structural standard.

None of these examples illustrate artistic standards, not even the last: to say that this is a 'good example of a sonata', meaning that it conforms to a defined sonata form, is very different from saying 'this is (artistically) a good sonata'. But there are two preliminary possible senses in which there might be artistic standards to which art can conform, and which, though distinguishable from particular works of art, are artistically relevant to them. They are (*a*) the 'canons' which may guide the making and understanding of art and (*b*) the basic philosophical categories applying to all art, within which an aritfact must fall if it is to *be* a work of art at all.

(*a*) There are plenty of canons, normative rules derived from the successful practice of art. Historical examples would be, recommendations to observe the 'unities of place and time', the 'grand style', the 'plain word'. More particularly, there is a prescriptive 'logical' form of the sonnet, empirical rules about the use of glazes in paint, or about composition or 'direct' painting, the 'laws' of harmony and counterpoint in music, and so on.

These 'canons' are useful. The artist, in learning his job, usually pays some attention to the practice of the masters. Sometimes, as a student doing exercises, he may treat them as rules strictly to be followed: he tries to put them literally into practice as well as he can, making, as it were, models to exemplify the rules. On the other hand, this is obviously a stage, an artificial if justifiable experiment in the process of learning to become an artist—if one may for the moment accept this disputable phrase. It is the stage of what R. L. Stevenson called 'playing the sedulous ape'. The student's aim, as a would-be artist, is not to go on doing these exercises, but rather to assimilate what is of importance in them, with a great deal of intelligent discard, in order to find his own 'style'. The 'style' of the masters can be analysed up to a point; 'style' can be talked about: on the other hand, if the generalizations about style continue to be observed as strict rules, the student never grows beyond the stage of the sedulous ape. Although the professional artist has generalizations in his background, they do not remain, for the intelligent artist, as generalizations logically applied: they remain with him rather as effects of lessons learnt and assimilated, transformed for his own individual use in so far as they are found relevant to his purposes. They are elements in, and contribute to, his 'experience', so that the experienced mature artist has a much wider range of possibilities at his command through having assimilated and learnt from the successful experience of others, than has the crude beginner or the self-made artist who has never bothered about learning from others. A real genius might dispense with such learning, and it is impossible to say that his work *might* not have a freshness because of his relative freedom from the influence of others. (Blake's paintings might be an example.) This does not, however, contradict the general trend of what I have been saying.

To put it more objectively, 'canons' are standards, empirically derived, distinguishable from individual works of art, statable in general language, which are (at any rate at sometimes) relevant to the making and appreciation of individual works of art. And, in a sense, individual works may of course 'conform' to these standards; this painting, e.g., conforms to accepted rules of composition. Nevertheless, although conformity to rules is sometimes a condition of artistic merit, it is never enough to constitute it. No work of art is ever first-rate as art just because it is an instance of a complex formula. As has been said, conformity to anything *else*, which seems to be the ordinary sense of conforming to a standard, is never sufficient as a criterion for the goodness of art. If so, this raises an acute problem, for if a work of art does not conform to a standard which is distinct from itself, how can there be said to be 'standards' in art at all? And if there are no standards, everything

is as 'good' as everything else. Learning to discriminate, education
in art, seems to go by the board. Surely there must be standards of
some kind? But what kind? This I shall return to.

(*b*) Can basic philosophical categories of aesthetics in any sense
function as 'standards'? If so, how? I suggested in Chapter I that
if there is such a thing as general aesthetics, if there is a general
aesthetics which is valid at all, then there must be certain categories common to anything which is 'art'; these might sometimes
be used in a normative fashion. Mrs Langer, affirming that the
general principles of art are very few, mentions 'organic unity',
'livingness', 'articulation'. There is, too, the 'unity of form and
content', which I have called 'embodiment'. If I am right, wherever
the aesthetic is, wherever there is art in any degree, wherever
there are works of art, there is embodiment of meaning. Embodiment is a defining characteristic formulated after careful examination of all kinds of art. Although it is a generalization open to correction, I do not know of any exceptions to it. If valid it may be
taken as an assumption which operates (as a rule unconsciously)
whenever we come across anything which claims to be 'art'. If
there is *not* aesthetic embodiment, if, e.g., meaning is separable
from symbol, as happens in the ordinary use of language, something will seem wrong. Again, in so far as embodiment breaks
down—e.g. in the use of clichés or stereotypes or the introduction
of extraneous devices, such as purely moral exhortations or happy
endings or trick sentimental effects—in so far as these things occur,
it will fail as art.

On the other hand, although the formulated concept of embodiment may influence the understanding of art by someone who
is a philosopher (and might even, as a theory, influence a philo-
sopher-artist) 'embodiment' is not a practical rule, like a canon,
which guides an artist to do something specific (like composing
according to rules) or which directly helps us much in our discriminating understanding of individual works of art. A canon may
profess to tell us how to make, or recognize, certain nameable
characteristics (like having unity of place and time) in a work of
art: an aesthetic category like embodiment cannot tell me how to
make the embodiment which is art, or how to know it when I see
it. Only by being an artist, or by possessing aesthetic sensibility,
can I make, or know, the embodiment which is art. A category
may be in our minds or at the back of our minds; but we have to
make from these 'the aesthetic leap'. If (in some conscious philo-

sophical mood) I recognize this piece of art as an exemplification of embodiment, I can only do so by first exercising an act of aesthetic intuition; 'embodiment' is one name for what I apprehend through aesthetic intuition which, as I have repeatedly said, is a *sui generis* form of indwelling knowledge.

There are two further important differences between canons and philosophical aesthetic categories. (1) Canons are particular rules, relative to a particular art, often to a particular period or to certain 'schools' of art. They are relevant to art, but not everywhere or always. The few categories of art, on the other hand, are, *if* valid, valid universally. (This does not preclude 'openness'.) Nothing which does not fall into a valid category of art, need be considered as art. That it falls into a valid category of art is presupposed when anything is considered *as* 'art'.

(2) The canons or rules of art can be quite clearly stated, and stated so that they could be understood (though possibly not adequately or with full intelligence) by anyone, whether they understand art or not. 'Do not write consecutive fifths or octaves.' 'Do not divide your composition exactly into two.' Anyone can quickly learn the meaning of such injunctions, whether he is an artist or not—though learning them would never make him an artist. And the canons can be understood clearly by anyone for the reason already mentioned—that they refer to the conditions of (some) art, and not directly to the aesthetic of art itself. To say that this work does or does not obey such and such rules is to talk *round* art (perhaps relevantly and importantly), not to talk of inner aesthetic significance. Talk of a category like embodiment, on the other hand, can only be understood by someone who is not only a philosopher, but who already knows art intuitively from the inside; it means nothing whatever to a philistine or an artistically raw person. The word for the category, as we have so often said, is only an imperfect symbol for something unique, of its own kind; it can be 'cashed' only in genuine aesthetic experience. Because it refers to something unique which has to be intuitively known to be understood, it cannot be clearly stated in the neutral public language with which canons are stated.

Because, if valid, a category like embodiment is a universal criterion of the very existence of anything as art, and because it refers to the inmost nature of art known only in artistic experience, it seems, *prima facie*, to satisfy the peculiar, indeed unique, requirement of a 'standard' in art—that the standard should be

H

distinct from that of which it is the standard, and at the same time not a purely *external* 'yardstick' to which it must conform. We approach, at least, that rather peculiar notion which requires careful examination, of a standard of art in which art 'conforms to its *own* standard'.

CHAPTER XIII

STANDARDS AND TRUTH, IN ART AND SCIENCE

CHAPTER XIII

STANDARDS AND TRUTH, IN ART AND SCIENCE

§1   *Truth to 'its own standard'*

So far, in discussing 'standards' and 'truth', I have been referring to 'art' and 'works of art' indifferently, without making much distinction between them. I have argued for a general complex category of 'embodiment', the *sui generis* emergent unity of meaning with form, which anything must fulfil if it is to be called 'art' at all. In a sense this can be called a 'standard' intrinsic to the aesthetic aspect of art in the sense that it defines its nature; it is— a little artificially—a 'standard' in a conceptual sense. It is a 'standard' of achievement or attainment, not a standard in the sense that anyone but a philosophically minded artist or critic (who had, perhaps read this book!) would consciously aim at or think of—though some unformulated version of it might be assumed.

But now a more particular problem presents itself. If a work of art is to be in itself in any sense 'true' (as distinct from containing, assimilating, and transforming truths in more ordinary senses), it cannot be true, we said, by conforming to anything which is *other* than, external to, itself. If not, and we are to call it 'true' at all, the only thing left is for it to be true to '*itself*'. The measure of its truth must, somehow, be intrinsic to it. This is a difficult notion. An artist or a critic may say 'It comes off', or 'It doesn't quite come off'. Here there seems some sort of comparison of the work with an ideal or standard, so that there must be a distinction between the two: yet the 'standard' seems to be its 'own' standard, whatever that means. It sounds nonsensical, or tautological: is it? Is there here just a verbal play with words? I don't think so. I believe the acceptance of it leads us straight back to the centre of art.

What is the 'it' which is true to 'its own' standard? What is the 'standard' which belongs to 'it'? One might say of the 'it', in the sentence 'It is adequate (or true) to . . .', that the 'it' refers to the *concrete work*, and 'its own "standard" ' to the *conception* of the standard which it (so to speak) prescribes for itself. I believe this is so; but the difficulty is, as I have suggested often enough, that the conception can't be adequately stated in words. It is a most peculiar sort of conception because it is not, as other conceptions seem to be, something which can be properly formulated in words at all. If we look at a successful work of art as a whole, and ask what it intends, aims to be, it is a not unfair answer to say, 'Just *this*'. If one is making a surgical instrument, or a chair, there are ideas or patterns existing beforehand with which we can compare the article; the intention is clear at the outset. But in making a picture or a poem or a symphony, the artist does not fully know his intention till he realizes it in a successful drive towards concrete form. No concept or system of concepts beforehand can fully forecast the meaning, which has to be discovered in the work, where content is united with form. The 'conception' has to be known in the living through of this individual work. The 'conception' is inseparable from the embodiment; the 'conception' of the poem is never, strictly speaking, what the poem is about, but the poem *speaking*. The 'conception' of this intermezzo is only known concretely, as we listen to it. If the 'conception' is a universal, it must be a kind of concrete universal, not an abstract one. If it could adequately be stated in abstract form, say in words, there would be no need for the poem, or the music. So it looks as if, when we say 'this poem, piece of music . . . achieves its own standard' we just mean, 'it is good, perfect . . . in being itself—and that is all there is to it'. And in experience, we all know that it is not only difficult, but it seems superfluous, to talk about a work which seems perfect. Beholding, being—that seems enough.

I believe that all this is true, but that it does not enable us to dispense with the notion of artistic truth, or 'its own standard' but forces us to accept its unique character. It is perhaps easier to understand this if we realize that perfection, 'truth to itself', is a limiting case, in which the actual work and its own 'standard' are indeed one and inseparable—but not therefore without distinction in idea. If we consider other works—even important and great ones—which are not quite perfect and do not in all respects attain their 'own standards', we can see that it is only by what the artist *has* achieved in this individual work, that we can judge that it falls down a little here and there. 'Only by what he has shown us, only by what he has achieved here, are we enabled to judge him. Even his imperfections point to the perfections from which they, here and there, may fall short.' From what he has achieved, we learn the perfection possible in such a work. I am not, of course, saying that a work has to be imperfect in order that we should pronounce on its artistic 'truth'. I am only drawing attention to instances of imperfection to reinforce the point that there is at least an intellectual *distinction* between the standard of artistic truth and the actual concrete work as we appreciate it. The distinction seems to disappear (as witnessed by our dumbness) in the limiting case of perfection, because the 'standard', that to which the work is 'true', has been made wholly (and not as in the case of the imperfect work, potentially) concrete. But the distinction, and the standard, is still implicitly there, though it can never adequately be stated in words, for the work itself has become the embodied 'statement'.

This analysis may not seem adequate. I doubt whether it can be carried much further, because the discoverability of the 'standard' *in* the individual work seems to be one of the basic facts of life in art.

Further, though it may seem to make nonsense of 'standards' in the usual sense (where there are general rules to which particulars must conform), it does *not*, in the emphasis on the individuality of art and art standards, imply that 'individuality' can justify anything, or even that individuality as such is an artistic justification at all. A work of art is individual, and prescribes its own standard, but of course it does not follow that anything that can be called an individual, because it is an individual, achieves any artistic standard whatever. Artistic perfection is individual, but it is not individuality which in itself constitutes artistic perfection; there are many 'individuals' which have no artistic merits or make claims to them. No, the artistic standard, though individual, is *artistic*, *sui generis*, and it demands an obedience, a discipline, it prescribes an imperative which is as absolute as the discipline of history, or science, perhaps more so. However queer the philosophical status of artistic standards as individual may be, they are there, as a fact. And the true doctrine of the individuality of artistic standards cannot be held responsible for the malpractices of some artists who think they can artistically get away with anything because it is the expression of their own [*sic*] 'individuality'!

§2   *The critical testing of art*

The artistic is *sui generis*, and individual, 'its own standard', etc. But it can be analysed by the critic, and can be *tested*. The work is a complex unity of parts, and the testing can be broken down into critical judgments that this, that, the other part . . . every part, is artistically meaningful and related to (or not related to) the other parts and to the whole. Sometimes the term 'organic unity' (an analogy) is used; the work can be looked at bit by bit to see how 'organic' it is, or isn't. (As we have seen, it is sometimes easier when it isn't quite.) 'This passage (in a poem, or painting or piece of music) is not "organic", "fits awkwardly", is "extraneous" or "irrelevant".' The work is not quite 'true to itself'.

I have, here and there, suggested brief examples of critical testing (e.g. in Chapter VIII, §2). At this point it may be helpful to quote some extracts (necessarily arbitrarily selected) from only a part of a very full and first-rate critical analysis of one of Donne's 'Holy Sonnets' (already mentioned). It is by Robin Mayhead.[1] I quote the whole sonnet:

> Thou hast made me, and shall thy work decay?
> Repair me now, for now mine end doth haste,
> I run to death, and death meets me as fast,
> And all my pleasures are like yesterday;
> I dare not move my dim eyes any way,
> Despair behind, and death before doth cast
> Such terror, and my feeble flesh doth waste
> By sin in it, which it t'wards hell doth weigh;
> Only thou art above, and when towards thee
> By thy leave I can look, I rise again;
> But our old subtle foe so tempteth me,
> That not one hour my self I can sustain;
> Thy Grace may wing me to prevent his art,
> And thou like Adamant draw mine iron heart.

After pointing out some facts about the sonnet-form, the skill it requires, the personal nature of this poem, the author proceeds to a fine analysis of the relation between the verbal forms and the meaning they embody. 'The opening line falls into halves, the first of which is a statement: "Thou hast made me". Directly addressing his God, the poet is asserting something which he, as a Christian, believes. Whatever else may be confused and uncertain, *that*, at any rate, gives him a feeling of complete assurance. Try actually speaking the words aloud. You will find that you cannot comfortably say them quickly. It is quite easy to see why this is so. There is no difficulty about saying the words "Thou hast" quickly, one after the other; but it is not possible to say "hast made

[1] Robin Mayhead, *Understanding Literature*, C.U.P., pp. 112 *et seq.*

me" in the same way. Or rather, it is not possible to do so without making the words sound clumsy and awkward. The explanation lies in the movements we have to make with the tongue and lips in order clearly to articulate the words. Passing from the "t" at the end of "hast", to the "m" at the beginning of "made" forces the reader to make radical changes in oral positioning . . . There is a similar change when we move from the end of "made" to the beginning of "me". Instead of saying all the words quickly together, then, we have to move deliberately, and detach them from one another. . . . It is in fact impossible to overestimate the importance to poetry of the effects produced by the speed or slowness with which words can be distinctly articulated.'

'In the second line, Donne calls upon God to "repair" him, to make him fit to confront death and judgment. It is useful to take the second, third, and fourth lines together:

> "Repair me now, for now mine end doth haste,
> I run to death, and death meets me as fast,
> And all my pleasures are like yesterday;"

Which words stand out most obviously in these words? Plainly they are "now" and "death", simply because they are repeated. Donne is not making these repetitions for lack of something to say. The repetition of "now" gives an impression of great urgency. It is as though Donne were saying "If anything can be done to save me, it must be done NOW!" In the same way, the repetition of "death" brings home to us just how terrifyingly close death seems to the poet . . . Death and despair are so dreadfully real to him that they seem like physical shapes which he would see if he dared to gaze around. Now much of the force of the lines comes from the slow, clogged movement. Instead of moving with the speed and impetuosity of "I run to death", the first line of this group is for the most part slow and heavy. It is easy enough to say "I dare not" and "any way" quickly, but to say "not move my dim eyes" properly requires quite an effort. Even "any way" has to be said quite slowly if we are to bring out the meaning correctly. For the words do not mean the same thing as "anyway". The same is true of "dim eyes". Nothing could be easier than slurring one word into the next: "dimeyes". But how silly and slovenly it sounds!' There is much more in the same vein; the whole sonnet is analysed with great insight, with some attention, later on, to the metrical form.

H*

Any good criticism such as this—and of any art—is a confirmation of the absolutely crucial importance of embodiment, though the word itself may never be used. And it shows not only how sound and sense are united, but how each part is integral with other parts and with the whole. It shows the inescapability of the idea of 'truth to *itself*', of the uniqueness of the 'standard' which each work must attain.

§3 Testing in art, and testing in science

The procedures for testing the truth of art to itself are *public*, in the sense that they can be displayed, written about, communicated, and are not simply ejaculations of private, subjective, incommunicable feelings. On the other hand, although public and transpersonal, they are not *im*personal, offering formulated techniques which any Tom, Dick or Harry could apply without the presence of something else, namely personal aesthetic intuition. The procedures are not like an instruction which might say 'Go and look at the pointer on the scale and you will see whether the results of the test are positive or negative'. In this case the ordinary use of the senses is all that is required: in the case of the aesthetic testing of art a special sort of personal involvement is required, and one which is not isolated and confined to what is immediately before the attention like the pointer on the scale or a specimen on the object glass; in testing the work of art, what is immediately there has always to be apprehended in relation to the whole. Since, because of the influence and success of scientific testing, there is a tendency to assume that 'public' testing must be impersonal, 'neutral' testing, it is particularly important to look at the differences between the public critical testing of the truth of art to itself, and the testing of scientific claims to truth.

Scientific hypotheses, and observations which test them, are in one sense and in some contexts external to and isolable from one another. In another sense, and in other contexts, the two are seen as internally related. They are *externally* related in that 'the facts' (in observation of fact) are, or are bound up with, something obstinately independent of the observer and all his thoughts and hypotheses. This is the strength of science. On the other hand, a character of scientific thinking is that its speculations and hypotheses and guesses must be followed up not only by testing in observations and (in some cases) experiments but by the *relating* n thought, in the formation of scientific theory, of the showings

of the observations and experiments to the thought which suggested them (the hypothesis), and more generally to the rest
of scientific knowledge so far as it has developed. If the observations and experiments were not intelligibly related to the thinkings,
the hypotheses, they just would not *be* scientific observations and
experiments. (One of the mistakes of logical positivism was its too
exclusive isolation of 'verification in sense experience'.) In this
sense, hypotheses and observations are *internal* to one another
(and may later be synthesized in scientific 'theory') in that they
must be seen as different aspects of one systematic whole of scientific thinking.

The first glance at science tends to emphasize the *externality* of
the relationship between the hypothesis and what tests it. The first,
and perhaps the second and the third, glance at art tends to emphasize the *internality* of relationship of all aesthetic judgments about
a work of art. The very particular judgments about a phrase or a
passage (*very* roughly analagous to particular observational judgments in science) seem to be internally related to more general
judgments about the whole. A work of art is, aesthetically, an indivisible individual where division of labour and qualitative diversity of attention (like the diversity between making observations
and working out, say, a scientific—mathematical 'theory') is
hardly possible. In science one can and often has to do one thing
at a time. In art, the one is involved in the many and the many
in the one, and this demanding unity dominates and interpene-
trates all the distinguishable parts of art and criticism. All this
gives aesthetic judgment the look of tautology or vicious circularity which can lead to the rash conclusion that there are no real
tests of artistic truth comparable to the independent empirical
tests which check the judgments of scientific hypotheses. The
mutual internality of relationship between aesthetic judgments of
art as it has been expounded here must certainly be maintained
without compromise, as must the distinction in science between
the hypothesis and the facts 'external' to them. But all 'circularity', all mutuality of check and support, is not *vicious* circularity. It is not so in the critical testing of artistic truth. It is not so in
science, either.

Even if, in science, the externality of relation between hypothesis and what tests it, stands out, the mutuality of support, the
internality of relation between hypothesis and facts in the general
systematic theoretic thinking which is science, is the more

important. It is the integration of what is at one stage of scientific procedure 'external' to the hypothesis, namely experiment and observation, with the hypothesis (or, more generally the larger systematic thinking of science), which is the major aim. In *this* sense, the verification of science, or the developing judgment of its integrity, is internal to science. In this sense, art and science have something important in common. One can say of both art and science (though of course with radical differences of detail) that each has to be tested from *within* its own internal 'integrity'. The 'integrity' of the one (art) is the integrity of an autonomous individual. The integrity of the other (science) is the integrity, ideally, of a self-contained system of thought about fact.

§4　*Contributory factors in the assessment of art*

I have been trying to show that, in *principle*, claims to artistic 'truth' can be tested, that the testing has a 'public' and communicable aspect, though the tests have to be applied by each person for himself in renewed intuitive experience of the work of art. And I have briefly compared and contrasted the testing of artistic with the testing of scientific truth.

But all this does not imply that the testing of artistic truth, 'truth to its own standard', is simple, or easy, or that its results are secure or certain or universally acceptable. In spite of the fact that scientific truth is in a large and important sense 'open', many scientific truths are accepted as 'facts' which no one wants to dispute. There is no exact parallel to this in art criticism. Many of the great works of the great masters of the past can be said to be pretty securely established—but their 'establishment' has a very different status from the status of established scientific truths, and has been arrived at in very different ways.

It is true that each work of art is an autonomous individual, and that its artistic truth can be known only by personally entering into its inner life. To say this is to emphasize the central importance of what has been called the 'intrinsic' element in criticism. But in emphasizing it, it can be too easy to forget the vast complexity of art, and the complexity of the motives and influences which may be at work—some of them perhaps blinding as well as some illuminating—when one is making what looks like a direct and straightforward assessment. For this reason disagreements about assessments of works of art are not significant unless the precise points of difference are made clear and precise. 'Good' or 'bad' are global evaluations, but they depend upon the perception of the parts of the complex unity, and the aesthetic discernment of any part of a picture or poem or piece of music may be affected in an indefinite number of ways. I shall not attempt to survey these, for it could be an endless task which even the detailed history of criticism could not cover. But a few arbitrary examples will illustrate the point.

One's own personal and temperamental dispositions affect what one notices, what one naturally tends to appreciate, like or dislike. My sense of colour or sound may be different from yours; I may need more, or less, stimulation than you, naturally liking or disliking softer, or stronger, hues and sounds. One's metabolism affects the impact of what one perceives. So, of course, does one's personal history, general or recent. A tragedy may be too 'near' to some recent harrowing experience to be contemplated aesthetically, or not 'near' enough to one's experience to make a vital impact, and subconscious and unconscious influences are always at work. Again, one's objective perception of the work itself is affected by background knowledge or ignorance of the influences which produced it. Knowledge (or ignorance) of prevailing rules and canons, of historical background, of the 'school' to which the work belongs, of the influence of contemporaries, of experiments in techniques (e.g. in Impressionism, Neo-Impressionism, or Fauvism), of sociological or psychological or moralistic influences (e.g. in drama or novels)—these and many other factors affect our intuitive aesthetic judgments of art. To learn—at different stages of our artistic education, certainly not necessarily identical with the moments of intense aesthetic perception—to be aware of the many factors which affect judgment, is to enrich experience and sharpen discrimination, giving complex content to art's 'truth to itself' which is the objective of our understanding.

Each person can learn much by himself, experiencing, re-experiencing, analysing, criticizing, self-criticizing, synthesizing; there is a sense in which all education has to be self-education. But of course self-education does not take place in a vacuum; it is nourished by reading, and by conversation with like-minded friends—or with unlike-minded friends so long as we share with them a common humility and genuine desire to understand. It is illuminated by listening to and talking with persons more expert than ourselves. Learning to discriminate the truth and falsity of works of art is a social and not merely an individual process. Moreover, as just hinted, it is one in which *disagreement*, so long as it is reasonable, knowledgeable, and not clouded by irrelevance, point-scoring, opinionated dogmatism, can be of the utmost value. It is superficial nonsense to suppose that disagreements about art imply that there are no standards or that 'there's no disputing about tastes'. We have to establish, by careful analysis, that the disagreements are *real* disagreements—and with a complex object like a work of art it is easy for two people who hastily think they 'disagree' to find that they are talking about, and emphasizing, quite different things, so that their talking has been at cross-purposes. But with this caution, there are of course genuine disagreements, even among discriminating experts. And these, if they are pursued reasonably intelligently and with good temper, can often be of the utmost help to understanding, on both sides. One does not necessarily have to 'convert' the other, though it may happen in that way. Each may acquire a sounder, modified, more mature view. Genuine conversation in (or perhaps after) the immediate presence of art is one of the most profitable ways of learning.

There are, however, many disagreements, genuine disagreements, particularly about contemporary art, which cannot be resolved, or resolved quickly. And here what has been called the 'verdict of time' becomes important. This is not a coward's way out or a matter of counting heads. The 'verdict of time' at its best comes about through the slow sifting out of irrelevancies, the conservation of what is essential and important through continual testing in the sensitive experience of many different people, who have learned through their differences with others, and who can because of it all see more steadily in perspective and in proportion. If you or I may much learn from our personal conversations, all men (if they are able to understand and are willing to listen) may learn from the conversations of mankind. If the truth of science in its own way is a treasury of inheritance, so the mature understanding and deep enjoyment of what is permanently good in art is a gift which we learn to participate in by learning from its critical history.

This is all, essentially, a *rational* process or—if 'rational' be thought too limited because of its association with discursive reasoning—at least a *reasonable* one. We are much 'involved', in all sorts of ways, in art-experience, so that it is more difficult to be reasonable about our judgments than in the—relatively—more impersonal knowledge of science. But reasonable in its own way the judgment of art certainly is, or can be, if we take the long view. It is difficult, but not impossible, to be reasonable about what we are involved in. (A good example of this is the established possibility of being *morally* reasonable.) I have tried to show some ways in which it is possible. I have not tried to say that judgments of the truth of art can be certain, much less infallible. Disagreements and uncertainties about some things will probably always remain. But they can be reasonably tested—though the testing process is never finished.

§5   *Art and Games*

There has been a good deal of discussion in recent philosophy about *games*. And the fact that art is a self-contained unity, with its own internal order, has suggested to some that art may be a sort of game, played according to self-prescribed rules.

To *argue* that art is a game because there is a resemblance between a work of art and a game in one respect, would be argument from analogy with a vengeance and of course quite fallacious. In terms of the old formal logic it would be the fallacy of the undistributed middle.

A game is a self-contained unity, with its own exclusive rules and with no purpose beyond itself.

Art is a self-contained unity, with its own exclusive rules, and with no purpose beyond itself.

Therefore art is a game.

But although as an argument this is a fallacy, there still might be some game-like features in art which make the comparison of art with a game interesting and important. I think there is very little in this; but perhaps the suggestion ought to be dealt with briefly.

The first part of the two premises, about self-containment and rules, refers only to a most superficial resemblance. A game is a self-contained unity and each game has its own rules, certainly. But the rules of a game are laid down independently, and prescribed for every game of that class. Every game of chess or cricket is an *instance* of the application of the set of rules. One *must* play according to the rules for the playing to be an instance of that game. A work of art, as we have seen, is a self-contained unity which prescribes its own standards. The standards *could* be called 'rules' exclusive to the art, but this is artificial, since standards are individual not general. And we have seen that, although there are some rules and canons of art, these are not artistically prescriptive, and a work, we said, is never art because it obeys the 'rules'. The making of a work of art is not an instance of the application of rules, as the playing of a game is.

The playing of many games (not games of pure chance) involves skill. The game must be played according to the rules, but it is not rule-obedience in itself which makes any good game; one may play chess or cricket according to the rules without the 'game' being worth the playing. It might be said that it is in the skill required in the making (or enjoying) of a work of art that makes art resemble a game. This however only needs saying to be shown as self-evidently absurd: art requires *artistic* skill for which skill in game-playing is useless: and if one talks of the 'art' of playing chess or cricket, one is using a word which, though it may have aesthetic overtones, is employed in a context which has no bearing on the making and enjoyment of fine art. And as we said, the skill of the game necessarily includes playing according to the rules; the skill of art does not. Every particular played game has an individuality of its own; but its individuality does not make it a game (nor an art). There is a story, probably apocryphal, of the great and much beloved philosopher, the late Professor G. F. Stout. Stout, it is told, used to play golf at St Andrews with his wife. He was very deaf, and had no sense of spatial direction. His wife and he, so the story goes, would go off in entirely opposite directions. It was a highly individual performance which took place on the one and original golf course, the *Royal and Ancient*; but it was hardly the *game* of golf according to the book. (I am not of course saying that it was 'art' either because it was very individual or because it was not according to the rules!)

One might put the general contrast between games and art in another way. It could be said that it is what is done over and above the rules which makes a game a good one, and that likewise it is what is over and above the canons which makes art, and that therefore they are exactly on a par. But whilst there may be a good work of *art* which as we say 'breaks all the rules', a particular game—say chess, is not even that game if it breaks all the rules: still less can chess be *good* if it is not chess! A game *must* at least obey the rules. Art may do so; but it need not.

It is the difference between the second parts of the two premises, however, which bring out the most important distinction between games and art. The playing of a game has no essential purpose beyond itself—though of course it may be recreative and refreshing. Of art this is true in a sense too, but only in a very special sense: the game is isolated from the rest of life and culture in one way which it would be profoundly false to predicate of art.

That art is an autonomous individual, an end in itself, need not be argued all over again—and it is this aspect of it which gives most point to the suggestion that art is a kind of game. But if art is autonomous, it is also an embodiment of meaning, and artistic meaning, we know, is a transformation of meaning which is drawn from all sorts of sources in the life beyond art. Moreover, this artistic meaning, once discovered and made, is something which remains and permeates the whole life of human culture. Games and pastimes do not embody meanings from beyond themselves, and they have no repercussions upon life and culture which are comparable with that of the arts. They have their origins in, and influence upon culture, of course. But of the heights and depths and expansiveness of human experience they know nothing as life through art knows it. Art is serious as games are not.

CHAPTER XIV

REVELATION AND THE AESTHETIC

CHAPTER XIV

REVELATION AND THE AESTHETIC

§1 *Aesthetic revelation? The particularity and individuality of the aesthetic*

I have stressed the autonomy of embodiment and the truth of art 'to itself'. I have also affirmed that expressions of life enter into much, if not all, art, though they are transformed in embodiment, and that art functions in the context of life and experience of reality, personal and trans-personal.

The first of these two emphases, on autonomy, may seem, at times, to have been made at the expense of the second. This Chapter will discuss some rather puzzling questions which arise partly out of the second: any answers to them can be valid only if not inconsistent with the first—that aesthetic significance is always embodied significance. I want to look at claims, sometimes made, that art is a kind of 'revelation', that in and through some art at least we come to know facets of the 'real world', it may be of 'ultimate' reality.

That the arts—or more broadly, the aesthetic aspects of any-thing—are revelatory, is a special form of the view that aesthetic experience in art and elsewhere is cognitive: these knowledge-claims have taken various patterns, in a very long lineage. Dance, drama, visual arts, literature, in their origins are inextricably bound up with religion; they served to express and expound religious ideas, images, intimations of religion, to the senses and imagina-tion. In spite of Plato's fundamental distrust of the perceptual particularity of the arts as knowledge-giving, in favour of the Forms apprehended by intellect, philosophers generally have given strong support to the idea that the arts are media of *noesis*, so long as this is not identified exclusively with intellectual noesis. In very different ways Aristotle, 'Longinus', Plotinus, St Thomas, Francis Bacon, Schopenhauer, Schliermacher, William James, Heidegger . . . all give credence to the idea that what we now call the 'aesthetic' is not only pleasing, but gives insight—and insight in some manner or degree into the nature of things. We experience, through the imaginative sensible apprehension of the appearances of things, the conviction that we are being brought into contact with the supersensible, the universal, the transcendent, even the eternal. In certain forms of this experience, it may be claimed that knowledge of works of art have a close parallel with religious experience, sometimes mystical experience.

Some of these claims are large; without an intolerably long excursion into history and the philosophy of religion it would be impossible to deal with them adequately. Our concern is with aesthetics, and we shall, in the main, have to confine ourselves to the question whether, or how far, the nature of aesthetic experience is consonant with any of the (several) senses of 'revelation'.

There are a number of reasons why the aesthetic as such might truly be called revelatory. One is its aspect of particularity. Professor H. D. Lewis[1] suggests that in art we have 'an awareness of reality in a form that is least reducible to the categories of our own thought, the world being thus presented in a way that has clearer traces of a sphere beyond that of finite experience itself'.[2] (I ought to point out that he is writing in a context of ideas about religion.) Again[3] 'For what is made plain to us in art is not the rational connectedness of things which we apprehend in science and everyday thought. Art concerns not the universal, but the individual, aspect of reality. It is for this reason that it does not follow any predeterminable course or admit, in essentials, of rational analysis. Art uncovers for us the character of particular things in the starkness and strangeness of their being what they are. It is mercilessly intimate.' This is just why Plato took such a poor view of art. The particular historical event, the unique specific reality, had little importance for him. 'But this is just what fascinates the artist, and however much he may draw for his purpose on harmonies detected for him by reason, this is always in the service of some quite independent way in which he puts himself and others in touch with reality in its more distinctive individual aspect.'

This is important. I have, throughout this book, insisted both on how impossible it is to state clearly and adequately in rational language the content and meaning of art which has to be known in its own way, and on its immediate presentational nature. If art does indeed 'reveal', it must do so in a medium in which there is direct presentation of meaning in an individual. We must emphasize the irreducible difference between the ideas, the concepts, with which we are familiar and over which we have control,

---

[1] *Morals and Revelation*, pp. 208–9 (Allen & Unwin, 1951).
[2] I shall later question the latter part of this statement.
[3] *Morals and Revelation*, pp. 211–12.

and the otherness of the presented particular which can never be exhaustively expressed in terms of a complex of universals and concepts—though some philosophers have thought otherwise.

Speaking of poetry as a form of art, Lewis writes: 'What do we learn? Just this: that poetry has to do with reality in that concrete and individual aspect of it which the mind can never tackle altogether on its own terms, with matter that is foreign and alien in a way in which abstract systems, ideas in which we detect an inherent pattern, a structure that belongs to the ideas themselves, can never be. On the contrary its function, the salve which it brings to mankind, the need which it meets and which has to be met in some way in every age that is not to become decadent and barbarous is precisely this contact with reality as it impinges upon us from outside, the sense that we can touch and feel a solid reality which does not wholly dissolve itself into the conceptions of our own minds. It is the individual and particular that does this. And the wonder and mystery of art, as indeed of religion in the last resort, is the revelation of something 'wholly other' by which the inexpressible loneliness of thinking is broken and enriched.[1]

This is eloquently said, and of great importance not only in itself but for education—as I shall show more particularly later (Chapters XV and XVI). Under the overwhelming influence of Plato, the stress upon conceptual thinking as almost the only mode or medium of knowledge has successfully inoculated the scholastic mind against the impact of the particular. It has led to a kind of academic escapism. It is not the artist who lives in an 'aery-faery' world. If it is true of anyone, it is true of some almost exclusively-intellectual academics who live in a world of ideas which in time become more real to them than the impacting world from which the ideas are originally abstractions. It is not an overstatement to say that sometimes this un-realism has poisoned the spirit of liberal education. Intellectualism of this sort had its apotheosis in the philosophy of Hegel; from intellectualism, empiricism in philosophy and the natural sciences on the one hand, and existentialism and pragmatism on the other, have been healthy revolts. Exclusive concept-centredness has been an obstacle to the understanding of knowledge in the widest sense. It is, as I have suggested elsewhere, an occupational disease. The academic mind is uneasy about what it cannot categorize, about what is not reducible to the logical organization of symbols.

[1] *op. cit.*, p. 241.

But, of course, if the impingement of particularity is essentially important, the importance of particularity cannot be isolated from the *meaning* of particulars. A particular is always apprehended in a context of meaning, whether it be the context of ordinary perception or of scientific thought. And the art-object, although a particular, is, as we know, far more than a particular. It is charged with meaning in a peculiar way in which the object of ordinary perception, or the object of science, is not. For this reason it is, as we have said repeatedly, appropriate to call the work of art an *individual*.

The word 'individual' expresses the nature of the work of art better than 'particular'. It is partly a matter of terminology. The word 'particular' has two related meanings. One of them lies in its distinction from the abstract or universal or general: 'this is a particular, as distinct from a concept'. The other sense occurs when it is used to distinguish one particular from another—this as distinct from that. Both of these are negative characterizations. The word 'individual', in turn, *can* be used as synonymous with 'particular', but it is capable of bearing a richer meaning. This is when 'individual' stands for a complex internally integrated being and the quality arising from its integration. It is in this sense that we speak of the individuality of a person, not simply as an individual distinct from other persons, but as having a quality of organized character and personality. The work of art is an individual in this sense, that is, not merely as distinguished from the universal 'work of art', or from other examples of works of art, but as having, through its organization, unique aesthetic quality.

The individual is particular, but it is, then, as qualitative individual charged with meaning and not just as particular, that art is able to 'reveal' in its own important way. It is in this that the aesthetic is, *qua* aesthetic, always revelatory, in major and minor ways. As Professor Lewis puts it[1] 'All things are made new in art, they are made for the first time, they count for their own sake instead of being pointers by which we move about in our own orbit.' The revelation of aesthetic newness may occur, too, in the familiar in nature suddenly seen as for the first time, or seen strangely in an unusual fall of light, or symbolically, as in the slow, gentle, relentless falling snow, measured, inevitable, unhurried as time itself. As Lewis says, 'There must be a miracle. Whereas we were blind we now see'. 'The artist hits on the right symbol, some way

[1] *op. cit.*, p. 242.

of arranging colours or sounds or words in a way that makes the
real nature of the world break upon our mind.'

What is this but revelation? As always in these things, there are
two levels, though one continuum. There is the level of ordinary
perception and thought, describable shapes, colours, patterns,
images, concepts. The other level is that of emergent aesthetic
meaning belonging to a different dimension of being, illuminated
by the 'light that never was, on sea or land'.

§2   Aesthetic and Religious Revelation

Our approach to the question of aesthetic revelation has been, so
far, exclusively from the side of aesthetics. The aesthetic in its
own unique way may be called revelatory. But it is possible to
approach from another side, the side of religion. ('Revelation' is
an everyday word of religion.) This is legitimate, so long as it is
compatible with all that has been said about the integrity of the
aesthetic. I now want to look at the problem from this other
angle: in so doing I shall make use of the writings of two authors
whose approach is religious and who at the same time thoroughly
understand the aesthetic. One is Professor H. D. Lewis, whom I
have already cited. The other is Professor F. David Martin[1]

Lewis asks[2] 'How does the relationship of art and religion
appear, and what is its importance?' He writes: 'Its importance
lies, I submit, in its bearing on a certain mode of religious awareness.' 'The relation between art and religion in which I have an
interest is that which has a bearing on our knowledge of God,
and I doubt whether any relation between them which is not
derived from this has any importance.'[3] (I quote this not necessarily with approval.)

The *immediacy* of art is a clue to its relationship with religion.
But it is not just immediacy, 'merciless intimacy', but the strange
union between what is immediate or intimate, and what is also
alien. 'The more the artist invests the commonplace reality of
ordinary experience with the significance of his peculiar individual
impression of them, the more starkly do they also present to him
an alien irreducible nature. The finer his appreciation of objects
the more is their distinctiveness stressed; there are no essential
grips, no claims to be staked, but only a relationship which, in
becoming more intimate, is in that measure also more precarious

---

[1] The Aesthetic in Religious Experience in *Religious Studies*, October 1968.
[2] *Morals and Revelation*, p. 207.   [3] *op. cit.*, p. 206.

and fortuitous; the closer the artist moves to reality the more it is alarmingly aloof, and so, paradoxically but unmistakably, in art there is an unveiling which is at the same time a concealment; in the very process of clarification there is also a deepening of mystery, not in the sense that there is a mystery at the end of every scientific truth, the sense, that is, that the solution of problems sets us "*ad infinitum*" new problems to solve, but in a more absolute immediate sense that that which is made peculiarly plain to us is itself proportionately more enigmatic. Mystery and illumination are one in art.'[1]

Lewis argues (and I cannot discuss the validity of his arguments here) that there is, in the exercise of human reason, an essential demand for wholeness which yet cannot be met at the rational level. 'Rational processes have an incompleteness in which reason cannot rest content, and we are brought in this way to the notion of a transcendent nature of reality.'[2] This approach, however, has its 'sharp and severe limitations' which attains only 'a purely formal knowledge of some ultimate ground or principle of reality of whose nature we can form no conception. This falls very far short of the needs of religion . . . It is here that the consideration of art is important. For we have in art an awareness of reality in a form that is least reducible to the categories of our own thought, the world being thus presented in a way that has clearer traces of a sphere beyond that of finite experience itself.'[3] In stressing the view that our knowledge of God is not known as (in Brunner's phrase) 'a truth that already lay in the depths of reason' but which is 'alien and other, bearing in what is most distinctive of it the stamp of outsideness'[4] he adds: 'in conjunction with our view of art, this will, I think, eventually bring us to the view that art is itself a divine revelation, although it need not always be acknowledged to be such'.[5]

I shall, a little later on, consider whether, or how far, these claims can be justified. For the moment I will content myself with a question. From the aesthetic point of view (as distinct from that of the religious believer), is not Professor Lewis, in claiming that the aesthetic reveals religiously 'transcendent' meaning, overstating his case? Aesthetic meaning may be meaning 'in depth', and it can never be adequately stated in words: in that sense it certainly 'transcends' conceptual categories, transcends the seeing

[1] *op. cit.*, pp. 212–13.   [2] *op. cit.*, p. 207.
[3] *op. cit.*, pp. 208–9.   [4] *op. cit.*, p. 214.   [5] *ibid.*

of the eye, the hearing of the ear. But from all this (which I myself have argued fully) is Professor Lewis justified in saying that the world is 'thus presented in a way that has clearer traces of a sphere beyond that of finite experience itself'? 'Transcendence' is an ambiguous concept: aesthetic meaning is certainly in one sense 'transcendent' of ordinary perception and conceptual thought. But is he not sliding over from 'transcendent' in this sense to 'Transcendent' in a much more metaphysically-religious sense? I shall return to this.

The parallel between religion and art (e.g. poetry) is, it is argued, very close. In both, mystery and illumination are one. In both, the content of meaning is untranscribable. Of this untranscribability Lewis asks[1] 'Is not this also how we think of religious experience and revelation; is it not in just the same way that God is said to be at once a "hidden" God, an absolute mystery, and yet also "light" and the "source of light", a God whose ways "are not our ways" but whose word is yet "nigh thee, even in thy mouth and in thy heart"? ' This may be so; yet it is not enough, as Lewis truly says, to establish a religious view. 'I do not know how such a view could be established had we not already implicit in all our thought . . . the notion of some ultimate ground of all being.' But *given* the religious assumption he does think that art is an important point of contact with religious reality, though both he and Martin emphasize repeatedly that the concept and life of religion is much wider than this point of contact.

Martin[2] also holds that what he calls 'participative' aesthetic experience can be a form of religious experience. 'Religious experience' requires explanation. Martin's conception of religion is in part a revision of that of William James. It involves '(1) uneasy awareness of the limitations of man's moral or theoretical powers . . .; (2) awe-full awareness of a further reality—beyond or behind or within; (3) conviction that participation with this further reality is of supreme importance'.[3] This of course is not all. Religious conviction seems to be always accompanied by feelings of ultimate concern, reverence and peace, or feelings closely allied. Martin is not, in his article, concerned with the theoretical, practical or social sides of religion but only with 'empirical' grounds, the religious experience. And on this he says very much the same

[1] p. 13.
[2] 'The Aesthetic in Religious Experience', *Religious Studies*, October 1968.
[3] *op. cit.*, p. 1.

kinds of things as Professor Lewis, though with special attention to Heidegger's position and terminology.

Much of the language about art and religion is already familiar to us. 'Being as revealed is always inseparably mixed with concealment. Nevertheless, the work of art corners and illuminates Being. And so we cling with rapt gaze on both the unveiled and the veiled.'[1] Again[2] 'Art is a gift of Being. That is why art, despite its autonomy, has always served as the principal sacred bridge . . . to the religious experience, and continues to do so even in these apparently post-religious times.' Or, 'The gifts of the artist focus to a fine point that aboriginal light of Being, present to us all, but usually as concealed or confused, that illuminates beings.'

Following Heidegger, Martin calls sense-data and objects, beings or things, and the world of beings or things, 'ontical' reality. This reality can be subjected to the procedures and uses of science. 'Ontological reality', on the other hand, is composed of 'Being' which reveals itself, if at all, not as a being or beings but as a 'presence' in our experience. Being is that temporal and yet permanent reality, a continual coming and an endless origin, that is the source or ground of objects, and yet Being is not an object. Nor is Being a sense datum or data, for Being is that intangible matrix and power that makes possible the existence of any sense datum at all. Nor is Being the common denominator of all beings. Rather Being refers to the to-be of whatever is, whereas being refers to anything that is as revealed by sensation. Being is that which renders possible all 'is', that familiar copula implying existence. Being gives beings their 'is'. Being is the primordial power that conditions and makes beings possible. Being is the depth dimension of all beings that both surpasses and includes them. Thus Being is a further reality. Furthermore, beings get their enduring value, their ultimate significance, from Being.[3]

Experience of Being is in some degree religious. 'If in an experience only beings or ontical reality come into explicit awareness, then that experience is non-religious or one-dimensional. If in an experience Being or ontological reality also comes into explicit awareness, then that experience begins to take on a religious or two-dimensional character. The religious character of the experience deepens as the ontological awareness brings with it conviction or belief that ontological reality is of supreme importance.

[1] *op. cit.*, p. 23   [2] *ibid.*   [3] *op. cit.*, p. 3.

The stronger the experience of Being, the stronger the conviction and the feelings of ultimate concern, reverence, and peace, as well as the need for theoretical, practical, and sociological forms of expression; and in turn, the more sharply the religious divides from the non-religious experience. Many experiences, however, cannot be neatly catalogued as either.'[1]

§3 *Criticism. Is aesthetic experience 'religious'?*

I will not stay to criticize this language—of the ontical and the onto-logical, being and Being. (I dare not: once inside Heidegger's terminological web the fly despairs of ever getting out!) The language can be as dangerously persuasive to some as it is repellent to others. Nevertheless the general position does need critical examination. Martin as we have seen repudiates the idea that Being is the 'common denominator' of all beings. But it is very easy to slip from the logic of a common being to the affirmation of Being which is the source and ground of all things. I do not accuse Martin of con-sciously doing this; he is talking of the impacting and significant-seeming *experience* of Being, and not of logic. But the inter-pretation of this experience has pretty clear metaphysical *nuances*: 'Being *gives* beings their "is".' Some call Being 'God'. Being is the 'lighting process by which beings are illumined as beings. Yet the light does not appear by itself as a being but only in the beings it enlightens. Being contracts into the beings it makes manifest and hides by the very fact that it reveals. The lighting of Being is a hidden light, always immersed in darkness. Being is a congenital concealment that permeates every self-disclosure. This is the mystery of Being.'[2]

All this is *highly* metaphysical language; there is a lot more of it: the claims need scrutiny.

The main question is whether aesthetic experience in depth is, as such, 'religious' in character, whether it reveals the transcen-dent in any religious sense. Even if it does for some, is it so for all? Is there not a danger in suggesting that an aesthetic experience may in some sort and degree be religiously 'revelatory' without its being in any way 'recognized' (Lewis's word) as such?

§4 *Religious assurance and religious truth*

Meantime, let us look more closely at Martin's general position.

[1] *op. cit.*, pp. 4–5.   [2] *op. cit.*, pp. 3–4.

He seems on the one hand to separate off quite sharply the 'ontological *experience*' (of which some aesthetic experience might be
an instance) from all *statements* about things, and almost in the
same breath to suggest that all sorts of religious-metaphysical
statements (see the quotations given) not merely arise directly out
of the ontological experience, but in some sense seem to be
validated by it. 'When the coercive quality of this experience is
strong, we have an awe-full awareness and in turn belief in Being
as in some sense ultimate and transcendent reality.' This reality
is 'felt . . . as the source of all enduring values'. 'The ontological
experience is the Good for the religious.'[1]

Being is 'felt . . . as the source of all enduring values'. And
'whereas the truth about beings is demonstrated truth, the truth
about Being is "felt truth". Whereas, too, "demonstrated truth"
produces belief *that* or belief *about*, felt truth is belief *in*. The
ontological experience must be its own assurance. And no
reason can supplant this ultimate pre-cognitional intimacy and
affirmation.'

This is one side—or it emphasizes one side, the important de-
liverances of feeling. I would certainly not wish to deny deliver-
ances of feeling as such. I have argued that feeling and some forms
of cognition are indivisible. Feeling may have a very rich and full
content which is never *adequately* statable in words. Religious
people (for example the mystics, to whom I shall refer later)
may become aware through ineffable feeling of something which
may be of utmost importance, which carries 'its own assurance'.
I do not deny either that there may be possible ways of testing and
validating this assurance, which are not the ways of discursive
reasoning or ordinary empirical tests. On the other hand, when
things are *said*, and particularly when metaphysical propositions
are made, then one has entered upon the realm of discursive
reasoning. This demands its own rational investigation. Convictions of feeling do not validate the succession of metaphysical
statements which arises out of them. Perhaps (as Martin says)
'reason' cannot 'supplant' the immediate intimations. But the immediate intimations have to be examined, with sympathy and
intuitive understanding albeit, by 'reason', 'reason' in some sense.
Perhaps Being is apprehensible 'in a more primal mode of thinking'. But metaphysical affirmations require the support of metaphysical reasoning. The 'feeling' is a hint, perhaps a very impor-

[1] *op. cit.*, p. 7.

tant one; but *what* the experience is 'felt' to signify must inevitably depend upon the theoretical structure of one's beliefs, worked out (*inter alia*) in open philosophical debate. Whatever the impressiveness of immediate experience, we know pitifully little about the structure of the universe or the nature of God. And there are, familiarly enough, opposite sorts of experience to set against those of conviction—the terrible impersonality of the natural world with its disasters of earthquake or tempest or flood, the cruelty of so much human feeling and behaviour, and, if we believe in a loving providential God, 'his' apparent indifference, or absenteeism. I am not pretending that these too-familiar difficulties are in themselves arguments. They are simply some of the other data of human experience which have to be put side by side with the ontological 'convictions' in attempting to construct any coherent system of belief. On the one hand there are the moments of exalted inspiration, on the other the world seems saturated with indelible evil.

§5 *Religious-aesthetic experience, and the religious sceptic*

How then as aestheticians are we going to interpret some of the following statements (for example) in the concluding paragraph of Martin's paper? 'Both the participative (aesthetic) experience and the religious experience spring from the same empirical grounds; both involve love for Being; both are attuned to the call of Being; both are reverential to things as well as persons; both give a man a sense of being united with "that with which he is most familiar"; both give enduring value and serenity to existence; and thus both are profoundly regenerative. The participative (aesthetic) experience, then, always has a religious quality, for the participative experience penetrates into the religious dimension. How deeply into this dimension the experience delves depends upon how seriously the participation with Being is believed to be of supreme importance, and this in turn, in so far as it is not a groundless belief, depends upon the convictional power of the participative experience itself, the pressure of the presence of Being. From the coercive character of the participative experience flows religious belief and the feelings of ultimate concern, reverence, and peace, and in turn the various theoretical, practical, and sociological forms of religious expression.'[1]

[1] *op. cit.*, p. 24.

There is a great deal of ambiguity here. I will put some of my doubts in a number of short questions.

Does the aesthetic experience spring from the 'same' empirical grounds as the religious 'love for Being'? Does *any* aesthetically sensitive perceiver (including the possible atheist) of a piece of music or a picture have an experience in some degree religious? Is the aesthetic experience of *any* sensitive percipient really the same in kind as the aesthetic experience of a highly religious person? Does the sentence, 'both involve love for being' have the same meaning in each case? Agreeing that the aesthetic is revelatory in its own way, this might be said to be an experience of 'being' which in most of the transactions of ordinary life we miss, or are unaware of. Some might be prepared to use the capital B for being, to say that the experience is 'reverential' in feeling, that there is some sense of 'union', 'value', 'serenity', 'regeneration'. But for others this would be distasteful language. How far then *is* aesthetic experience for everyone, in some degree 'religious'? This is a very important question for aesthetics as well as for philosophy of religion. Martin seems—at least verbally—to speak with two voices. On the one hand: 'the participative (aesthetic) experience always has a religious quality'. On the other, 'how deeply into the religious dimension the aesthetic experience delves depends upon how seriously the participation with Being *is believed* (my italics) to be of supreme importance'. Which is right?

There seem to be two questions tangled up here. One has a more subjective emphasis—whether aesthetic experience can be religiously revelational, whatever one's beliefs. The other, related, question is philosophical. It is, How far does one's conception of the *nature* of religious revelation affect the answer to the first question?

Though distinct, the questions *are* related. On the face of it, it would seem absurd, as well as perhaps presumptuous, to insist that someone having an experience of genuine aesthetic insight, must be having at the same time a 'religious' experience (or to say that his aesthetic experience is a form of religious experience, if this person is, say, a convinced atheistical secular humanist. In *his* sense of 'religion', his experience could not be for *him* religious in any sense of revealing the divine, or some spiritual dimension of Being, the belief in which he strongly repudiates. On the other hand it is just possible that his strong disbelief and his very definite, perhaps limited, philosophical ideas of what religion is, might blind him, might close his mind, to the possibility of valid religious truth-claims. He might be in fact having a religious experience, but not calling it that. Before one could finally decide that his aesthetic experience could not now possibly be 'religious', one would have to investigate further possibilities outside the atheist's present acknowledgement. So, the concept of religious revelation might affect one's answer to the more psychologically loaded question.

Without attempting the impossible task of discovering an agreed definition of 'religion,' or touching, in a page or two, the bewildering mass of literature on the subject, we can pinpoint two (or three) outstanding senses of what 'religion' and 'religious revelation' may mean, at least in the West.

§6 Religious revelation and the aesthetic: two senses of revelation

'Revelation' may mean very specific revelation—often called 'special revelation'—given on authority, for example, the Jewish-Christian religion, or Islam. In the theology of the Jewish-Christian religion a very sharp distinction is drawn between what God reveals to man and what man discovers for himself. In 'special revelation' it is not man who discovers God, but God who declares himself and speaks to man. One form of this is exemplified in the story of Moses descending from the smoke-topped mountain, with the Ten Commandments given by God, complete; its corollary is the belief in the Word of God delivered in verbal inspiration. In the Christian transformation, the Word is made Flesh in Jesus who is God incarnate, atoned for men's sins on the Cross, rose from the dead . . . On orthodox views the person, life and teachings of Jesus Christ are invested with divine authority. The Church, through its Councils and Creeds affirms divine revelation, albeit necessarily expressed in the propositional language of men.

It needs no argument to show that for a religious *unbeliever*, no art could be religiously revealing, in this sense of revelation. If the definite revelation is rejected, it could not enter into art.

For the believer—the more or less orthodox Christian believer for example—the believed religious subject-matter, entering into a religious poem or drama or Mass, may well provide something of religious experience; it might in a sense be a 'revelation'—and I am assuming here that in such experience the religious is united

I

with the aesthetic. The reading of the religious poems of Donne, Vaughan or Herbert, for instance, may certainly be said to be aesthetically-religious. This would be true similarly of religious pictures, music with religious words. Of pure music, nothing need be added to what has already been said at length. It is not of the nature of pure music to expound (or assume) specific concepts such as are implied for instance, in the Creeds. Pure music could not 'reveal' in the present sense of 'revelation'.

But 'special revelation' is only one sort (or theory or concept) of religious revelation. 'Revelation' as used by Professor Martin and some of the other writers mentioned, is very different. Revelation now is not defined as orthodox Christianity defines it—though this does not imply that these writers discard the theology or history which any developed religion must take into account. But for them, it is fair to say, revelational religious insights are continuous with the whole of the rest of life; religious meaning enters at many points, and there are degrees in which this may happen. There is the 'uneasy awareness' of man's limitations, the 'awe-full' aware-ness of further reality, of the importance of this awareness, of reverence, of 'ultimate concern'. Religious feeling in this sense can be present at any time, and a great variety of names are given to its object—God, the Holy, the Other, the Transcendent, Being, Being-in-itself. . . .

In this sense of 'revelation' the chances that art might 'reveal' religious meaning are much greater than in the case of a theologi-cally defined religion. Many who could not possibly assent to, say, the credal affirmations of Christianity, might admit to some sense of 'otherness', 'transcendence', 'numinousness' . . . —though not necessarily using these words. Art might be, up to a point, religiously revelatory without their recognizing it as belonging to the category of religion.

Many, or at least some—but certainly not all. There are the radical sceptics. And the question arises whether for them an aesthetic experience could be a religious experience without, in Professor Lewis's word, 'being acknowledged'? The answer turns, I think, on whether one uses 'religious revelation' with a subjective or an objective stress.

'Religious' and 'religion' are ambiguous words. Etymologically, the possible derivation from *ligare*, 'to bind' gives a clue to one side of its meaning. With this stress of meaning, no experience, includ-ing the aesthetic, could be 'religious' except through acknowledgement, i.e., unless the person concerned were in some way or degree 'bound together' in belief and feeling, with religious ideas or objects. On the other side, the word 'religion' includes, not only this idea of a subjective relationship with the idea or objects of religion, but a claim to truth and objective fact, the claim that the 'objects' (or Object) of religion are indeed real, more real than anything else. God has been called by philosophers the *Ens Realissimum*. If in fact these religious claims *were* true, then the Real (etc.) would in fact be impinging upon human experience all the time whether 'acknowledged' or not. Revelation would be in operation.

This might be so. On the other hand it would seem very strained and unnatural to say that the atheist (let us suppose) was having a 'revelational' experience without acknowledging it. A man surely could hardly be having a religiously revelational experience if nothing 'religious' was being revealed to *him*? However dazzling and resonant in impact were the divine, how could he see if blind or hear if his ears were stopped? I conclude that aesthetic experience as such is not religious, and could only be religiously revealing to those who, in some degree at least 'believe'—in the very broad non-credal sense we have in this last part been assuming.

§9 (b) *Mystical experience and aesthetic experience*

It would be quite wrong to label any or all of the writers mentioned as 'mystics' or 'mystical'. 'Mystic' is a technical concept in the philosophy of religion, controversial and difficult to define. But it may be of some interest now, in exploring a little further the notion of aesthetic revelation, to make a very brief and untechnical excursion into mystical revelational claims, with an eye both to resemblances and differences between the mystical and the aesthetic. Perhaps each can illuminate the other.

If, for non-mystical theological-type revelation it is fair to say that what 'God speaks' has to be done into human language-symbols, for the religious mystic 'speaking' is not a typical or an easy metaphor. The talk of the mystic is of intimate communion, sometimes of being and identity, rather than of 'speaking' in the limited language of men. The mystic constantly characterizes the ultimate achievements of mystic union as 'indescribable', 'un-speakable', 'ineffable'. The mystic's supreme joy of ecstasy, so overwhelming that everything else seems nothing by comparison with it, is in the end utterly beyond words. It is true that the mystic cannot keep silent about it; the talk of the mystics fills many library shelves; but it is always interspersed with protests that nothing which can be said can possibly convey the blessedness of union. Although no human language can be concept-free, the language of mysticism is not that of conceptual metaphysics: rather, it is metaphorical. It speaks of 'feeding', 'touching', 'marriage', 'immersion'. It is full of familiar paradoxes. There is self-loss, dying to one's own being, swimming in the ocean of the Divine, melting, merging, being reborn, being laid hold of by, or being infused with God. The flavour of the paradoxes is epitomized in the description of the 'Divine Abyss' as 'deep yet dazzling dark-ness'.

I am not at all concerned here with assessment of the religious validity of mystical claims to revelation, particularly in their final or consummatory forms. But the journey into mysticism has stages, and it is the similarity between some ways of mystical experiencing, and some ways of experiencing in art, which is of particular interest in the discussion of art-experience as a claimed form of 'revelation'.

I want to make it very clear that (in consonance with what has already been argued) I shall not be saying that art-experience as such is mystical: if for some people art may have been at times a way into mystical experience—that is another matter. The art object and the Object of mystical experiences are, phenomenologically and ontologically, two entirely different things, and if we suppose (for purposes of argument) that mysticism gives insight of an ineffable kind into ultimate Reality, there could be no inference from that to what it is that art-experience gives insight into, even if art-experience has some resemblances in form to mystical forms of knowing. Art-experience gives immediate insight into *artistic* meaning, not ultimate Reality. Nevertheless, it may be that exami-nation of some of the characters of experiencing which knowledge of art seems to have in common with mystical experience—par-ticularly noticeable in deep and intense experiences of great art—will throw light upon the conviction of 'revelation' in art.

(i) One resemblance which art-experience has with the mystical lies, we know, in its ineffability. *What* we know in art cannot be told—except by presenting art to be experienced. But the reason why the meaning of art is 'ineffable' (that it is meaning-embodied) is different from the reason which the mystics give when they say that their vision of the Divine is ineffable. For them it is so because it is God himself (or the Infinite, or the Absolute) with whom the mystic is in union. In mystical vision there is a (claimed) content of divine revelation not present in the aesthetic as such. Though as Professor Lewis stresses, there is union between the immediate and the 'other'.

(ii) Another resemblance between the two is in the concentrated attentiveness of contemplation which both involve. In each there is an outpouring of self into the object. Attention is intense. Barriers are broken down; there is a positive kind of openness—in mysticism of submissiveness—to the *fiat* of cosmic existence, or of art. And in each case the complement of some degree of self-elimination is new insight. The mystic (Julian of Norwich) from the self-effacing contemplation of 'a little thing, the quantity of a hazel nut', comes to see life in its wholeness, or to hear 'the music of the world'. In the outgoing contemplation of art, meaning is revealed: we 'see' the wholeness of *The Madonna of the Rocks*, 'hear' the wholeness of the *Double Concerto*.

(iii) But perhaps most important of all in both types of experience is immediate contact with what is *given*: *existence, things, being* . . . in contrast to commerce with the dialectic of symbols and concepts. Sometimes the impact is more than impact: there is a claim of mystical identification with Being, or God. Or the language is the language of love. The author of *The Cloud of Unknowing* writes '. . . Of the works of God's self, may a man through grace have full-head of knowing, and well he can think of them: but of God himself can no man think. And therefore I would leave all that thing that I can think, and choose to my love that thing that I cannot think. For why: He may well be loved, but not thought. By love He may be gotten and holden; but by thought never.' 'Knowing' here (pretty plainly) means the knowing of 'thought', 'Unknowing' the knowing of love.

Manifestly, this language cannot be transferred straight over into art-experience. The mystic is talking about a union of love with God, about the Universal One and Many, about Being interpenetrating time and yet timeless. *Our* talk is about art experience. But there is some transfer possible. It is by a kind of unsentimental 'love' that musicians 'know'. With a fair understanding of the changes of language required (particularly the words 'think' and 'love') one could use here too the words of the author of *The Cloud*: 'Therefore I would leave all that thing that I can think, and choose to my love that thing I cannot think. By love he may be gotten and holden; but by thought never.'

There is too, in mystical and in art-experience (iv) the knowledge of the many in the one, and (v) of the 'that' which permeates through and is permanent in, process and change. For art it is not the universal One and Many, or the Being of the universe; but there is an analogy. It is pretty evident once it is pointed out.

We do talk often enough about the 'one and the many' in art: yet the thing in itself remains mysteriously and always freshly challenging, whether in a piece of sculpture, or a picture, or a poem or a fugue. The knowing is a temporal process (even in the visual arts). We have to 'live through' the art-object, bit by bit; without this, 'unity' would be empty. Yet the 'bits and pieces' are not bits and pieces; they have their aesthetic meaning only as functioning within, and constituting, the whole which is both over and above them in one way, yet organic with them all in another. This is, of course, just talk again. It is the *experience*, both temporal and time-transcending, which is freshly mysterious and revealing.

The analogy of art with mystical experience is only an analogy, though it is helpful. It is Universal Wholeness, the Many in One (or God, in some language), with which the mystic claims communion. *Art* is not the universe, still less God, but each work of art is a microcosm, complete and whole in itself once made. And the knowledge of art's many-in-one, the permanent through change, has a completeness within its frame which is found nowhere else in the finite world. (The living organism is a unity, but its very continuing life exists in dialogue with its independent environment.) So a completely fulfilled art-experience might even be regarded—on one side—as a *model* of mystic experience.

It could be a model, of limited value, like all models. Another, similarly limited, model of mysticism would be that of the work of art as drawing into itself (and transforming in the unity of embodiment) meaning from an indefinitely large reservoir of human experience. In that sense, the art, and the experience of the art, is, though self-contained, a focus of potentially unlimited meaning. The frame of (some) art is necessary, as is concentration within the frame, and that is one thing. The other is that the experience of what is necessarily limited within the frame in part derives from a totality of experience to which there is no set limit. This could account for the feeling of revelation particularly in some art-experiences: it would have some, though limited, resemblance to the mystic's experience of 'eternity within an hour'.

There are, too, the after-effects, changes in the quality of living, which may supervene upon the revelations of mysticism and art-experience. For the great mystics the experience is not only supremely prized as an event; it can change life for ever afterwards, illuminating all else. One may not want to use such extreme language of the experiences even of great art. Yet great art is not only revealing in itself; its influence transcends its boundaries; it can and sometimes does enable us to see and feel after it as we did not see and feel before, to be newly sensitive and aware. The great drama can be educative so that after it we can apprehend *nuances* of love, of human tension, suffering, tragedy, as we did not before. We come to know more of 'the piece of work' that is man. Of pure music it is not possible to speak in exactly the same way; yet after the self-loss in music there is the silence; something remains: we are changed, enlarged and expanded perhaps, breathing freely in a purer air. Put in more objective, though still halting, language, the sense of music at times seems to expand beyond itself into the sense of universal reality continuous with it, its temporal quality transcended in timeless peace.

> Words move, music moves
> Only in time; but that which is only living
> Can only die. Words, after speech, reach
> Into the silence. Only by the form, the pattern,
> Can words or music reach
> The stillness, as a Chinese jar still
> Moves perpetually in its stillness

The claims, then, that the aesthetic in art is 'revelation' are not spurious if they are cautiously stated and carefully sifted. Certainly the aesthetic as such does not reveal conceptual truths or metaphysical verities, nor is it in and by itself religious insight. If Browning meant when he wrote

> The rest may reason and welcome,
> 'Tis we musicians *know*

that musicians know what others know by reason, he is plainly wrong. But art can fairly be said to be revelation in a number of ways, some of which I have tried to indicate.

PART V

THE ARTS IN EDUCATION

CHAPTER XV

THE AESTHETIC IN EDUCATION

CHAPTER XV

THE AESTHETIC IN EDUCATION

§1 *Introductory: the Arts in School*

'Children's Art' has a public image. It is 'news'. In recent years there have been many exhibitions of children's art of various ages. These exhibitions represent a great change of attitude from the past; what were once dismissed, with kindly adult indulgence, as childish daubs or the products of childish play, are now displayed on walls and stands, admired, enjoyed, sometimes goggled at or gushed about.

In education itself a great deal of attention has been paid to the drawings, paintings and modellings of children. Many psychological and other studies have been made of 'child art', and for generations now teachers have learned to speak of 'education through art' —a term which has become almost a slogan, derived from an important idea pioneered by Cizek, presented and developed in England through the influence of Marion Richardson and the enormously wide-ranging work of Sir Herbert Read—particularly by his *Education through Art*. The effects of this interest is seen mostly in attention to the work and education of younger children, where the 'permissive' atmosphere which is now taken as a *sine qua non* is as yet not violently threatened by the menace of immediately approaching examinations.

Attitudes to aesthetic education in the later years of school, as adolescence approaches and arrives, are a rather different story. Several things make it so. One is an inference (which I shall contest) from the fact that adolescents tend to be shy, self-conscious, critical about their own efforts, desiring communication yet wary of too much self-revelation to others. It is sometimes supposed, therefore, that they have ceased to be *interested* in the aesthetic and the arts, or that their 'creativity' for some reason disappears at adolescence. This belief may be strengthened because some adolescents spurn 'art' as what 'kids do' (and what they themselves earlier did quite happily); they aspire after new things belonging to the adult world but cannot attain them, because these require techniques as yet unmastered. So they may seem to give up trying —but are not the less frustrated. The most important reason, however—or perhaps it should be called 'cause'—for (a very common) lack of attention to aesthetic education in the later years of school, is that the arts (with the possible exception of literature) are simply not taken seriously by many teachers and educationists as a necessary component of all liberal education. This is seen in actions rather than in words. Everyone—except perhaps a few dyed-in-the-wool philistines—is ready to give lip-service to education in the arts. But when their importance is weighed against the need to pass examinations in the 'serious' subjects, the arts are found wanting. It is 'nice to have them about'; they are refreshments, relaxations, recreations, to be relegated (hopefully) to the hours of leisure, to 'out-of-school' activities. They are the ornaments of life rather that a part of its vital tissue. The view that they are estimable hobbies, a most respectable kind of play, is perhaps derived from the one-sided view that art is only a sort of 'self-expression'. The idea that the making and appreciation of art is a unique kind of *insight* and discovery, certainly not (pursued seriously) inferior to science, or history, or moral judgment—is not only alien to the minds of many teachers; it is an idea of which there is little clear or explicit recognition anywhere. (Were it not so, it would hardly have been necessary to labour the argument of this book—that art is indeed a form of discovery, of knowledge *sui generis*.) So at the later stages of school, the arts, always with possible reserves about literature (which is, after all 'about life'!) tend to get elbowed out of the way. There are exceptions, of course. Individual schools here and there in Great Britain take them really seriously. In some places they are thought to be integral to education. In New South Wales in Australia, for instance,[1] every public school pupil, from the beginning to the end of his or her school life, is actively engaged in the study and practice of some art or craft (including music). But generally speaking, the arts still get a pretty poor deal in the central educational curriculum of this country at its later stages. The less 'academic' pupils may get a chance in the art room; for others art is thought to be good 'therapy'. But the 'brighter' pupils, by and large, have to stick to the pressing work of knowledge-getting: art, it is assumed, is no such thing.

§2 *Different stages—and different ideas—of art education*

Education is a continuous, single, undivided process—though of course it has its stages at which markedly different things happen.

---

[1] Under the enlightened initiation of Dr Harold Wyndham and his able Director of Art, Mr Dabron.

Its progress—though continuous—is not a perfectly smooth curve, but more like the rhythmic rising of the tide whose waves

Begin, and cease, and then again begin.

The rhythm of this rising tide, too, and its span, is individually different for each individual child; each tide has its small individual moon.

Though nowadays it seems an utterly commonplace truism to say that what is appropriately done for, and by, a fifteen-year-old is quite different from what is appropriately done for and by a five-year-old playing with blocks, clay or water—this truism, so far as it applies to aesthetic education, was, not so long ago, surprisingly ignored, and in two opposite ways. In former times, in my own childhood, for example, about the only 'art' which was allowed to young children was the kind of thing which Leonardo recommended that young *professional* artists should learn to do, namely, draw with accuracy. The difference was that the models for drawing given to these children sixty years ago were less inspiring than Leonardo's. The 'art lesson' consisted of exercises such as learning to draw perfectly straight lines of exact length, or the symmetrical curves of a vase, or flower pots or buckets and mops or doorplates. 'Expression', nowadays taken for granted, was unheard of, at least in ordinary schools. On the other hand, when 'expressiveness', 'freedom', 'activity', 'permissiveness' (in a dubious sense) caught on, many of the rank and file of the teachers of older children became so obsessed with the fear of 'imposing' anything that they fell into the trap of another kind of imposition— the imposition upon *adolescents* of methods suitable only for young children. They overplayed in the years of adolescence a very proper sensitiveness to the need for children to experiment and develop in their own way, standing off from helping these older pupils to learn the techniques which they obviously wanted and needed at *their* stage of development. Confusedly importing into adolescence the image of young children and their needs, they fancied that they were helping adolescents to develop. In fact they were impeding development. Artistic development at this stage requires, and asks, sometimes urgently, for experienced help in the mastery of techniques and the use of materials, necessary for the development of expression and embodiment. Denied this help, it is little wonder that feelings of frustration sometimes arose.

Further, we may fairly say that both these mistakes show failure to understand the *continuity* of education. The old formalism was ignorant of development. The young child was regarded as just a potential, rather crude, adult; it was not understood that if you starve him of what he needs at his particular stage of growth, his later growth may be jeopardized also; to treat the young child as a crude adult may condition him into becoming later in fact just that, a crude adult. Formalism tends to prevent development at all stages by its rigidity, and permissiveness to thwart its own avowed purpose—to foster the development of young people— by not being realistic about the appropriate help that young human beings need (at any stage).

§3 *Philosophical questions about art education: plans*

My concern, in this last *Part*, is a wide one—the place and function of aesthetic education (including, importantly, art education) in what is usually called 'liberal' education. Since education is a continuum, we have to keep in mind the whole range of school life. On the other hand, because younger children's needs are so different from those of later years, I shall discuss them first.

I ought perhaps to make clear what I conceive to be the function of the kind of writing which follows. It will certainly not be a potted treatise or digest of the theory of the practice and methods of art education. There is a large literature on this subject (varying very much in quality) in books, magazines, society proceedings, etc. Most of it does not deal with philosophical principles at all, but either with psychological studies of children and their development, or with educational methods and techniques of teaching in art and craft, music or literature. The latter is usually practical in emphasis, written with special age-groups in mind, offering specific examples drawn from the experiences of teachers of pupils with particular backgrounds, tastes, talents and temperaments. Here and there some 'philosophy' may pop up, and plenty of general assumptions are made. It is some of the more important assumptions which I want to dig up and scrutinize.

There are questions about the aims and purposes of art teaching in education. Some of them are very general: What is the function of art education as a whole and how is it justifiable? Other questions of aims are more particular. Are they different for children in the earlier years as distinguished from later? How? Why?

Again, what is the distinction, and what the relation, between aims and methods? There is a 'permissive' *method*. Is permissiveness a final *aim*? Then there are many assumptions about young children's art. We assume that children's drawings, paintings, modellings are 'art' in that we use the name 'art'. Is it necessarily so? May we not be lumping together by the use of the same word a whole assortment of different things—'expression' (in many senses), discovery of self in the world, therapy, exciting (but not necessarily aesthetic) physical experience, aesthetic experience, the doing of something which could be called 'art', the making of 'works of art'? Are there confusions about children's 'art' due to a kind of word magic, things having the same name being equal to one another?

Although the distinctions to be made are mainly philosophical, to make them can have a positive bearing upon the actual work of art education. Philosophy may be, in the current jargon, a 'second order' activity—which (to translate) implies that the philosopher is not, *as such*, either an expert in art or art education, or, *as such*, competent to give practical advice to teachers of art. But as conceptual confusions can, without doubt, mislead practice, so can conceptual clarification, indirectly, make possible sounder practice. There is no infallible deduction from general principles to what ought to be done in particular practice. But good practice ought to be compatible with sound principles, and practice incompatible with sound general principles, or compatible with unsound general principles, will be bad practice. So, thinking about principles is of vital importance, though principles can only be expressed in sound practice through the mediation of good teachers who have assimilated a good deal of the knowledge (e.g. psychological knowledge of development) necessary for their art of teaching.

A last preliminary observation. As this Part is an essay not a treatise, I shall, in what follows, concentrate mainly on the so-called 'visual' arts and crafts as they relate to education. (The adjective 'so-called' is added not only because in general the 'visual' arts are perceived with much more than the organs of vision, but because both at the earlier and the later stages of education the so-called 'haptic' experiences are important in themselves and as modifying visual experience, as well as the drawings, paintings, and models and sculptures, which express it.) Discussion of arts other than 'visual'—for example music or literature—although they are equally important, would take up far too much space and time. I shall therefore (in the later part of this discussion) refer to these other arts only now and again.

§4 *The aesthetic and the educaton of younger children*

What happens, and what should happen, in the so-called 'visual' education of younger children? Our answer will depend on whether or not we distinguish clearly between two quite different questions —the question of the general psycho-physical development of these younger children, and another—whether and how far what they do in their developmental adventures is properly called 'aesthetic', and whether and how far any of it is 'art'.

Wolfgang Groezinger, a sensitive observer of young children, in his book *Scribbling, Drawing, Painting*[1] criticizes those adults— parents or teachers—who in effect interfere, often with the most innocent and loving motives, with the natural development of young children by forcing their scribblings into their own categories of 'writing', or 'art', often prematurely introducing into the child's mind adult ideas of artistic representation when they are after something of their own which is quite different. They are in effect confusing two quite different issues. Groezinger insists that what they should be primarily concerned with is not art, but the child's normal development. The question that adults should ask is not, 'What do we like?' or 'What do we find beautiful?' but 'What phenomena can be observed in the normal child?' 'What is useful and what is damaging to its development?' 'What is the aim of this development?' His answer is that 'the aim of the child's apparently artistic development is not art, but reality. At each stage in its drawing and painting, except at the scribbling stage, the child is a realist and thinks it is portraying the world perfectly.'[2] Groezinger's use of 'realism' might be questioned. The 'realism' is not the 'realism' of the constructed world of the adult (all our knowledge is in terms of a construction of one kind or another). It is the imaginative construction of the child himself, which is neither bare fact nor merely subjective, but a compound of the impingement of the world upon him, and his own attempts to come to terms with the world in his own various ways. (This is my statement, not Groezinger's.) Groezinger asks significantly,[3] 'Can we adults simply walk into the child's world?' Not perhaps so

[1] English Translation by Kaiser and Wilkins.
[2] *ibid.*, p. 20.
[3] *ibid.*, p. 27.

easily, though perhaps we may come to understand some things with love, sympathy, *and* study. Intuitions, even of the most loving mother, may be mistaken. Mother says with pride, 'Baby is writing' (not well, perhaps, but he will learn a little later!). 'In reality, however, the words "Baby is writing" are the prelude to little tragicomedy in which the tragic element is the adult's delusion that he or she understands the child, and the comic element is the child's readiness to enter into this "understanding" game, which is the same time a game of hide-and-seek.'[1] The child is interested in the activity, the possibility of expressing, or rather impressing, movement and rhythm on the paper by means of a tool, whereby something comes into existence that was not there before, and which opens up all sorts of possibilities. Moreover, 'the fact is that the primal pattern of scribbling is *not* those well-known zig-zags which pretend to be grown-up writing and which belong to a slightly later stage of development, but circular movements, spirals, skeins and tangles, from which we infer that the small child has a *rotatory* sense of space and that its hand is, as it were, impelled by a dynamo'.[2] The child—only some two years ago lapped in the waters of his mother's womb—was, in being born, left high and dry, compelled to adapt to 'a blaze of light, contact with the soft and hard, the warm and the cold, and the gnawing extremity of hunger'. 'But it also has its triumphs behind it: grabbing and holding fast, throwing away and picking up, crawling, the first attempt at pulling itself up, standing on its own feet, and walking— victory over the force of gravity.' The child is still living within himself, a sensitive sphere on the periphery of which the stimuli of the outer world impinge. Groezinger works out the development of the space sense through the making of circular movements in scribbles, spirals, zig-zags, criss-crosses, boxes . . . Scribbling is a kind of walking, standing upright, perpendicular and horizontal movement. By expression on paper the child is liberating himself from his world of endless ages ago (two years!) in a new rhythm of life itself. A conversation is going on privately between the child's inner life, his body, and the external world. (This again is my own interpretation, not necessarily Groezinger's; he says, 'Scribbling is autocommunication', a dialogue between inner self and body. I prefer to extend it.)

This all happens naturally and inevitably. Then the loving, sympathizing, improving adults poke their fingers in. 'What *is* it?'

[1] English Translation by Kaiser and Wilkins, p. 27.   [2] *ibid.*, pp. 27–8.

they ask. This question, says Groezinger, 'is like a lasso, with which we try to catch the child and pull it over to our side. Is it the cunning of love? Is it the force of habit? Whatever it may be the child obliges us and produces some explanation or other. Giving names is a good game, and in an instant a circle has become Daddy, the moon, a potato, or a balloon, whatever happens to occur to the child. But by doing this we have brought about something which is laden with heavy consequences: we have established a connection between the primal realm of scribbling and the already far advanced realm of language, and the only effect this can have is to speed up and shorten the child's pictorial development, so that it does not come to organic maturity. For language names things and thus objectifies forms that have not yet detached themselves from the child. Objectivity will enter into the drawing one day of its own accord, but it is only the child that knows the right moment, not the adult. Even years later the child will remember the names it has itself found for its pictures; those extorted by questioning change from moment to moment.'[1]

All this deals with a very early stage. Groezinger discusses later developments: the correlation of eye and hands, the importance and implications of 'haptic' and 'eidetic' experiences. Only when 'the hands have reported back, like scouts, to see how far away things are, does the eye know something of the world'. He deals with representation, with two-handed drawing and the danger of suppressing (by insistence on using the 'proper hand') the haptic contribution to the development of the sense of three dimensions by the use of the whole body. Moreover, the importance of all these and related factors, though particularly relevant to the earlier years, does not cease there; it persists into adolescence and through-out life into the life of art itself. There is a dialectic of develop-ment—self, external world, the synthesis—and this is a condition of maturing into art. But 'only when the adolescent has found him-self through art, through gaining freedom, does he know what *art* is'. (My italics.)

Sir Herbert Read did not always, I think, clearly distinguish between the needs of the total natural development of children, and the disciplines of 'art'. In an article, 'Education through Art'[2] speaking of the discipline of art, he said, 'It is a discipline inherent in the natural order and in conforming to this discipline the child

¹ English Translation by Kaiser and Wilkins, p. 35.
² In *Education and Art*, Unesco Symposium, 1953.

finds perfect freedom'. Two things—opposite and complementary —can be said of this. One is that it is questionable whether the discipline of *art* is a discipline of the *natural* order. The other, related, observation (more important in this context) is the opposite one that the 'discipline inherent in the natural order' is by Read being assumed to be the discipline of *art*. But if one does say this, one is forcing one of the basic aims of the education of young children— of allowing and helping them to grow up normally according to their general and individual needs (which includes finding the need for many different 'disciplines')—into a much more limited category, that of disciplining them in art.

If an assumption of this kind is a mistake or confusion, it will not only be an intellectual mistake or confusion. Being an assumption about aims of education, it will adversely affect (as suggested above, p. 273) the practice of education. If 'art' has a specific meaning (and does not, for instance, include *anything* children do in the way of painting, modelling, etc.), art-education will have a specific meaning too, and will move in specific directions. And if the carrying out of these specific aims in these directions should happen to conflict with broader, more basic aims of development, then something will go wrong.

My point in these last few pages has been to consider (in of course the sketchiest way) children's scribbling, drawing, and such like, as fulfilling *general* developmental needs, and not as 'art' or 'art-education'. But this leaves quite open certain other questions. Has what children do in these ways, sometimes at least, aspects of aesthetic value? Do they sometimes produce 'art', or even 'works of art'? And if the answer is, in any particular case, 'Yes', how far should the recognition of this affect our educational procedures? How far should they be encouraged and guided to cultivate the aesthetic? Let us assume that what has already been said about the broad educational need for all-round development is true. Is there, within this, a place for incorporation of specifically aesthetic —perhaps art-education? I have been arguing throughout the book that the aesthetic is of unique importance as a form of knowledge and experience. If this is valid, it would seem odd to leave it entirely out of consideration at any stage of education—though it is agreed that we ought not, educationally, to force the issue.

There are two sorts of question here. One is a question strictly for aesthetics: the other is a question for education. Let us take them in that order.

§5 *Is it 'art' that children do?*

Here it is helpful to recollect and to remake some distinctions, between the aesthetic, art, and the work of art. These are not divided by lines from one another; they overlap and intertwine: but they are distinguishable, and to keep the distinctions in mind is useful in trying to understand the development and education of young children.

Aesthetic pleasure occurs wherever—to use our own technical jargon—embodied-meaning is contemplated and enjoyed; this aesthetic enjoyment, we know, has an almost indefinitely large range of possible operation, certainly much wider than the range of the aesthetic in art. And it seems quite beyond doubt—from affectionate and informed observation of children as well as from the recollections of our own childhood—that children have what are in fact aesthetic experiences from very early days, though obviously they give no labels to it. A child may get intense aesthetic delight from things that *happen* to him, from the feeling of cool or warm water on his skin, of falling raindrops splashing upon him, from the sight of the whimsical hide-and-seek of falling snowflakes. Or it may be the delight just of what seems to happen when he *does* things—scuffle his feet deliciously through the crackling or sodden autumn leaves with their intoxicating smell, or plays with (to adult ears) those terrible drums, trumpets, tin whistles, or just keeps beating a tattoo with hands, feet, or stick. It may happen when he is doing something rather more deliberate, as scribbling, or dropping ink on wet paper, or feeling the resistance of a bit of clay, or the smooth yet softly resistant matt texture of a piece of chalk being cut with a penknife, or even contemplatively breaking down with his tongue a piece of lemon jelly.

It may well be said that all this is merely the enjoyment of sensation, legitimate and enviable sensuality. (If enviable, why? Why should it be assumed that adults may not go on discovering and rediscovering the pleasure of sensuality for the whole of their lives?) Sensational (or perceptual) it certainly is. But it is more too. It is, or it can be, intensely aesthetic. Think back to the early dynamic 'writing' experience. Such scribbling is at least expressive, a 'getting out' of energy, an enjoyment of dynamic feeling, the feeling of rhythm, *and* perhaps, moments of the contemplation of it as form. It is also physical contact with the external world, the holding of a pencil or crayon, moving it against the resistance of the paper, seeing the marks which are the externalization of all this. The enjoyment is certainly sensational, but it is an embryonic experience of embodiment which is more than sensation. It is the discovery of a new meaning known as the pencil or crayon moves along the paper, and in the perceived marks on paper which are the final outcome of this continuous process. It is delight in the fresh meaning which comes of the union between the seeking active self of the child, and the medium whose independent characteristics are a facet of the independent external world. The meaning is discovered in this vital encounter, and it is certainly a very simple instance of aesthetic discovery. Henri Matisse,[1] writing of his own mature experience, says: 'We have . . . to nourish our feeling, and we can only do so with materials derived from the world about us. This is the process whereby the artist incorporates and gradually assimilates the external world within himself, until the object of his drawing has become like a part of his being . . .' And though this is mature experience speaking, the experience is not different in kind from that of the child. Or the child's experience is not different in kind from the exciting discovery of which Barbara Hepworth speaks (in the passage quoted on p. 108) when she describes incising upon a resisting medium. The child, with his body-and-mind, is discovering the independent world through his interaction with the medium. His contemplative enjoyment of the new meaning which he finds in this, even if it is only momentary, is aesthetic, and has a common character with the aesthetic in all art making, a discovery in union.

These rudimentary experiences can have an aesthetic quality; but they are not 'art' in any serious recognized sense. 'Art' seems to imply some measure of intention, at least in a loose sense of the word—intention to make and give form to something; it involves some element of self-criticism: if the thing is not quite right, it must be altered or modified or done again better. The making does not of course exclude accident, things happening which were not planned or intended: but it is the *use* of accident, not just aesthetically pleasing accident, which distinguishes the aesthetically pleasing in itself from the aesthetically pleasing in art. 'Intention', as I say, has to be taken here in a loose sense. But it is intention at least to give, or to find, form which is aesthetically satisfying. It may range from experiment which is a sort of play, the dropping, say, of waterproof ink upon wet paper, first just in order to see what happens, then with some more or less deliberate manipula-

---

[1] Unesco volume, *op. cit.*, p. 21.

tion of the dropping to get an arrangement which is aesthetically pleasing. This can fairly be called the beginning of art—and of course children begin to do it, sooner or later. In so far as they do, they can fairly be called embryonic 'artists'. Some will be much more particular than others, taking great care to find out what is aesthetically pleasing to them, eliminating the failures.

From this to the making of 'works of art' there is no division but only a difference of degree—the degree of planning, complexity, insistence on unity. Very young children do not attain this and are not interested in doing so. Older children may go a long way towards it, though distinction in it can only be expected at a fairly mature age. (I am being deliberately vague about ages; children vary enormously individually; the experts are very careful to emphasize this, and also to insist that stages of development are not clear-cut.) Further, the distinction of degree between 'art' and a 'work of art' is of course not just a matter of maturity, and a 'work of art' is not necessarily superior to a bit of 'art' which is not a completed work. In the adult world, would we say that, for instance, the sketches of Constable or Turner are 'works' of art? And may they not, sometimes, be better, more spontaneous and free, than more laborious 'work'?

The question, then, whether all younger children are 'artists', whether their drawings, paintings, modellings should be looked at as 'art' in an omnibus way, whether their teachers are educating them through 'art'—is not capable of a single, simple answer, and if, biased by our interest in art-education, we give it a too simple answer, harm may be done both to our understanding and judgment and even to children themselves. In a process of education, including self-education, in which many things are happening all at once, where many sorts of discovery are being made, there are very often present aesthetic elements; sometimes the children are small artists producing art or even works of art of their own kind.

But, as we have said, the total process of becoming educated is much wider than aesthetic or art education, and our interest in children as artists, combined with a eulogistic use of 'art' and 'artist', may lead us to confuse these things with the others. Children and children's work is refreshing; the work has spontaneity, charm, a directness which we older people admire and perhaps envy. Marion Richardson wrote:[1] 'Art is not an effort of

---

[1] Introduction to Exhibition of Children's Drawings and Paintings at the County Hall, London, 1938. Quoted in Tomlinson and Mills, *op. cit.*, p. 2.

will but a gift of grace—to the child at least, the simplest and most natural thing in the world.' She is right in saying that much of what children do is 'a gift of grace', a natural thing. I think however that in her great love for children and their work she over-simplifies at this point, in *identifying* this early spontaneity with art, in effect confusing the wider concept of 'natural' child de-velopment with the more specific cultivation of art. This is shown by the fact that a few lines later in the same piece she does more specifically refer, not to natural spontaneity but to the *discipline* of art. 'Work such as we see here', she says, 'is not "free expression" as generally understood . . . but a disciplined activity in which the teacher's own imaginative gifts play a very important part.'

These two things, however, 'nature', the gift of 'grace', on the one hand, and discipline on the other, need not in the end be at all contradictory. We may truly say that the difficult discipline of art at more mature stages is the very way to discover, and win, new freedom at a higher level. We learn to do new, creative things not by 'first' nature but by 'second nature'. We learn how to *become* 'natural', to acquire a new kind of spontaneity through passing through stages of hard discipline. We have to learn how to use the 'gift of grace' in a mature way so that the potentiality of 'grace' is far more fully realized. I have argued elsewhere (*Philo-sophy and Education*, pp. 125–7) that the attainment of freedom at a high level (I called it the 'third' freedom) is the aim not only of art but of other studies too, and further that the attainment of freedom through discipline is a major aim of all education.

The too-exclusive emphasis on the 'art' of young children, again, may lead us to place too much emphasis upon their final product, may indeed blind us to even the *aesthetic* discoveries made by children in their active, progressive experiments. Jane Cooper Bland,[1] writing of children of three, says: 'The child at this age does not usually regard what he has made as a painting or a piece of sculpture. He lives through a series of experiences as he paints or models and his final creation might be compared to a motion picture of which we see only the last frame. The finished product reveals very little of the variety and richness of experience the child has gained in the process.' Again, 'They often keep chang-ing the colours on their papers by painting one over the other until the result is a mass of brown paint. Although this may make the painting less attractive to the adult, the value for the child has been

[1] *Art of the Young Child*, pp. 7–9.

his growing power to change colours. This is an important part of learning.'

§6 The aesthetic education of younger children: a note on teaching method

Having now suggested that there *are* aesthetic elements in some of the work and experiences of younger children, and having insisted that this must be seen in relation to their total educational development, we can return for a moment to the strictly educational question—as distinct from that of aesthetics (referred to on p. 277 above). It was, 'How far, within the general aims of development, should the specifically aesthetic aspect be encouraged and developed?'

The question, put in this way, and in the context of all that has been said in the last few pages, really answers itself. Everything said supports the contention that the aesthetic is important at any stage of education. If so, it *should* be cultivated for itself, *so long* as it is kept in proper proportion within the general aim of all-round development.

The cautious emphasis here is upon the 'aesthetic', rather than upon 'art'. I would hazard a guess that all young children—all normal children living under reasonable conditions at any rate—enjoy aesthetic moments, little moments of delighted contemplation. These are very precious and potentially of great importance in a self-education which can go on throughout the whole of life. The teacher of young children should be sensitively aware of these significant moments and should be careful not to bustle a child who is absorbed in what for him is his own kind of contemplation. He may seem to be idle; he may be dubbed an 'isolate'; but if he is not allowed, within reason, to 'stand and stare', he may be deprived of something necessary to his development at that moment, hard to re-initiate later on if it is not allowed to happen now.

There are *aesthetic* moments, experiencable perhaps universally by children, and to be distinguished from 'art'. Some children are (but not, without far more investigation, all) or are potentially, artists. They may or may not show signs of it in very early years but as time goes on they may need help in their artistic development.

And it is here that a mere note may be added on teaching method, particularly about the controversial question of teaching techniques to children at this earlier stage. It has to be a mere note, partly because the present writer is no expert in the teaching of young children, and partly because much of it is application of educated common sense.

The desirable method seems to be, very broadly, a blend of permissiveness, with tactful encouragement and readiness to help when help is needed. The very use of the metaphor 'tact' indicates that only the teacher on the spot, the teacher who is intelligent, educated, informed, as well as sympathetic and intuitive, can judge of the right moment to offer help, or the proper time to provide the material conditions which will help the pupil to help himself. Experienced teachers are agreed that the positive help should be there when needed. Jane Cooper Bland instances obvious things at the very early stages—how to wash brushes, hold them, keep them clean, how to mix colours or stick bits of clay together or use paste. But further, as she says,[1] 'Experimenting is not (*just*) finding out what paint, clay, or other materials can do. A child also experiments with expressing in concrete form his ideas and feelings about what is happening to him in his own world. . . . Painting or modelling may be pleasurable but it is also serious business.' Herbert Read points out[2] that 'the degree of enjoyment does depend, to some extent at any rate, on the degree of skill which the pupil has developed'. Broadly speaking, interest in skills, feeling of the need to acquire techniques for mastery, increase as the child grows older. More will be said about this in the next chapter.

It is impossible to lay down rigid rules; children are sensitive plants, and things which are generally good may do harm on some occasions. Sometimes even encouragement of younger children— not to say positive praise—may do harm, since the child may feel an urge to please Mummy or Teacher! There is no general formula for perfection, and mistakes are inevitable sometimes, mistakes of commission *or* omission. What may be wrong for a child this week may be right next. And individual adult teachers vary in their bias: some topple over backwards in an almost morbid fear of 'interference' with the individuality of the child: others have to fight with themselves to keep their mouths shut or their hands still. Each has to find his or her own way, guided only by the assimilated general principles learned by teachers with

---

[1] *op. cit.*, p. 37.
[2] *The Growth of Child Art*, *op. cit.*, p. 22.

sound educational training. Intelligent tact goes a long way to fill up gaps. Fortunately children are resilient; were it not so, most of us, the older generation, would be aesthetically damned for ever!

All these observations would, I think, apply, *mutatis mutandis*, to the teaching of other arts and crafts.

CHAPTER XVI

THE ARTS IN LIBERAL EDUCATION

CHAPTER XVI

THE ARTS IN LIBERAL EDUCATION

§1 *Some characteristics of 'liberal' education*

Although we can talk, in some sense, of a 'liberal' (or an 'illiberal') education at any stage of growing up, the word 'liberal' comes to have a more specific meaning when subjects in the curriculum have become increasingly differentiated, and—with the 'academic' pupils at any rate—increasingly specialized. Then the question arises: Which subjects should be included, which left out, what is the proper 'balance'? And so on. It is here, in the competition of subjects, that the arts tend to be squeezed out.

'Liberal Education' can mean a good many different things. It can be used in a very wide sense indeed so that it is almost equivalent to 'good education', or in a more restricted, technical sense. I shall follow a more restricted usage. What this liberal education is, and what it should contain, is a highly complex, controversial, and as yet unsettled question. I shall not begin to attempt to cover it as a topic in itself, but shall confine myself to several, mainly three, aspects of it which are relevant to the claims of the arts to be included in a liberal curriculum.

A preliminary question, in a potentially crowded curriculum is: What should the *range* of any liberal education include? Clearly, if we are thinking, as we are, in the immediate context of school education, it could not be confined to the specialized study of *one* subject. Nor, at the other extreme, can it include simply *everything*. There must be selection of some kind. On what basis should we select?

Many answers can be given, some of them 'subject'- or 'field'-biased, perhaps conservative, based upon the traditional curriculum; 'we know, well enough, what is it best to hand on to the younger generation'. Others would call 'liberal' that education which helps a person to live in present-day society. (The validity of this would depend upon what one means by 'living' and upon what one thinks of 'present-day society'. Learning to drink, to drive a car, to play bridge, to 'swing', to be politically astute? In another sense of the word, a 'liberal' education might lead one to dislike much of what goes on in present-day society.) There are more fundamental philosophical analyses: it is some principles of these which I shall now briefly discuss, under the three headings mentioned. Though distinct, they very much overlap. The first (1) is based upon an attempted analysis of the fundamental forms of human knowledge, or as I prefer to say, ways of knowing, experiencing, understanding. The second (2) is concerned with the way in which studies based upon such forms or ways tend to expand beyond themselves, to open up new vistas of knowledge and experience, to develop wide perspectives. The third (3) concerns the *manner* in which becoming educated must take place in order to be liberal; it must be something which so takes hold of a person that his outlook is transformed by it. Being instructed or well-informed is not enough. I shall first outline these overlapping distinctions in order to see, a little later, how far the study of the arts fulfils what each insists on.

(1) In my book, *Ways of Knowledge and Experience* (1961), I distinguished several fundamental modes of knowledge and experience—the arts, religion, morals, knowledge of persons, with some reference too to scientific knowledge. The present work has concentrated further upon art-experience as a kind of knowledge. Professor Phenix, of Teachers' College, Columbia, has, in his *Realms of Meaning*[1] attempted 'to elaborate a philosophical theory of the curriculum based on the idea of logical patterns in disciplined understanding'.[2] His distinctions are elaborate; I need not here expound them: they are given technical names—Symbolics, Empirics, Esthetics, Synnoetics, Ethics, Synoptics. All the main, curriculum materials, he thinks, should come from these disciplines.

A recent—and very able—attempt to work out in outline the conception of liberal education in terms of basic forms of knowledge, is that of Professor P. H. Hirst. His thought was first published in an essay, 'Liberal Education and the Nature of Knowledge'[3] and has been developed since.

A liberal education is concerned, he says, with the development of mind. (If liberal education is going to include aesthetic education, then, since sense-perception is an essential part of most aesthetic experience, we ought, I maintain, to think of the term 'mind' as having attached to it '-and-body'.) But mind is not a ready-made entity, a kind of organ or muscle, with its own inbuilt

---

[1] Philip H. Phenix, *Realms of Meaning*, 1964, McGraw-Hill.
[2] *op. cit.*, p. x, Preface.
[3] In the volume *Philosophical Analysis and Education*, ed. Archambault, Routledge.

forms of operation which if developed will function in a pre-determined way. There is a real sense—as we saw with young children—in which mind comes into *being* through its encounters with the world. And as it develops, to 'have a mind' basically involves having experience articulated in various ways by means of what Professor Hirst calls 'conceptual schema', the basic 'forms of knowledge'. Examples of forms of knowledge (which can have various sub-forms) are: mathematics, physical and human sciences, history, religion, literature and the fine arts, philosophy—all of them objectified and progressively developed over millennia. By a 'form of knowledge', he says, is meant a distinct way in which our experience becomes structured round the use of accepted public symbols. The use of these symbols, again, can be publicly tested. So knowledge is developed. Each form—mathematics, the sciences, history, the arts and the rest—has (it is argued) its own central concepts, its distinctive logical structure, its special tests, its special skills. Mathematics depends upon deductive demonstrations from certain sets of axioms, the sciences upon empirical experimental and observational tests. The arts too have their 'distinct forms of critical tests though in these cases both what the tests are and the ways in which they are applied are only partially statable'. Hirst adds significantly '(Some would in fact dispute the status of the arts as forms of knowledge for this very reason.)'

The reservations are, I think, significant and ought to be noted carefully. Professor Hirst came to Philosophy of Education by way of mathematics and logic, and his treatment of the 'forms of knowledge' is strongly influenced by these interests, as is his language. Words like 'forms' of knowledge, 'conceptual schema', 'accepted public symbols', 'publicly tested', 'distinctive logical structure' . . . may work very well for mathematics, the natural sciences, perhaps history. The *manner* of their application to human sciences (or more safely, human 'studies') is at least open to question. Again, it would, I think, be dangerous to use this language, without very careful critical qualification, to religion. And Professor Hirst's own *caveat* 'Some would dispute the status of the arts as forms of knowledge for this very reason' is very serious indeed. He is himself provisionally willing to include the arts in 'forms of knowledge', but has not, I think, as yet worked out his position in relation to the arts. The doubts he describes might very well be crucial for him, *so long as* this language, clearly derived

K

from the logic of discursive understanding, is strictly insisted upon.

It would be out of place to go into this in detail now. But it has to be said that any really open account of ways of knowing (or 'forms of knowledge') has to face the basic challenge, nowhere better stated than by Mrs Langer (in *Mind: an Essay on Human Feeling*, Part II), of the *radical* difference between the 'logic' (the relational structure) of art, and the 'logics' of various kinds of discursive reasoning. (This was discussed above but is worth fresh attention.) It is a complete mistake, according to Mrs Langer, to think of art as though it were like other systems of thinking, a *symbolism* made up of a system of 'significant elements which may be variously compounded'. 'A work of art is a single symbol . . . Its elements have no symbolic values in isolation. They take their expressive character from their functions in the perceptual whole.' (p. 84, *op. cit.*) Discursive thinking, on the other hand, *is* a symbolism. 'What can be stated has to be logically projectable in the discursive mode, divisible into conceptual elements which are capable of forming larger conceptual units by combinations somehow analogous to the concatenations of words in language. The principles of verbal concatenation are few enough to be formally known as the rules of syntax and grammar . . .' Again, 'A symbolism to be currently manipulated as a tool in practical life must have a single set of rules; and the units deployed by these rules, the words of the language, must be as unequivocal as possible.' (*ibid.*, pp. 102–3.)

This is absolutely necessary for clear discursive thinking. But these very characteristics, the atomistic structure and singleness of projection 'set limits to the expressive power of language. It is clumsy and all but useless for rendering the forms of awareness that are not essentially recognition of facts' (p. 103). Examples of such forms are the life of subjective feeling, and the 'life' of art. The elements of art have to seem 'organic', and 'living'; they 'have no existence apart from the situations in which they arise; but where they exist they tend to figure in many relationships at once . . . A work of art is like a metaphor, to be understood without translation or comparison of ideas; it exhibits its form, and the import is immediately perceived in it' (pp. 103–4).

Speaking for myself, I have, for the last thirty years or so, both in writings and teaching, explicitly advocated the study of the various 'ways of knowing' as a contribution to the better understanding of liberal education. Naturally, therefore, I welcome Professor Hirst's fresh investigations into the 'forms of knowledge'. The idea of liberal education requires this, and much more, study. But if the study is to be really productive, it must criticize, with the utmost rigour, any attempt to import bodily the logic of discursive thinking into non-discursive, non-propositional fields, and particularly the field of art.

With these, vital, reservations, let us return to the notion of liberal education as worked out in terms of 'forms' (or ways) of knowledge. The contention is that the cultivation of the fundamental forms of knowledge *is* the basis of liberal education. (This is the restricted, and prescriptive, usage. In this usage 'liberal education' falls *within* 'education': it is not the *whole* of education.) To build up a liberal curriculum, examples of each of the different areas must be chosen. The forms of kowledge give a *general* principle of selection. The need to select is not *simply* a consequence of the vast growth of knowledge and the limits of time; it is inherent in what a liberal education is aiming at—neither encyclopaedic information nor on the other hand specialist knowledge. What is required is sufficient immersion in the concepts, 'logic', and critieria of a discipline, for a person to come to know the distinctive way in which the discipline works by pursuing these in particular cases, *plus* sufficient generalization over the whole range of the discipline. A pupil will then be able to recognize an 'empirical' assertion, or an 'aesthetic' judgment, for what it is. This understanding should be supplemented by an outline of major achievements in each area. Sufficient intelligent critical understanding is the aim; this will, of course, involve some selected participation in the work of the discipline. The good teacher will very carefully choose 'paradigm' examples to illuminate the discipline and educate in it: the aim of this 'liberal' education is quite different from the aim of highly specialized education. The actual choosing of which particular areas to study *within* a form of knowledge, the order in which it should be presented, how it is to be done for such and such pupils at their particular stages and with their particular interests—these are matters which no philosophical analysis can determine: it is the educated teachers on the spot who have to decide.

One corrective note is offered by Professor Hirst in conclusion. The forms of knowledge must be distinguished—and hitherto the philosophical distinctions have been only dimly grasped in a muddled way. Their *interrelations* are as yet little understood. Yet they have common roots in the common world of persons and things which we all share—and what Professor Michael Oakeshott calls the 'conversation of mankind' is a vitally important way in which the distinctive contribution of each 'form' to the common whole, may better come to be felt and understood. Liberal education and understanding of the 'unity of knowledge' (as I have argued elsewhere) requires the life of the community of liberally educated people.[1]

I have then—to recapitulate—some reservations about certain parts of Professor Hirst's arguments. 'Liberal education', was, in the paper alluded to, too exclusively described by him in conceptually cognitive or intellectual terms. Liberal education is education of feeling, too, and of 'persons' as well as 'minds'. Again, though Hirst includes the arts as among his forms of 'knowledge' (as I have argued in this book one must), he is a little hesitant about it and some of his arguments are not clearly compatible with it. I have argued, too, that experience of art, though knowledge, is *more* than knowledge. But, with reservations, I find Hirst's comments illuminating and challenging.

(2) The other two headings (referred to on p. 288 above) represent somewhat different educational emphases. I do not think they are incompatible with anything which has so far been said. They can be explained quite briefly.

The first refers to the way in which a subject may be taught and studied so that it opens up questions, speculations and explorations, which lie beyond its own immediate content. It should develop what Professor R. S. Peters[2] calls 'cognitive perspective'. A man may, for instance, be a very highly trained scientist, caring about science, having grasped scientific principles. But he may have a very limited conception of what he is doing, showing little interest in the connection of science with other things, failing to think of its place in a coherent pattern of life. One would hardly say, in such a case, that he was a very 'educated' man or—to use the term in a complimentary way—a 'liberally' educated person. He would lack 'cognitive perspective'.

If the arts are to be accepted fully as part of liberal education,

[1] See also Chapter XV, 'Persons, and the Unity and Variety of Knowledge', in my *Ways of Knowledge and Experience*: also my 'The Community of Scholars', *Teachers College Record*, Vol. 65, No. 5, February 1964.
[2] Professor R. S. Peters, *Ethics and Education*, p. 31, Allen & Unwin.

they must be studied in such a way as to increase cognitive perspective. The discriminating and critical appreciation of the arts should not stop just at that, but should open up the pupil's mind to explore the whole wider world of culture in which the arts have always played an important role. If a boy or girl is encouraged to paint, or model, or work in a craft, the aim will not *exclusively* be to teach him a skill, or to give him an insight into what it is to be something of an artist. It will also be to open up his mind, through the inspiration of these insights, to a broad vista of the arts in their setting through time. The exploration of a medium in depth might initiate this wider interest. Or his own experiments might lead him in consultation with the work of the masters who have done like experiments, to the history of art and to the lives and times and cultural backgrounds of men far removed from his own age. I shall return briefly to this later.

(3) The third emphasis which any education, and any liberal education, must insist on is a certain feeling and manner and method of it, the ways in which subject-matter is learned and taught. A pupil must participate freely in what he is learning, must himself feel it to be valuable, must be taught in such a way that he comes to appreciate its form and structure and development from the inside because he is committed to it through his own choice. He learns through his own involvement in it, discovers its disciplines and accepts them because it is they which challenge him. His motives are intrinsic; the subject is studied for its own sake, not because it is externally required or because it is a means to some end outside itself. A liberally educated person in this sense is freed or emancipated through what he does. He may also have much information and be well instructed, but his education consists not in this but in what he *possesses* and has made peculiarly his own.

These three emphases reinforce and supplement one another; they are not, I said, exclusive; they overlap. In what follows I shall try, without sticking too closely to the distinctions between the different emphases, to illustrate a little how art education may achieve its liberalizing mission. But before developing this it is necessary to say something about the relation of art to *craft*. I have referred almost exclusively throughout this book to the experience of the arts, and it has been art-experience which has staked its claim to be a form of knowledge and so an integral part of liberal education. Yet—particularly when we are thinking of school education—'arts and crafts' are usually said as though they were one word. What is the distinction between them, and how are they related?

§2   Art and Craft

Though all art implies craft in some sense, since art involves skilful manipulation of tools and materials, it is possible for some purposes to distinguish between art and craft. Thus Collingwood, in his *Principles of Art*[1] affirms craft as a skill which is knowledge of the means necessary to a given end. The craftsman knows what the end is—for example a chair to sit on or a cup to drink out of—and his job is to make the chair or cup according to a design which is given to him, and which he carries out as well as he can. Collingwood, quite usefully, distinguishes between the artist, who does not know beforehand exactly what he is going to do, and the craftsman who has a set pattern before him to follow.

This is up to a point legitimate, because there is craft which is not as such art. To plane a piece of wood square, or to shape the spokes of a cart wheel to given dimensions, or to make a watch according to a precise plan—this is craft which is not in itself art in the sense of 'fine art'. On the other hand, the distinction is dangerous too, encouraging a rigid separation of art and craft which need not exist at all. It is dangerous for several reasons. First, though the wheelwright's or watchmaker's work may not, as such, be art, we cannot exclude *a priori* an *aesthetic* element in a great deal of craft. Anyone who has used a plane or spokeshave skilfully and felt the clean cutting of steel through wood to a given dimension—or who has even watched the craftsman—must know this. Secondly, the entire separation of art from craft is not true of many crafts. The chairmaker (of a hand-made chair) within the limits of the purpose of the chair, gives his own individual touch to the work as it goes on: *he* does not know exactly beforehand what the 'touch' will be. Thirdly, the craftsman traditionally has often been the artist, designing as well as carrying out his own work. Historically speaking, it is impossible to deny that art and craft overlap at least along much of the line.

It is true that craft, as distinct from art, does essentially contain the idea of the distinction between end and means. There is, in craft, an end or purpose beyond the object made. A jug, a spoon, a chair, a rug, all these are made to be used, whereas a work of art

[1] Chapter II.

as such has no purpose beyond itself; it is made to be contemplated. But, as I have been saying, in craft in the generous sense end and means overlap and have to be experienced in relation to one another. We enjoy, aesthetically, contemplatively, the very form of the instrument of use. The craft-object is both of use and is an expression of the human spirit, the body-and-mind of the craftsman. As Seonaid Robertson puts it,[1] the craftsman 'knows that the innermost core of everyone demands an immediate satisfaction, in the spoon no less than the food, in the instrument as well as in the music . . . In craftsmanship, in its fullest form, the craftsman creates the object from its inception to its finished shape, responsibly controlling the work at every point, holding the final purpose, the nature of the raw material, and the traditions of its use balanced, as it were, within the magnetic field of his own personality. The peculiar alchemy of this evades definition.'

This may be developed by putting it in a slightly different way. A craftsman potter makes a cup and saucer for sale. Can he be called an 'artist' as well as a craftsman? (Part of the answer will depend on some of the things already said, and I need not repeat them.) It will turn partly upon definition. If an 'artist' is someone who makes an artifact to be aesthetically contemplated, an end in itself, then the craftsman who makes a cup and saucer for a purpose 'outside' itself, and not just to be looked at, is not, by *that* definition, an artist. (Of course he might be partly an artist, in that, for some of the time at any rate, he does make it, with beautiful shape, colour, decoration, to be looked at in a moment of contemplation. In that sense, we do sometimes enjoy cups and saucers as works of art. And, short of 'work of art', we could have plenty of aesthetic enjoyment in the cup and saucer, apart from its use.) But if we think of the cup and saucer, not as a unit which is a means to an end outside itself, but as cup and saucer-being-*used*-contemplatively-with-aesthetic-pleasure, then this total thing can not unfairly be called in some sense an art object, perhaps even a 'work' of art. The total thing is not of course displayed on a stand (it could not be) nor could this hang on a wall like a picture to be looked at. But its shape, weight, balance, colour, operating functionally so that this enjoyment is part of the total holding, pouring, drinking situation—surely *this* is a good in itself (as a picture is) and not merely a means to something else. It is not

---

[1] *Craft and Contemporary Culture:* see the whole Chapter on 'Towards a definition of Craftsmanship'.

cup and saucer (full stop) as means to use, but cup and saucer-in-use, a totally aesthetically pleasing thing, and designed as such; it is a thing ingredient in a process of life—a fragment of art in living, a piece of the art of living. Whatever one thinks of the exact status of this peculiar situation, it makes the craftsman who thinks of function imaginatively in this way, an artist. And, in so far as craft is art, all the things which have been said of the implications of art as being a form of knowledge, can be said of the craft which is art.

This argument, that there is craft which is truly art, should not lead us to depreciate, educationally or otherwise, craft which is not art. The craft which is not art may not be part of *liberal* education in the special and limited sense in which we have been using it: but it can be (like many other things not coming within the special definition) of great educational value. And craft, both for its own sake and as initiation into art, can widen the outlook of both children and their parents. The children can make things for use with an eye all the time to their use. They can take home the things they have made with loving care; they can experience their qualities in use—as well, no doubt, as their defects! They can weave their own cloths, dyeing them perhaps with dyes made from collected vegetable materials; they can make scarves or garments—and wear them. They can make pots and plates and ash trays, or pieces of furniture. There is perhaps some education-propaganda value in this, for parents and children. 'Art' is no longer 'queer', but a relish in ordinary life. The children are making real things, not just 'works of art'! The emphasis on things, too, is sometimes healthy; the *thing* that Johnny has made, rather than the 'expression' of Johnnie's personality, is what counts.

§3 *Pottery, and 'cognitive perspective'*

Whilst on the subject of craft, it may be worth suggesting that out of the study of some crafts at least—for example pottery—can be developed a special form of the 'cognitive perspective' which we spoke of earlier. Seonaid Robertson in her book, *Rosegarden and Labyrinth*[1]—starting from her experiences with children in the classroom who were working with clay for the first time, expressing in it the feelings of crawling through a cave, the feelings of being down a 'mine' (constructed in the classroom), of making a garden—is led to explore the history and symbolism of gardens and laby-

[1] Routledge, 1963.

rinths in pictures, romance, allegory, poetry, Jungian psychology ... This is, of course, a development worked out (in a very striking way) by a sophisticated and mature teacher. But under the care of such a teacher, there are no set limits to the expansion of perspective which children may attain.

Further, one must not, when talking of a craft like pottery, allow oneself to be bullied too much by the intellectuals. There is a 'cognitive perspective' which, although it may have its *extensive* aspect, is attainable not so much by going beyond or outside the art or craft itself, as by *intension*, by going deep down inside it. It is expansion of outlook by cultivation of aesthetic depth, an increase of understanding through the feeling of the involved body-and-mind. The feeling of, and through, clay is so elemental that it has to be known in experience—or very lively sympathetic imagination—to be understood at all. The 'intellectual' is, as we have already seen, often self-deprived of this understanding because he is over-dominated by his concern for (very necessary) abstractions, with the sophisticated languages which they require. The construction and manipulation of conceptual abstractions is, no doubt, one of the top achievements of man. But the top cannot exist without a base, and man's base goes deep down into the earth, of which clay is a form as well as a symbol. Some academic intellectuals quite badly need at times the experience of what Hillaire Belloc once described as 'carousing in the dirt'.

This is really quite serious. Not to take it seriously is to be deficient in one kind of 'cognitive perspective'. Miss Robertson, in a chapter 'On being a Potter' in her book *Craft and Contemporary Culture*[1] puts the case for a direct approach to what I am here calling the 'cognitive perspective' of the primeval and universal, through working with clay.

'One takes a lump of clay, the very stuff of this earth—clay which was once hard granite, thrusting in sharp blocks out of windswept moors; granite which softened through countless ages of time, and which eventually decomposed into clay which was washed down by the rains into the beds of rivers spreading at flood-times over the flat valleys, where, among the coal-seams or the gravel-beds, we now find it.

'To be a potter means to take a lump of clay, plastic from its damp, thousand-year-long journey to the potter's bench, and to work it to increase that essential plasticity.' Families of Japanese

[1] Unesco, Harrap, 1961.

K*

potters, we are told, used to lay down clay for their grandchildren as European connoisseurs laid down wine. 'A good clay, like a good wine, has a bouquet.' Describing one way of working the clay by 'walking' it, the potter, she writes, stamps 'up and down, treading the soft, squelchy mass underfoot till it grips the heels and almost seems threatening to engulf one. By this time one's body is becoming deeply aware of the clay, and other awarenesses are falling away. One seems to have gone down into something unformed, primeval, and almost given oneself to it.' Describing throwing and centring: 'Here, laved in more water, the lump is centred between the hands but with the whole body. The weight is taken on the ball of the foot and one is conscious of the force of the solid earth, which is felt through the muscles of the calves, of the thighs, of the loins, of the shoulders, a force drawn up and directed downward through the arms so that beneath enveloping hands the thrust of the earth is poised against the thrust of the centrifugal force of the wheel. To learn to use one's body thus as a mediator without strain, to centre the lump of clay until it spins like silk beneath the fingers, that is the perfection of co-ordination, an exquistite sensation of wholeness.'[1]

There is much more of this very realistic poetry of the dialogue between man and the earth, and of the other processes of pottery—drying, glazing, decorating, submission to the fire . . . Some of it may sound like sheer sensationalism yet, though the experience is certainly sensational, it is much more, the dialogue. Through sensation comes an elemental knowledge—something utterly different from anything which is known by the intellect, and which goes far beyond art. It is, indeed, a 'revelation'.

In insisting on this sort of knowledge as a neglected aspect of liberal eduction, I am not of course saying that everyone should do pottery (any more than that because science is an ingredient in liberal education, everyone must do physics). Pottery is simply one very good instance of discovery of meaning through working with the physical body (of the body-and-mind) in a physical medium, a discovery which takes place, in different ways, in all art making.

§4 *Literature, and the overcoming of stereotypes*

As a way of knowing, experience of art is knowledge of a unique individual. As we have already said, it is not uniqueness by itself

[1] pp. 21, 23.

which distinguishes works of art from other things or events. There is an obvious sense in which any stick or stone or falling snowflake is 'unique' in its existence here and now; this thing is itself and not another thing; this event has never happened before, and will never happen again. These are examples of spatio-temporal, or quantitative uniqueness. A work of art, like anything else, of course has uniqueness in this sense. But the importance of the uniqueness of art is not quantitative but qualitative: the embodiment-symbol has a unified single meaning which it alone can possess. This makes it an individual in a sense in which other matters of fact—the stick, the stone, the snowflake—cannot be called individuals. It is as qualitatively an individual that art is peculiarly precious and important. Another way of stressing the same thing is to remind ourselves of what was said earlier (Chapter XII, §6), that art is never important aesthetically simply because it is an instance of anything. Although every work of art includes being an instance of many concepts (e.g. being of such and such a period, of such and such school, style, of work in such and such a medium . . .), its aesthetic value as a work of art is never exhaustively assessed in this way; it is an *individual* rather than merely a *particular*, or complex of particulars, an individual rather than an *instance*. One attends to and 'addresses' a work of art as an individual, as one does not address a particular or an instance.

I am recalling these things now, because of their special bearing on literature and drama, which has particularly to do with the individuality of human persons, their interrelations, their actions. The cultivation of understanding of such individuality is in itself liberalizing; it is also important in a world in which we tend, increasingly, to be dominated by stereotypes, in which, for instance, the individuality which ought to belong to persons and personal relations is more and more overlaid by the often crude images of mass media. Art education, particularly in literature and drama, can be a good corrective of this. The sensitive portrayal of character, whether in novels or plays, films, or TV, illuminates our understanding of it as individual—in sharp contrast to the manipulative use in popular media of impoverished, fixed images, for advertisement purposes or for entertainment.

We cannot, of course, do without general images of some sort, and we are imitative animals. Each epoch, each generation, today each quickly changing age-group, has its own general images of what is beautiful, ugly, ethical, masculine, feminine. What is

important is that the images should have some subtlety, some complexity, some basis of discriminating experience in depth, that
(negatively) they should not be exclusively dominated by the
publicity-inflated, oversimplified, fashionable stereotype of the
moment. Professor Harry S. Broudy points out[1] how the existence
of powerful mass media, 'able to shape the values of multitudes
possessing political and economic power, but ututored taste, is as
explosive a threat to rational democracy as an unlettered public
was thought to be fifty years ago. Aesthetic illiterates are just as
dangerous as intellectual ones.'[2] Popular art tends to substitute
the caricature and the cartoon for the many-dimensional realities
of love, duty, loyalty, truth.[3] 'A long tradition of art history and
criticism leaves little doubt as to the possibility of some works of
art being more complicated, more sophisticated, more dedicated,
more serious, in short, more significant artistically than other works
of art. Such art objects, therefore, present value models and feeling
possibilities more discriminating, more cultivated, more reflected
upon than do the popular arts. For serious art, love is more than
moon in June and death more than two shots at high noon.
Popular art in our culture tends to express life as felt by the adolescents of all chronological ages; serious art by its sophistication
tends to probe levels of experience that the young may not yet
have undergone.'

Professor G. H. Bantock, similarly,[4] shows how works of bad
popular literature, whether of crime or love, are not to be condemned because they incite to violence or rape, 'but because the
attitudes they involve in important matters of human relationship
and moral choice are obstructive to finer or more subtle responses.
The expectations about human behaviour aroused by the ordinary
work of popular fiction or popular magazine story involve grossly
oversimplified stereotypes which to addicts must to some extent
interfere with their ability to understand those with whom they
have to live in close personal contact, as in family life. At the very
least, they debase the medium of social intercourse, language . . .'
So much cinema and TV is daydreaming, emotionally trivial,
crippling to the apprehension of the real world. I. A. Richards[5]
wrote of bad literature, art, the cinema, as 'fixing immature and

---

[1] *The Journal of Aesthetic Education*, Spring, 1966.
[2] *op. cit.*, p. 17.   [3] *op. cit.*, pp. 17–18.
[4] *Pelican Guide to English Literature*, Vol. VII, 'The Modern Age'. The
quotations which follow are taken from this.
[5] *Principles of Literary Criticism*.

actually inexplicable attitudes to most things. Even the decision as to what constitutes a pretty girl or a handsome young man, an affair apparently natural and personal enough, is largely determined by magazine covers and movie stars.' And D. H. Lawrence: 'The girl who is going to fall in love knows all about it beforehand from the books and the movies. She knows exactly how she feels when her lover or husband betrays her or when she betrays him: she knows precisely what it is to be a forsaken wife, and adoring mother, an erratic grandmother. All at the age of eighteen.' Hannah Arendt stresses the potential human catastrophe of all this. It is 'as though individual life had been actually submerged ... and the only decisive requirement of the individual were to let go, so to speak, to abandon his individuality, the still, individually sensed pain and trouble of living, and acquiesce in a dazed "tranquillized" functional type of behaviour . . . It is qute conceivable that the modern age—which began with such an unprecedented and promising outburst of human activity—may end in the deadliest, most sterile passivity history has ever known.'[1] The dangers seem even greater now than when this was written. And if we add to this the apparently gleeful anticipation with which some writers look forward to increased powers of conditioning and control of human nature by scientific technology—without any thought of the human values (or absence of them) involved—the prospect is nightmarish indeed. *Quis custodiet ipsos custodes?*

§5 *The aims of art education: Appreciation and making*

Having said something generally about liberal education and the place of study of the arts in it, we may now ask more specifically, What is the basic aim of art education within liberal education?

The term 'critical understanding' was used of the liberal study of the ways of knowing or forms of knowledge. There is nothing wrong with this as applied to experience of the arts. But it might be misleading as suggesting too much detachment or too intellectual an approach. For this reason I shall say that the function of art education in liberal education is 'to develop discriminating apprehension and understanding of the arts'.

In the first Chapter of this book I wrote[2] 'The study of the arts in the fullest sense—dance, drama, music, literature, the visual arts and crafts . . . architecture—may draw from the understanding of magic, myth, religion; archaeology, anthropology, social

[1] Hannah Arendt, *The Human Condition.*   [2] Above, p. 18.

and political history, "conscious" and "depth" psychology, in fact from all the sources of human experience and culture.' But I added that when one is talking about the arts seriously, to focus upon the *aesthetic* aspects of them, to keep it constantly in mind, is not just a matter of temperamental bias; it is *logically* necessary if the talk is really to be about art. This is equally valid for art education. The possible or potential cognitive content of the study of 'the arts', over and above the cognitive content of actual aesthetic experience, is enormous, in fact indefinitely large. But it can only be part of education *in* art if it is constantly related in feeling and thought to the intrinsic aesthetic experience. If this does not happen, there is the danger that it will become a clutter of so much information *about* art, learned and reproduced, a lumber room of 'inert ideas'. If on the other hand, the centre of it all, from which the rest branches out, is aesthetic knowledge and feeling, then everything which is learnt *about* art becomes not only an extension of informational knowledge but at the same time a deepening and enriching of artistic experience itself. Art education must, as a first principle, initiate people into what it feels like to live in music, move over and about in a painting, travel round and in between the masses of a sculpture, dwell in a poem by reading and hearing it with understanding. These 'paradigm' experiences are the basis of an illumination of much that is beyond themselves, livening the mind and making it hospitable.

Aesthetic insight, feeling from the inside what an art is—this is the central starting and expanding point for everything else. How best can it be developed? For the practical teacher no encyclopaedia of practical advice could ever be complete. But some general questions of principle can be stated.

For the central aim, 'discriminating apprehension and understanding', might be substituted 'critical appreciation'. But in the application of these terms there is an ambiguity. 'Appreciation' of art normally means intelligent looking, listening, reading . . . in general, *contemplating* works of art already made and given to us by the artists. That is, very clearly, an indispensable part of all adequate art education. But there is another sense of 'appreciation' —or at least another application of it. In the art teaching which is a part of liberal education, we have agreed that we do not aim to turn out potentially professional artists. But unless there is some degree of real insight ('appreciation' in a wider sense) into what it means to *make* art, to be an artist, our understanding of art will be very one-sided. Not only this; appreciation in the other, first, sense, is likely to be constricted, perhaps superficial. One must not be too dogmatic here. Some people may certainly learn much about how to look at pictures and sculptures or about how to listen to music, without having tried to paint or sculpt or compose or play, and some good critics of the arts seem to have had little experience of the 'making' side. But it is a limitation, and I do not think that omission of practical artistic experience could be recommended as sound education. It is true, of course, that looking or listening is not passive reception; done intelligently it is highly active. Artistic perception implies implicit construction, or re-construction, of art. This is not the *same* as the construction of the artist actively working in his medium, but it is a kind of *virtual* imaginative 'creation'; it is being a sort of 'artist after the artist'. Virtual creation, when a person is looking or listening, is not externally observable (or not wholly so), but that it happens is sufficiently indicated in the intermediate case of interpretative art—of the sensitive reading of a poem or the understanding playing of a piece of music.

The two kinds of appreciation—or appreciation applied to apprehension of finished works of art, and to the making of art— are very different. Appreciation of a masterpiece, however actively one may apprehend it, has a peace of contemplation which has a timeless quality. It is an intuition of wholeness which is in sharp contrast to the sometimes very long processes of art making, with their rhythms of desire and fulfilment, frustration and success whilst in intercourse with the medium, in labour with the embodiment. Art education, I am affirming, must include both, so far as it is feasible. Of course we do not expect pupils at school to produce masterpieces (though work of great significance is sometimes found); but they should have some first-hand experience of working in a material medium, according to abilities, tastes, opportunities. This is not only educative in itself; it helps the pupil in his understanding of the masters and of the problems they have solved. A wise teacher will feed one kind of experience with the other. It is difficult to know when, and how, to do this. The educational aim of 'appreciation' has, as I have suggested, two sides. (a) When a pupil is learning to appreciate the masters, it is a help if he has some experimental experience of his own to bring to his looking. This experience must, obviously, be very limited. The range and complexity of the material and technical problems which artists past and present have had to meet is so great that not even the most experienced professional can know at first hand more than a few of them. So much the less, then, the mere pupil in school. The most one can hope to attain in a general art education is an openness to and a broad awareness of these problems, so that the appreciative understanding of the works of others becomes more illuminated. Even a little first-hand experience can help. On the other hand (*b*), whilst a pupil is *actually in process* of himself actively experimenting in the making of something, it may be premature to show him, *at that point*, how some master has dealt with a problem similar to his own; the pupil might give up the effort to find his own solution, and merely imitate. This danger could be lessened if the teacher were to show him examples of a number of different ways in which masters had dealt with his particular problem. (A colleague has suggested the example of different ways in which painters, eastern and western, have approached the problem of 'perspective'.) In such a situation he has at least to choose for himself. Even so, the danger of imitation remains—though whether imitation is absolutely and always a bad thing is still a matter for some debate. In the end, the sensitive teacher has to judge what is right here and now. There are times to act, and times to refrain from acting!

§6   *Methods: the teaching of techniques*
We have already entered upon the controversial questions of general principles of method, and of the place and danger of teaching techniques.

In Chapter XV I referred to the opposition between the older (yet not completely dead-and-buried) emphasis on Formal education and its opposite extreme of Laissez Faire. Formalism, *inter alia*, insisted on the learning of particularly limited sorts of techniques, for example perspective, accurate drawing of models, etc. The children had to learn their techniques before they were allowed to 'do art'. They had to learn how to make a perfect wash with watercolour before using washes in painting. Formalism was authoritarian; do as teacher says. In reaction against this, some teachers went to the opposite extreme—complete freedom to express, no restraint, nervous and rather grudging technical help. It is easy now to see where both extremes are wrong, and yet how each is asserting an element in art education which cannot be ignored. The earlier way of teaching techniques in isolation was rigid and wrong, on aesthetic grounds. The cart is put before the horse: techniques are the servants of creative art. It was education-ally wrong too: it had no relation to the stage of development of the child, and showed no understanding of the importance of freedom. But—and much more obviously now at the adolescent stage which we are considering—laissez faire is wrong too, and on both grounds. At some stage, when 'art' begins to be explicitly taught, it becomes necessary to master some techniques. Educa-tionally, too, children begin to need to learn techniques. They certainly need a lot of freedom if they are going to develop their own creative powers: but they also want, and need, technical help at the right times. And adolescents are self-conscious as young children are not; they want, not only to express themselves, but to do it effectively; sometimes they are after representation; generally speaking, they want to achieve the thing which we have called embodiment, which implies understanding and some mastery of the media.

Victor Pasmore, speaking (on both educational and artistic grounds) of the danger of thinking that what is suitable to young children will do for adolescents, of transferring 'free' methods suitable at an earlier stage straight over to adolescence, says: 'The term "child art" . . . in its primitive form, cannot be applied to the adolescent. Nevertheless it is evident from the unsatisfactory response of the adolescent to the new [i.e. *laissez-faire*] art teach-ing, that the imagery and technical limitations of the small child are being imposed on all children irrespective of their age and development. Two unfortunate developments arise from this error: (1) both teacher and adolescent pupil tend to mistake sloppiness for freedom of expression and (2) those teachers who realise something is wrong tend to abandon the new teaching directly the child reaches adolescence, and revert to the old, imi-tative approach. Whereas the former represents a travesty of the principles of the new teaching, the latter is a negative reaction to the problem, depriving the adolescent of the benefits of his earlier teaching.'[1]

In the last chapter I referred to the opinion—still current here and there—that somewhere about puberty children lose their 'creative' ability and cease to be interested in painting, drawing and other forms of art. It was articulated long ago by Cizek and has often been repeated. But, though there are certainly special

[1] Victor Pasmore, *The Growth of Child Art, op. cit.*, p. 28.

and difficult problems at the adolescent stage, there seems now not the slightest reason to think that the apparent loss of interest is anything but appearance, or that there is anything inevitable about it. What seems to be lack of interest is, teachers and psychologists tell us, a phenomenon due to the many uncertainties and insecurities of growing up, as well as to bubbling new ambitions. Adolescents no longer want to 'play' with wire or clay or paint, but to use these and other media in a purposeful more controlled way. Not only is it not true that the adolescent is 'not interested': he— or she—is at a stage of unusual sensitiveness and creative desire. One obvious cause of this is pubescence; but it is certainly not true that sexual interests *replace* interests in the sort of satisfactions that working with material media can bring. It is rather that (*inter alia*) sexual stirrings increase and make far more complex these other, aesthetic impulses and desires. The sense of, and desire for 'beauty' (and not only the beauty of the other sex) at adolescence can be painfully intense. The apparent 'indifference' is often the result of sheer inhibition. They want to express their personal reactions and feelings; but they also need to define them in external symbols in order to come to terms with life and to communicate with others. This is not just a general, developmental, educational need (e.g. to release emotion) but an aesthetic one too, to discover meaning in embodiment—the essence of art. There is a new general desire for objectification, and also for the aesthetic ordering of it. But the means are so difficult. They have a lot to 'say', but it feels chaotic; how can it become ordered? The adolescent is now, we remember, highly self-critical; what might be satisfying aesthetically for some young children—is no longer enough; he wants more control. There is an increased awareness of standards in everything (the opposite facet of self-criticism), but young people growing up are afraid of being looked at in a superior way, and afraid of failure.

These phenomena are a challenge for the sympathetic and understanding teacher, and there are many ways in which it may be met. Some think that it is better to ease the tensions by turning the pupil away for a time from these emotion-laden problems, stressing craft and design, rather than expression or representation. Others (and I would side with them) would grasp the nettle, offering the technical help that the pupils need and sometimes ask for— whether for the expression into more impersonal embodiment of their own ideas and feelings, their inner conflicts, or for the representative skills which they want to acquire. This would be accompanied by the making available of a large variety of materials and tools, with plenty of illustrations of their use in books or displays. Details of the ways in which teachers may solve these problems are, as I said, innumerable; they belong to the expertise of the teacher and the teacher of teachers; I have only tried to give a thumbnail sketch of some questions of principle.

§7 *History of Art, Criticism, Aesthetics*

Discriminating understanding of the arts, we said, has two sides, the enjoyment of the finished work, and insight into making, insight through direct experience of trying to be something of an artist: each enriches the other. Historical examples, for instance, chosen for their relevance to what a pupil is actively doing, can illuminate and help. But the use of historical examples does not, in itself, teach 'History of Art'; and some knowledge of this History (the history of whatever art it is that is being studied) would seem to be a requirement of liberal education in art.

I must make it clear that in speaking of 'History of Art', I am thinking of it in a very humble and limited form, in the context of pre-university, school education. 'History of Art', as it is taught in some distinguished university schools, coupled with highly specialized, often minute, research, is obviously, far beyond the scope of the school curriculum. History of Art in this advanced sense is a high discipline of its own, requiring a special initiation suitable only for persons of relative maturity. It is a study in itself, and whilst it could be expected, in opposite ways, both to be illuminated by and to illuminate direct artistic experience, it would not be cultivated simply as a means to any end other than itself. Here I am thinking of something quite different, an elementary sketch, given for the sake of increasing discriminating experience of art. And I am assuming, without any new arguments, that, well taught and used, it can do this.

History of art, in this limited sense, is sometimes condemned as a component of art education because it is all-too-easy to teach it badly. Certainly if learned as a string of facts, names and dates, isolated from the constant, direct, enjoyment of examples of the art of which it is the history, it can be profitless and dull. On the other hand, if presented in broad outline, with careful and limited selection of the best examples, from good reproductions, good slides —and, where possible, with visits to galleries to see selected originals—history of art can give a coherent background to the study of particular aspects of art, and to practical work. Putting it more positively, to possess a framework of knowledge of at least one of the arts—say, the visual arts, including architecture—is something which every liberally educated person ought to have as a right. This is truer than ever today when holiday travel is increasing, and museums, galleries, radio and television are offering more facilities to the public. Many of us, and certainly all who are likely to read this book, have no doubt acquired something of this background framework of knowledge. But unless we are exceptions, and were lucky enough to have had some initiation into it at school or university, we have had to acquire it by our own efforts, sometimes piecemeal. It has been chancy. Think, however, of the majority of children coming out of school with absolutely no fragment even of this framework of knowledge. In many cases they are unlikely to acquire it for themselves. It takes some imagination to picture what their blankness of mind means. What must it be like to have not even a hint of knowledge whether a great public building (or its remains) is Greek, or Roman, or Medieval, or Renaissance, or Modern, not to have any knowledge of the main 'orders' of architecture, not to be able to recognize the sculpture of the Parthenon as later than Greek Primitives or Egyptians, or Rodin later than Michelangelo, or that this is Chinese, that Indian, that African or perhaps Aztec, not to be able to recognize or to place roughly a Byzantine painting, a Leonardo, a Vermeer, a Cezanne, a Gainsborough . . .? Yet this is not an exaggeration of the condition in which a majority of pupils are turned out of school, having completed their 'education'. Everyone ought to have an outline of such history. And it does not matter that some of it has to be learned and remembered —always so long as it is related to actual experience and study of typical carefully chosen examples. (Needless to say what 'goes' for History of the visual arts, also 'goes' for the study of any other.)

What of *Criticism*, and *Aesthetics*? They are a different story. Whilst some outline of History of Art is essential as a framework, the history and theory of criticism are too advanced and specialized to be included in a general liberal education. Criticism in practice is another matter. It would naturally be involved (or, shall one say, it ought to be) in studying historical and contemporary examples. Appreciation of art is inseparable from criticism of it: a good teacher would be teaching both as two aspects of an indivisible whole. The same kind of thing is true, broadly speaking, *mutatis mutandis*, of the study of *Aesthetics* as such. Aesthetics as philosophy is far too difficult, far too advanced, too specialized, to be cultivated as a part of general liberal education. Undoubtedly, in critical study of the arts, some of the most intellectual pupils will find themselves 'doing' it, willy nilly: there is no reason why they should not be encouraged, though with caution and warnings. (But if the art teacher is to help the exceptional students to struggle along, he needs, himself, in his own teacher-education, to have had some guidance in aesthetics: this has been, at least until recently, unfortunately very rare: some beginnings have now been made.)

This cursory discussion has also been arbitrary. For reasons given I have confined myself mainly to the 'visual' arts. But of course each kind of art—literature, music, drama, dance and the rest—has its own unique contributions to offer which others cannot rival. One special thing which the 'visual' arts and crafts can teach is increased aesthetic sensibility, visual, tactile, to the textural qualities which lie outside the arts, in the *natural* world of perception. A whole new universe is opened up, micro- or macroscopic, animate or inanimate, in the beauty of land- or sea-scape, of growing things or shells and stones on the seashore or mountains. Woodland or hedgerow in mass or in detail, the flight of a bird or the structure of its wing, the minutiae of a flower or beetle or snow crystal—almost anything or everything can come to cast its spell upon us. Any teacher who sees his pupils awakening to these marvels of beauty in the natural world is well rewarded. The good art teacher sees it constantly.

§8 *Conclusion*

The discussion of education in the last two chapters may seem perhaps to be a straying away, a diversion, from the main subject of this book—embodied knowing of aesthetically embodied meaning. It has been, however, in its own way a support and reinforcement of the existence and importance of this way of knowing, so different from most of the knowledge which is stressed in school education largely to the exclusion of other forms—the propositional knowledge of science, history, and other subjects.

Embodiment, suggesting the essential incarnateness of human life, mind, and aesthetic meaning, is a very fundamental idea, stretching far beyond the strictly aesthetic: in a wide context it might be called archetypal. Man, 'the great amphibian', is a bodily organism which has to come to terms with a physical world independent of the organism, and a psychophysical organism for which the physical world is saturated with meaning which, very soon, even in the infant, comes to have much more than physical import. The young child comes to know the world, other people, and himself through his body—tasting, touching, moving, feeling . . . seeing, hearing. He begins to discover at one and the same time his unity with, and his distinction from, his mother through his groping conscious organism, his blind mouth, his seeking clutching hands moving restlessly over her breast to the gorged and engorging nipple. It is a basic knowledge, a basic discovery, inseparable from feeling and being, occurring well before seeing her face and hearing her voice become clearly differentiated from the rest of organic sensation. Because it is so undifferentiated, we can hardly say whether any elements in it could sensibly be called 'aesthetic', except in the strictly etymological sense. It is, certainly, biologically a thoroughly *practical* enterprise.

Our quick glance at the explorations or rather older children, however, showed that childish explorations, though cognitive and practical, are at times almost certainly aesthetic too, and that judicious sympathy is needed to encourage the attentive enjoyment of aesthetic meaning. In the earlier years, we must suppose, the physical world—of touch, smell, resisting mass, empty space, the hot, the cold, the coloured . . . —becomes strangely symbolic of what is far more than itself. It is debatable whether we should call this early symbolism in part 'aesthetic'. (From early memories, I think I would.) But however that may be, the actual or potential aesthetic element in it is a fragile, vulnerable, evanescent thing, easily overwhelmed by practical needs, needs to take sensuous data not as for sheer enjoyment of their qualities, but as *cues* for the practical action of living. Colours, shapes, sounds, patterns . . . become reference points, signals, signs, symbols of various kinds. To attend to them for their own sakes any more is for the most part theoretically or practically irrelevant, and it may sometimes be dangerously distracting. In 'science' a pupil may get into trouble for spending any appreciable amount of his time in contemplation of the beauty of what he sees under a magnifying glass or microscope, or for paying too much attention to the aesthetic quality of his drawing. A halted car driver may get into worse trouble if he attends to the patterns of oil on a puddle instead of getting on with his driving. Generally speaking, 'programming', the refinement and multiplication of cues, begins long before the appearance of the computer. It develops, of necessity, out of early childhood into the complexities of the peripheral stereotypes of adult life. More and more we live by these stereotypes, signs, symbols, abstractions, all very far removed from the direct contemplative enjoyment of the world which at times is experienced by the child.

Every bit of it is indispensable for the development of mind, for the practical and theoretical necessity to know conceptually, to get on practically, to come to terms with and control the world. But there is always the danger, in the pursuit of any particular mode of human excellence, that other modes may be neglected, and that the wholeness of the incarnate life may be broken up, perhaps in part lost. We can be cut off from our roots. The cultivation of the aesthetic, and particularly of the arts, is a corrective of this, a restorative, or, perhaps better, the discovery of new meaning to be achieved only when body, imagination, intellect are working together as one whole.

I am, therefore, making no plea for a holiday now and again into regression to some childish or infantile state, nor for any supression of intelligent understanding. The plea is, rather, a positive one, for the education of intelligent understanding of a different *kind* from that which is cultivated in the abstract discursive studies. This other understanding is of a whole expanding world of meaning which is revealed through aesthetic feeling for, and of, the forms of things. It is the understanding of the 'embodiment-symbol'. It is understanding which, in its developed forms, requires intelligence and intellect: but these have to function through the body, its breathing, heart-beats, pulsing blood, inner rhythmic motions.

The general development of mind and understanding from the early years is development *from* the blind gropings of the infant or the symptomatic expressions of the young child, towards clarity, distinction, intelligent understanding and mastery of the external world of things and other persons. It is, as we have seen, a development towards the achievements of *abstracting* intellect and the imaginative constructions of intellect including—for some at least—the constructions of mathematics and science. The other line of development, which I have been saying is insufficiently recognized, is the development of the *concrete* intelligence involved in the contemplative apprehension of a world to which we are personally much closer. It is a world of aesthetic perception, in art or outside it—once again of the embodiment-symbol.

There can be no doubt that the world of art—of Shakespeare, Bach, Rodin—is a world which it takes high *intelligence* to construct and to understand. Much of it is intelligence in the very ordinary sense, the intelligence involved in distinguishing and seeing relationships of all kinds, in exercising sense of relevance, etc. Mathematics, physical science, philosophy, politics . . . require the use of intelligence in various ways. So, also, intelligent understanding must enter in various ways into the different arts. But the experience of art, as we have amply seen, is intuitive embodied experience of embodied meaning which, though it requires intelligent thinking, is much more, and, moreover, is never adequately understandable in discursive terms. If the understanding of art presupposes, as it does, the exercise of general intelligence in an ordinary sense, it also requires a special *sui generis* aesthetic intelligence, which might be called the intelligence of (aesthetic) *feeling*. This intelligence implies an ability of the embodied person to pour himself into the experience of art.

The metaphor 'pour himself into experience' does not mean to relax in a welter of emotion as somnolently into a hot bath. 'Oneself' comes, let us say, to a highly complex work of art such as Bach's *The Art of the Fugue*, fully equipped and aesthetically sophisticated. Let us assume that a person has been through a good musical education, has done his analyses, understands fully the complicated structure and rules of the fugue, has given long thought to the study, on paper and with instrument (or instruments), of *these* variations upon these given themes. All this study does not remain in him as a load of inert ideas: the study alters the very stuff of his mind-and-body, so that now, educated in this way, he is able to perceive aesthetically with a discrimination and understanding which would have been impossible without it. This discriminating perception, necessarily preceded by the long discursive analyses, is not now discursive but richly intuitive, a total illuminated experience of the complex embodied meaning of the music into which he has to 'pour' himself to receive what it has to offer. The effects of the long study are there, but the previous study in its discursive form is no longer present to focal consciousness. In a sense it is 'forgotten' in the total attention to the work as it flows on, *and* as we both flow on with it and in the same process retain a time-transcending intuitive grasp of its structure. The intelligence which is involved all the time is the embodied intelligence, active as we 'live through' the embodied meaning which is developing in the music we 'hear'.

Music is, no doubt, a supreme example of the operation of the 'intelligence of feeling', of embodied intelligence participating in aesthetically embodied meaning. But it happens, in different ways, as I have tried to show, in all the arts.

One may, finally, put the uniqueness of the contribution of art to education in a slightly different way.

In the study of other subjects—mathematics, science, history . . . —we may view the understanding of the world as having a number of distinguishable aspects. There is (1) a self, in which the activities of intellect play a leading part; (2) symbols—linguistic or other—which express (3) concepts and propositions, which in turn, are ways of apprehending (4) an independent world. The world is apprehended—mathematically, scientifically, historically —in terms of concepts symbolized in language or other formulae. There is a proper detachment about all this, and some measure of impersonality. And it is, though quite certainly not a value-free process, in the main an attempt to understand and to come to terms with the *factual* structure of things. It is a mediated process, in which the symbols and concepts are vehicles of the understanding of aspects of the world.

The aesthetic symbol—in art or otherwise—functions, as we have seen, in quite a different way. It does not function as other symbols, by being simply a necessary vehicle. The embodiment-symbol *means* by drawing *into* itself—into its very individual shape and form—'the world'-as-felt in every kind of way—'things' known as loved, hated, marvelled at, enjoyed, felt with the sense of tragedy, comedy, disturbance, peace, dynamic portent . . . —in short an infinitely variegated world of values, personally felt. The embodiment-symbol draws these into itself and transforms them through its union with a medium into untranslatable new meaning which has to be known intuitively in aesthetic experience or not at all.

In aesthetic experience we come *directly* to know aspects of the world, value-orientated within the autonomous embodiment-symbol, individualized there. And in knowing meaning-embodied in this way, we are participating in *what* we know in a personally involved way which is quite different from the (relatively) detached way in which we think scientifically or mathematically. We not only 'know the world' in this special way; we are in intimate union with it. We have not only knowledge but being. We know, in being. A good deal of this due to the fact that it is in a physical medium that meaning is embodied aesthetically, and that we have to use our senses—which take hold of the *particular*—in our involvement with art, and not just our intellects—which emphasise the *general*—as we tend to do in other ways of knowing. A person involved in art has to come out of his enclosing, often self-protecting, shell, right out, through and with his body, into the physical world. Even if he is just 'appreciating' art he has to do some of this: but he does it best when he knows from personal experience what painting, or working in clay, or playing an instrument, or acting, or dancing, or reading literature aloud, actually feels like. The person whose education has been exclusively 'academic' is often far too introverted, made artificially safe from the turmoils of the physical world—or even from acute sensation of it. Physical education (in its great variety of forms) in one way, direct participation in embodied meaning in another, can do much to release him from his academic *gaucherie*, inhibition, maybe from unconscious fear of the physical world.

In once again emphasizing this physical side of art, it is perhaps unnecessary to repeat too that it is but one aspect, though essential. Entry into the life of art is not physical only, but a constant challenge to imagination. Since meaning in art is not the defined systematic meaning of some other symbols (e.g. mathematical or scientific), but open and richly ambiguous (so long as apprehended as aesthetically relevant to the forms of art as given), it is a constant stimulus to the active interpretative imagination. The 'meaning' of art is not finally given, once for all, by the artist as he intended it—in whatever century he lived or lives. Each new generation can, within the proper limits of aesthetic relevance to the form, discover for itself in its interpretative reconstructions, new meaning (as well as discover new meanings through the making of new art). But, as always, it is a direct, intimate and intuitive knowledge of meaning not quite paralleled in any other forms of knowledge, experience, or study.

For all these reasons, it is imperative that the arts should be a component of every liberal education. But how scandalous it is that it should have to be argued at such length!

INDEX

GEORGE ALLEN & UNWIN LTD

Head Office
40 Museum Street, London, W.C.1
Telephone: 01-405 8775

Sales, Distribution and Accounts Departments
Park Lane, Hemel Hempstead, Herts.
Telephone: 0442 3244

Athens: 34 Panepistimiou Street
Auckland: P.O. Box 36013, Northcote Central N.4
Barbados: P.O. Box 222, Bridgetown
Bombay: 103–105 Fort Street, Bombay 1
Buenos Aires: Escritorio 454–459, Florida 165
Beirut: Deeb Building, Jeanne d'Arc Street
Calcutta: 285J Bepin Behari Ganguli Street, Calcutta 12
Cape Town: 68 Shortmarket Street
Hong Kong: 105 Wing On Mansion, 26 Hancow Road, Kowloon
Ibadan: P.O. Box 62
Karachi: Karachi Chambers, Mcleod Road
Madras: 2/18 Mount Road, Madras
Mexico: Villalongin 32, Mexico 5, D.F.
Nairobi: P.O. Box 30583
Philippines: P.O. Box 157, Quezon City D-502
Rio de Janeiro: Caixa Postal 2537-Zc-00
Singapore: 36c Prinsep Street, Singapore 7
Sydney N.S.W.: Bradbury House, 55 York Street
Tokyo: C.P.O. Box 1728, Tokyo 100-91
Toronto: 81 Curlew Drive, Don Mills

Recent Titles in the Muirhead Library of Philosophy Series

SIR MALCOLM KNOX

Action

This study of moral experience is based on Gifford Lectures delivered in Aberdeen. It begins by describing the way in which the action of human beings rises from being instinctive to being chosen. Moral problems arise when man has to choose. At different times men act for pleasure, or to obey a rule, or to obtain some benefit, or to do their duty. All these reasons are considered in the book, and it is argued that they all have their place in such different levels of experience as play, law, economics, politics and personal relationships. Special consideration is given to the nature of action as such. The book ends with an examination of the relation between morality and religion. The wide range of the author's argument and his numerous concrete examples present a challenge to the contemporary linguistic philosophy which he rejects.

A Layman's Quest

This book, like its predecessor, *Action*, is a revised and enlarged version of Gifford Lectures delivered in Aberdeen. It begins by arguing that to have a religion is reasonable, but then asks: What religion? How much of orthodox Christianity is it reasonable to believe? The author thinks than an approach to answering this question must be through studying the course of New Testament criticism and considering recent theological developments which have laid less emphasis on historical facts and more on the proclamation of a Gospel. He begins with Reimarus, in the eighteenth century, and continues through Lessing, Kant, Hegel, and Strauss. English and Scottish ecclesiastical history in the nineteenth century is not ignored, and there are special appreciations of Modernism and Schweitzer. With contemporary theology, so much influenced by Karl Barth, and more recently by Rudolf Bultmann, the author has less sympathy. After a chapter in which he provides an answer to his main question, he concludes with an essay on philosophical theology, outlining implications of the belief which he has come to find reasonable.

LONDON: GEORGE ALLEN AND UNWIN LTD